THE MYSQL ENGINEER

Step-by-Step Learning of Essential Techniques for Efficient MySQL Database Development and Administration.

SOHAIL MOHAMMED

B.Sc. B.Ed. M.C.A

ISBN:9798314942604

DEDICATION

To all aspiring developers, database enthusiasts, and engineers who seek to master the art of data management—this book is for you.

To the beginners taking their first steps into the world of databases, may this guide be your solid foundation. To the seasoned engineers, may it serve as a valuable reference in your journey of continuous learning?

To my mentors, colleagues, and students whose questions, challenges, and insights have shaped my understanding—your curiosity and dedication inspire me every day.

And to my family and friends, whose unwavering support fuels my passion for knowledge-sharing—this book would not have been possible without you.

May this work empower you to build, innovate, and create with confidence?

Happy learning!

Table of Contents

ACKNOWLEDGMENTS

It's my pleasure to express my sincere gratitude to people who helped me successfully write this book.

I thank my friends, teachers, students for providing their valuable constructive feedbacks and suggestions without which this book would not have been in present form.

My special thanks goes to my kids Zakir and Zahid and my wife Anjuman for being patient and driving force behind my writing.

Preface

Welcome to *The MySQL Engineer* - *Step-by-Step Learning of Essential Techniques for Efficient MySQL Database Development and Administration*, a comprehensive guide to mastering MySQL, one of the world's most popular relational database management systems. Whether you are a budding developer, a seasoned database administrator, or an IT professional looking to deepen your understanding of MySQL, this book is designed to provide you with practical knowledge and industry insights.

In today's data-driven world, efficient database management is critical for the success of applications and businesses. MySQL, known for its reliability, scalability, and open-source nature, continues to be the backbone of many web applications, enterprise systems, and cloud infrastructures. However, to truly leverage its power, one must not only understand its syntax and functionality but also the best practices, optimization techniques, and advanced features that enable high-performance database solutions.

This book is structured to guide you from the fundamentals of MySQL to advanced topics, including database design, indexing strategies, query optimization, replication, security, and performance tuning. Each chapter is crafted to offer hands-on exercises, real-world scenarios, and practical insights that will help you apply the knowledge effectively in your projects and professional work.

As you embark on this journey, my goal is to make you a proficient MySQL engineer, equipped with the skills to design, implement, and maintain robust database systems. Whether you are building a small-scale application or managing large, distributed databases, the concepts and techniques discussed in this book will empower you to harness MySQL's full potential.

Thank you for choosing *The MySQL Engineer*. I hope this book serves as a valuable resource in your journey toward mastering MySQL and excelling in the ever-evolving field of database engineering.

Happy learning!

Sohail Mohammed

1 INTRODUCTION TO DATABASE CONCEPTS

In the modern digital age, the management and organization of data are paramount to the functioning of businesses, organizations, and even personal endeavors. At the core of this management lies the concept of a database.

1.1 What is a Database?

A database is essentially a structured collection of data that is stored and organized in a manner that allows for efficient retrieval, updating, and management. It serves as a centralized repository for storing and managing information, making it easier to access and manipulate data as needed.

1.2 Key Components of a Database

1. **Data**: At the heart of any database are the actual pieces of information, known as data. This could include anything from customer names and addresses to sales figures or inventory items.

2. **Tables**: Data in a database is typically organized into tables, which are structured sets of rows and columns. Each row represents a single record or entry, while each column represents a specific attribute or field of that record.

3. **Relationship**s: In many databases, data from different tables are related to each other in some way. These relationships help to establish connections between different pieces of information, enabling more complex queries and analysis.

4. **Queries**: A query is a request for information from a database. By writing and executing queries using a specialized language such as SQL (Structured Query Language), users can retrieve, manipulate, and analyze data stored in the database.

5. **Indexes**: Indexes are used to optimize the retrieval of data from a database by providing quick access to specific records based on certain criteria. They work similarly to the index of a book, allowing for faster lookup of information.

1.3 Types of Databases

There are various types of databases, each designed to serve different needs and requirements. Some common types include:

1. **Relational Databases**: These databases organize data into tables with predefined relationships between them. Examples include MySQL, PostgreSQL, and Oracle.

2. **NoSQL Databases**: NoSQL databases, or "Not Only SQL" databases, are designed to handle unstructured or semi-structured data and offer more flexibility than traditional relational databases. Examples include MongoDB and Cassandra.

3. **Object-Oriented Databases**: These databases store data in the form of objects, making them well-suited for object-oriented programming languages like Java or Python.

1.4 Traditional ways of storing data

In the days before modern digital databases, storing and managing data was a vastly different process. Here's a glimpse into how data was stored in the "olden days":

1. Paper Records:

• One of the oldest methods of storing data is through physical paper records. These records could include ledgers, journals, index cards, and other paper-based documents.

• Information would be manually written or typed onto these records, and they would be stored in filing cabinets, shelves, or other physical storage systems.

• Retrieving information from paper records could be time-consuming and labor-intensive, requiring manual searching and sorting.

2. Filing Systems:

• Filing systems were developed to organize and categorize paper records for easier storage and retrieval.

• Records were typically organized alphabetically, numerically, or by some other predefined system, making it easier to locate specific information.

• Different types of filing systems were used, including alphabetical, numerical, chronological, and subject-based systems.

3. Card Catalogues:

• Card catalogues were commonly used in libraries and other institutions to organize and index collections of books, documents, and other materials.

• Each item in the collection would have a corresponding catalogue card containing information such as title, author, subject, and location.

• Users could search the card catalogue to find specific items and locate them within the library.

4. Indexing and Cross-Referencing:

• To make it easier to find information within large collections of records, indexing and cross-referencing systems were often employed.

• Indexes would be created to catalogue specific information, such as names, dates, or topics, along with references to the corresponding records.

• Cross-referencing techniques would link related information together, allowing users to navigate between different records and documents.

5. Physical Storage Media:

• In addition to paper records, data could also be stored on physical storage media such as tapes, disks, and other magnetic or optical storage devices.

• These storage media were used to store larger volumes of data in a more compact and durable format than paper records.

• However, accessing and managing data stored on physical media still required specialized equipment and manual handling.

6. File System:

In a file-based system, data is stored in individual files on a computer's file system. Each file typically represents a specific type of data or a collection of related data, and these files are organized within directories or folders. Here's an example to illustrate how a file-based system might work:

Example: Student Records Management System

Consider a simple system for managing student records at a school using a file-based approach. In this system, each student's information is stored in a separate text file. The data for each student includes their name, ID number, grade level, and courses they are enrolled in.

File Structure:

• Each student's information is stored in a separate text file, named according to their ID number or some other unique identifier.

• For example, the file for a student with ID number "123456" might be named "123456.txt".

• Inside each file, the student's information is stored in a structured format, such as comma-separated values (CSV) or in a human-readable format like JSON or XML.

Directory Organization:

• All student record files are stored within a dedicated directory on the computer's file system.

• Within this directory, files are organized based on some criteria, such as grade level or last name.

• For example, files for students in different grade levels might be stored in separate subdirectories named "Grade9", "Grade10", etc.

File Content:

• Each student record file contains the relevant information about the student.

•The content of each file might include fields such as:

•Student name

•Student ID number

•Grade level

•List of courses enrolled, with details such as course name, teacher, and grade

Accessing and Updating Data:

• To access or update a student's information, the system would locate the corresponding file based on the student's ID number.

• For example, if a teacher needs to update a student's grades, they would locate the student's file, open it, make the necessary changes, and save the file.

Example File (123456.txt):

Name: John Smith ID: 123456 Grade Level: 10 Courses: - Mathematics (Teacher: Ms. Johnson, Grade: A-) - English (Teacher: Mr. Thompson, Grade: B+) - Science (Teacher: Mrs. Adams, Grade: A)

While file-based systems can be simple and easy to implement, they have limitations in terms of scalability, data integrity, and concurrent access. As a result, modern systems often use relational databases or other data management systems for more efficient and reliable data storage and retrieval.

Limitations of File Systems

File-based data storage systems have several limitations compared to modern database management systems. Some of the key limitations include:

Data Redundancy: In a file-based system, the same data may be duplicated across multiple files. For example, if a student changes their address, each file containing their information must be individually updated, leading to redundancy and inconsistency.

Data Inconsistency: Because data is stored in multiple files, ensuring consistency and accuracy across all files can be challenging. Updates made to one file may not be reflected in other files, leading to inconsistencies and errors.

Limited Data Integrity: File-based systems lack mechanisms to enforce data integrity constraints, such as unique constraints or referential integrity. This increases the risk of data corruption and inaccuracies, as there are no safeguards to prevent invalid or inconsistent data.

Limited Query Capabilities: Retrieving specific information from a file-based system often requires manual searching and parsing of data. Without a query language like SQL, complex queries or analysis tasks are difficult to perform efficiently.

Concurrency Issues: File-based systems typically do not support concurrent access to data by multiple users or processes. This can lead to conflicts and data corruption if multiple users attempt to access or modify the same file simultaneously.

Scalability Challenges: As the amount of data grows, managing and organizing files becomes increasingly cumbersome. File-based systems may struggle to scale effectively to handle large volumes of data, leading to performance issues and management overhead.

Limited Security Features: File-based systems lack robust security features to control access to data and protect against unauthorized access or tampering. This makes it difficult to enforce access controls and maintain data confidentiality and integrity.

Difficulty in Data Management: Managing data in a file-based system requires manual intervention for tasks such as backup, recovery, and data maintenance. Without automated tools and processes, these tasks can be time-consuming and error-prone.

Overall, while file-based systems may be suitable for small-scale applications with simple data storage requirements, they are generally not well-suited for modern data-intensive applications that require scalability, data integrity, concurrency control, and advanced query capabilities. As a result, many organizations have transitioned to more sophisticated database management systems to address these limitations and better manage their data.

2 INTRODUCTION TO DATABASE MANAGEMENT SYSTEM (DBMS)

A Database Management System (DBMS) is a software system that provides an interface for managing databases, including storing, retrieving, updating, and managing data efficiently. It serves as an intermediary between users and the database, facilitating the interaction with data while ensuring data integrity, security, and concurrency control. A DBMS allows users to organize and manipulate vast amounts of data in a structured and organized manner, making it a crucial component of modern information systems.

2.1 Components of a Database Management System

Database: The central repository that stores organized collections of data. Databases contain tables, indexes, views, stored procedures, and other objects to represent and manage data.

DBMS Engine: The core component responsible for managing database operations, including data storage, retrieval, manipulation, and security. It interprets and executes user commands and queries, optimizing performance and ensuring data integrity.

Database Schema: A blueprint or structure that defines the organization of data within the database. It includes definitions of tables, their attributes (columns), data types, relationships, constraints, and other metadata.

Query Processor: The component responsible for processing user queries and commands. It parses SQL queries, optimizes query execution plans, and retrieves data from the database efficiently.

Data Storage: The physical storage mechanism used to store data persistently. It may include disk storage, memory caches, and other storage technologies optimized for performance and reliability.

Concurrency Control: Mechanisms to manage simultaneous access to data by multiple users or processes. It ensures data consistency and prevents conflicts and data corruption during concurrent operations.

Transaction Management: The management of transactions, which are units of work performed on the database. Transaction management ensures the ACID properties (Atomicity, Consistency, Isolation and Durability) of transactions, maintaining data integrity and consistency.

Security and Access Control: Measures to protect the database from unauthorized access, data breaches, and security threats. It includes user authentication, authorization, encryption, and auditing to enforce access controls and maintain data confidentiality and integrity.

Diagram:

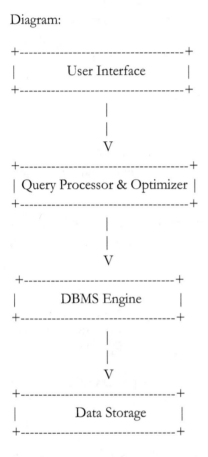

2.2 Advantages of using Database Management System (DBMS)

Using Database Management System (DBMS) software offers numerous advantages for organizations and individuals alike. Here are some of the key advantages:

Data Centralization: DBMS allows for centralized storage of data, providing a single source of truth for all organizational data. This centralization streamlines data management and ensures data consistency across multiple applications and users.

Data Integrity: DBMS enforces data integrity constraints, such as unique constraints, foreign key constraints, and data validation rules. This ensures that data stored in the database is accurate, valid, and consistent, maintaining data quality and reliability.

Data Security: DBMS provides robust security features to protect sensitive data from unauthorized access, tampering, and breaches. It supports user authentication, access control, encryption, and auditing mechanisms to safeguard data confidentiality and integrity.

Concurrent Access and Transaction Management: DBMS supports concurrent access to data by multiple users or processes while maintaining data consistency and integrity. It employs transaction management techniques to ensure that transactions are processed reliably and adhere to the ACID properties (Atomicity, Consistency, Isolation and Durability).

Scalability: DBMS systems are designed to scale effectively to handle growing volumes of data and increasing numbers of users. They support features such as partitioning, replication, and clustering to distribute data and workload across multiple servers, ensuring optimal performance and scalability.

Data Recovery and Backup: DBMS systems offer features for data backup, recovery, and disaster recovery planning. They allow for regular backups of database contents and transaction logs, enabling organizations to recover data in the event of hardware failures, data corruption, or other disasters.

Query Optimization: DBMS includes query optimization techniques to improve the performance of database queries. It analyzes query execution plans, indexes, and statistics to optimize query processing and reduce response times, enhancing overall system performance.

Data Analysis and Reporting: DBMS provides tools and capabilities for data analysis, reporting, and business intelligence. It supports SQL queries, data mining algorithms, and reporting tools to extract insights from data and make informed business decisions.

Data Consistency and Redundancy Reduction: DBMS helps maintain data consistency by minimizing data redundancy and enforcing normalization principles. By eliminating duplicate data and ensuring data integrity, DBMS reduces the risk of inconsistencies and improves data quality.

Ease of Application Development: DBMS simplifies application development by providing APIs, libraries, and frameworks for interacting with the database. It supports standard data access interfaces such as ODBC, JDBC, and ORM frameworks, enabling developers to build applications quickly and efficiently.

2.3 Applications of Database Management System (DBMS)

Database Management System (DBMS) software finds applications in various domains and industries due to its capability to efficiently manage, store, retrieve, and manipulate large volumes of data. Here are some common applications of DBMS software:

Enterprise Resource Planning (ERP) Systems: ERP systems integrate various business processes and functions such as finance, human resources, inventory management, and supply chain management. DBMS software is used to store and manage the data required for these processes, providing a centralized platform for information sharing and decision-making.

Customer Relationship Management (CRM) Systems: CRM systems help organizations manage interactions with customers and prospects, including sales, marketing, and customer support activities. DBMS software is used to store customer data, track interactions, and analyze customer behavior, enabling organizations to improve customer engagement and retention.

Healthcare Information Systems: Healthcare organizations use DBMS software to store and manage patient records, medical histories, diagnostic test results, and other healthcare-related data. This data is used for patient care, treatment planning, research, and regulatory compliance.

Online Transaction Processing (OLTP) Systems: OLTP systems handle large volumes of transactional data generated by online transactions such as e-commerce purchases, banking transactions, and airline reservations. DBMS software ensures the integrity and reliability of transactional data and supports high-speed data processing and concurrency control.

Data Warehousing and Business Intelligence (BI) Systems: Data warehousing and BI systems collect, store, and analyze large volumes of data from multiple sources to support decision-making and business analysis. DBMS software is used to store and manage the data warehouse, support complex queries, and provide tools for data analysis, reporting, and visualization.

Financial Services Systems: Banks, financial institutions, and insurance companies use DBMS software to store and manage financial data such as customer accounts, transactions, loans, and investments. This data is used for risk management, compliance reporting, fraud detection, and customer analytics.

Supply Chain Management Systems: Supply chain management systems track the flow of goods and materials from suppliers to manufacturers to distributors to retailers. DBMS software is used to store and manage inventory data, track shipments, optimize logistics, and coordinate supply chain activities.

Educational Systems: Educational institutions use DBMS software to store and manage student records, course schedules, grades, and academic resources. This data is used for student enrollment, course registration, academic advising, and institutional research.

Government Systems: Government agencies use DBMS software to store and manage a wide range of data, including tax records, census data, public health records, and law enforcement data. This data is used for policymaking, public services, law enforcement, and regulatory compliance.

Social Media and Content Management Systems: Social media platforms and content management systems use DBMS software to store and manage user profiles, posts, comments, and multimedia content. This data is used to personalize user experiences, target advertisements, and analyze user engagement.

3 INTRODUCTION TO RELATIONAL DATABASE MANAGEMENT SYSTEMS (RDBMS)

A Relational Database Management System (RDBMS) is a type of database management system that organizes data into tables, where each table consists of rows and columns. RDBMS software facilitates the creation, management, and manipulation of relational databases, which are structured collections of related data organized according to predefined relationships.

3.1 Key Concepts of RDBMS

Tables/Relations: In an RDBMS, data is stored in tables, also known as relations. Each table represents a specific entity or concept, such as customers, orders, products, or employees. Tables consist of rows (also known as tuples) and columns (also known as attributes), where each row represents a single record and each column represents a specific attribute or field of the record.

Keys: Keys are used to uniquely identify records within a table. The primary key is a unique identifier for each record in the table and ensures data integrity and uniqueness. Foreign keys establish relationships between tables by referencing the primary key of another table.

Relationships: RDBMS software supports relationships between tables, enabling data normalization and integrity. Common types of relationships include one-to-one, one-to-many, and many-to-many relationships. These relationships help reduce data redundancy and ensure data consistency across tables.

Structured Query Language (SQL): SQL is a standard programming language used to interact with relational databases. RDBMS software provides support for SQL commands and statements for querying, inserting, updating, and deleting data from tables. SQL also enables the creation and management of database objects such as tables, indexes, views, and stored procedures.

Data Integrity: RDBMS software enforces data integrity constraints to maintain the accuracy and consistency of data within the database. These constraints include primary key constraints, foreign key constraints, unique constraints, and check constraints, which prevent invalid data from being inserted or modified.

Transaction Management: RDBMS software supports transaction management to ensure the Atomicity, Consistency, Isolation, and Durability (ACID) properties of transactions. Transactions are units of work that consist of one or more database operations, such as insertions, updates, or deletions. RDBMS software ensures that transactions are processed reliably and safely, even in the event of system failures or interruptions.

3.2 Advantages of RDBMS

Data Integrity: RDBMS software enforces data integrity constraints to ensure the accuracy and consistency of data within the database.

Data Consistency: Relationships between tables help maintain data consistency and reduce data redundancy.

Data Security: RDBMS software provides robust security features to protect sensitive data from unauthorized access and breaches.

Query Flexibility: SQL provides a powerful and flexible language for querying and manipulating data in relational databases.

Scalability: RDBMS software is designed to scale effectively to handle growing volumes of data and increasing numbers of users.

Transaction Support: RDBMS software supports transaction management to ensure the ACID properties of transactions and maintain data integrity.

3.3 Examples of Relational Database Management Systems (RDBMS)

MySQL: MySQL is an open-source RDBMS known for its speed, reliability, and ease of use. It is widely used in web applications, content management systems, and e-commerce platforms.

Oracle Database: Oracle Database is a commercial RDBMS developed by Oracle Corporation. It is known for its scalability, security features, and comprehensive suite of tools. Oracle Database is commonly used in enterprise environments for mission-critical applications.

Microsoft SQL Server: Microsoft SQL Server is a commercial RDBMS developed by Microsoft. It is widely used in Windows-based environments and integrates closely with other Microsoft products and technologies. SQL Server is commonly used for enterprise applications, business intelligence, and data warehousing.

PostgreSQL: PostgreSQL is an open-source RDBMS known for its reliability, extensibility, and support for advanced features. It is commonly used in web applications, geographic information systems (GIS), and data analysis projects.

IBM Db2: IBM Db2 is a commercial RDBMS developed by IBM. It is known for its performance, scalability, and support for large-scale enterprise applications. Db2 is commonly used in industries such as banking, finance, and healthcare.

SQLite: SQLite is a lightweight, embedded RDBMS designed for simplicity and portability. It is commonly used in mobile applications, desktop applications, and embedded systems.

MariaDB: MariaDB is an open-source RDBMS derived from MySQL. It is designed to be a drop-in replacement for MySQL, offering improved performance, scalability, and features. MariaDB is commonly used in web hosting, cloud environments, and high-availability setups.

Amazon Aurora: Amazon Aurora is a cloud-based RDBMS offered by Amazon Web Services (AWS). It is compatible with MySQL and PostgreSQL, offering high performance, scalability, and reliability for cloud-based applications.

SAP HANA: SAP HANA is an in-memory RDBMS developed by SAP. It is optimized for real-time analytics, data processing, and transaction processing. SAP HANA is commonly used in enterprise resource planning (ERP), customer relationship management (CRM), and business intelligence (BI) applications.

Teradata: Teradata is a commercial RDBMS known for its scalability, parallel processing capabilities, and support for large-scale data warehousing and analytics. It is commonly used in industries such as retail, telecommunications, and finance for data analysis and decision support.

4 RELATIONAL DATA MODEL

The relational data model is a method of structuring data into tables (relations) consisting of rows and columns. Here's an example of a relational data model:

Consider a simple relational database for managing information about students and their courses. We can represent this data using three tables: Students, Courses, and Enrollments.

1. Students Table:

StudentID	Name	Age	Gender
1	John	20	Male
2	Emily	22	Female
3	Michael	21	Male

2. Courses Table:

CourseID	CourseName	Instructor	Credits
101	Math 101	Dr. Johnson	3
102	English 101	Prof. Smith	4
103	Science 101	Dr. White	3

3. Enrollments Table:

EnrollmentID	StudentID	CourseID	Grade
1	1	101	A
2	1	102	B+
3	2	101	A-
4	3	103	A

In this example:

• The Students table contains information about each student, including their unique StudentID, Name, Age, and Gender.

• The Courses table contains information about each course, including its unique CourseID, CourseName, Instructor, and Credits.

• The Enrollments table represents the many-to-many relationship between students and courses. It contains records of student enrollments in courses, including the unique EnrollmentID, StudentID (foreign key referencing Students table), CourseID (foreign key referencing Courses table), and Grade.

This relational data model allows us to represent complex relationships between entities (students and courses) using simple tables and establish connections between them using foreign keys. Queries can be performed across multiple tables to retrieve information, such as finding all courses a student is enrolled in or all students enrolled in a particular course.

4.1 Important terminologies used in relational data model

In the relational data model, several important terms describe the components and relationships within a database. Here are some of the key terms:

Entity: An entity is a distinct object or concept that exists independently and can be uniquely identified. In a relational database, entities are typically represented as tables, with each row in the table representing a single instance of the entity.

Attribute: An attribute is a characteristic or property of an entity. In a relational database table, attributes correspond to the columns, with each column representing a specific attribute of the entity.

Tuple: A tuple, also known as a row or record, is a single instance of an entity in a table. It consists of a set of attribute values that describe the characteristics of the entity.

Relation: A relation is a mathematical concept representing a set of tuples with the same attributes. In the context of relational databases, a relation corresponds to a table, where each row represents a tuple and each column represents an attribute.

Key: A key is an attribute or combination of attributes that uniquely identifies each tuple in a relation. There are different types of keys:

• **Primary Key:** A primary key is a unique identifier for each tuple in a table. It ensures that each row in the table is uniquely identifiable.

• **Foreign Key:** A foreign key is an attribute or combination of attributes in one table that refers to the primary key in another table. It establishes relationships between tables.

• **Candidate Key:** One or more attributes in a single table that have capacity to uniquely identify each record are known as candidate keys. Example- ID and SSN number in employee table.

• **Alternate Key:** The candidate key that has not been declared as primary key is called as alternate key. Example- If ID is declared as primary key, then SSN will be considered as alternate key.

• **Composite Primary Key:** When two or more attributes together in combination uniquely identify each record, they are known as composite primary key. Individual attribute of composite primary key may have duplicate values but not in combination.

Domain: A domain defines the set of allowable values for an attribute. It specifies the data type and any constraints or validation rules that apply to the attribute.

Normalization: Normalization is the process of organizing data in a database to reduce redundancy and dependency. It involves decomposing tables into smaller, more manageable structures and establishing relationships between them.

De normalization: De normalization is the opposite of normalization, involving the process of adding redundant data to tables to improve query performance. It is often used in data warehouses and analytical systems to optimize data retrieval.

Relational Algebra: Relational algebra is a set of mathematical operations used to manipulate and query relational data. Common operations include selection, projection, join, union, intersection, and difference.

Relational Calculus: Relational calculus is a non-procedural query language used to specify queries in terms of formal logic and set theory. It defines what data to retrieve rather than how to retrieve it.

Degree of Relation: Degree of relation is the count of number of columns in the relation/table.

Cardinality of Relation: Cardinality of relation is the count of number of rows in the relation/table.

Understanding these important terms is essential for designing, implementing, and querying relational databases effectively. They form the foundation of the relational data model and provide a common framework for representing and managing data in relational databases.

4.2 Important properties of relations (table)

In the context of the relational model in databases, a "relation" refers to a table containing rows and columns. The properties of relations define the characteristics and constraints that apply to the data stored within these tables. Here are the key properties of relations:

Uniqueness of Rows:

• Each row (tuple) in a relation is unique. There are no duplicate rows within the same relation.

Uniqueness of Columns:

• Each column (attribute) in a relation has a unique name. No two columns within the same relation can have the same name.

Atomic Values:

• Each cell (intersection of a row and column) in a relation contains a single, indivisible value. This ensures that the data is atomic and does not contain multiple values or data structures.

Fixed Number of Columns:

• The number of columns in a relation is fixed and predefined. Each row within the relation has the same structure, with the same set of attributes.

Fixed Domain of Values:

• Each attribute in a relation has a fixed domain of values, which defines the set of allowable values for that attribute. All values stored in the attribute must belong to this domain.

Ordering of Rows:

• The rows in a relation have no inherent order. The order in which rows appear in the relation is not significant and can change over time.

Ordering of Columns:

• The columns in a relation also have no inherent order. The order in which columns appear in the relation's schema (definition) is not significant.

Independence of Rows:

• Each row in a relation is independent of other rows. Changes to one row do not affect the values or properties of other rows within the same relation.

Independence of Columns:

• Each column in a relation is independent of other columns. Changes to one column do not affect the values or properties of other columns within the same relation.

Relationships between Rows:

• Relationships between rows in different relations are established using keys. Foreign keys in one relation refer to primary keys in another relation, establishing relationships between the data stored in those relations.

4.3 Keys in a table

In a database table, keys play a crucial role in uniquely identifying records and establishing relationships between tables. Here are the key types of keys commonly used in a database table:

Primary Key (PK):

• A primary key is a unique identifier for each record (row) in the table. It ensures that each row has a distinct identity within the table.

• The primary key constraint ensures that the values in the primary key column(s) are unique and not null.

• Only one primary key can be defined for a table.

• Example: EmployeeID in an Employees table.

Foreign Key (FK):

• A foreign key is a column or set of columns in a table that establishes a relationship between two tables.

• It refers to the primary key of another table, called the referenced table.

•The foreign key constraint ensures referential integrity, meaning that values in the foreign key column(s) must match values in the primary key column(s) of the referenced table, or be null.

• Example: DepartmentID in an Employees table, referencing the DepartmentID primary key in a Departments table.

Composite Key:

• A composite key consists of two or more columns that together uniquely identify records in a table.

• It is used when a single column cannot uniquely identify records, but a combination of columns can.

• The composite key constraint ensures that the combination of values in the key columns is unique.

• Example: (OrderID, ProductID) in an OrderDetails table.

Alternate Key:

• An alternate key is a candidate key that is not chosen as the primary key.

• While it is unique and can serve as a primary key, it is not designated as such for various reasons, such as preference for a different key or performance considerations.

• Example: EmailAddress in a Users table, where UserIDs are chosen as primary keys.

Super Key:

• A super key is a set of one or more columns that uniquely identifies each row in a table.

• It can contain more columns than necessary to uniquely identify rows, making it a superset of keys.

•Example: (EmployeeID, LastName) in an Employees table.

Candidate Key:

• A candidate key is a minimal super key, meaning it is a set of columns that uniquely identifies each row, and removing any column would make it lose that uniqueness property.

• From all the candidate keys, one is chosen as the primary key.

• Example: SSN (Social Security Number) in an Employees table.

Understanding and appropriately defining keys in a database table is essential for maintaining data integrity, establishing relationships between tables, and ensuring efficient data retrieval and manipulation.

Consider a table named "Employees" with the following attributes:

• EmployeeID (Primary Key)

• FirstName

• LastName

• Email

• DepartmentID (Foreign Key referencing Department table)

Primary Key (PK):

• Example: EmployeeID

• Each EmployeeID uniquely identifies a record (row) in the Employees table. It ensures that each employee has a distinct identity.

Foreign Key (FK):

• Example: DepartmentID

• The DepartmentID column establishes a relationship with another table, such as a Departments table. It refers to the primary key (DepartmentID) in the Departments table, linking employees to their respective departments.

Composite Key:

• Example: (FirstName, LastName)

• A combination of the FirstName and LastName columns can uniquely identify an employee. Together, they form a composite key ensuring that no two employees have the same first and last name combination.

Alternate Key:

• Example: Email

• While EmployeeID is chosen as the primary key, the Email column can also uniquely identify employees. It serves as an alternate key, offering an alternative unique identifier for employees.

Super Key:

• Example: (EmployeeID, Email)

• The combination of EmployeeID and Email together can uniquely identify each employee in the table. This constitutes a super key, as it contains more columns than necessary to uniquely identify rows.

Candidate Key:

• Example: EmployeeID, Email

• Both EmployeeID and Email can individually serve as candidate keys, as they can uniquely identify each employee. However, only one is chosen as the primary key, while the other remains a candidate key.

These examples illustrate how different types of keys function within a relational table, providing unique identification for records and facilitating relationships between tables in a database.

4.4 Referential Integrity

Referential integrity is a concept in relational databases that ensures the consistency and accuracy of data between related tables. It is enforced through the use of foreign key constraints, which maintain the integrity of relationships between tables by enforcing rules about the values that can be stored in certain columns. Here's an explanation of referential integrity with an example:

Consider two tables: "Employees" and "Departments".

Employees Table:

EmployeeID	FirstName	LastName	DepartmentID
1	John	Smith	101
2	Emily	Johnson	102
3	Michael	Brown	101

Departments Table:

DepartmentID	DepartmentName
101	HR
102	IT
103	Sales

In this example:

• The Employees table has a column named "DepartmentID" that references the DepartmentID column in the Departments table. This establishes a relationship between the two tables, where each employee is associated with a department.

• The DepartmentID column in the Employees table is a foreign key, while the DepartmentID column in the Departments table is the primary key.

To ensure referential integrity, the foreign key constraint is applied to the DepartmentID column in the Employees table. This constraint specifies that each value in the DepartmentID column of the Employees table must exist in the DepartmentID column of the Departments table. In other words, employees cannot be associated with non-existent departments.

Example of Referential Integrity in Action:

Suppose we attempt to insert a new record into the Employees table with a DepartmentID that does not exist in the Departments table:

INSERT INTO Employees (EmployeeID, FirstName, LastName, DepartmentID) VALUES (4, 'Sarah', 'Jones', 104);

Since the DepartmentID 104 does not exist in the Departments table, the foreign key constraint would be violated, and the database would raise a referential integrity error, preventing the insertion of the new record. This ensures that only valid department IDs can be assigned to employees, maintaining the integrity of the relationship between the two tables.

5 Structured Query Language (SQL)

Structured Query Language (SQL) is a specialized programming language designed for managing and manipulating relational databases. It is widely used in database management systems (DBMS) such as MySQL, PostgreSQL, SQLite, SQL Server, Oracle, and many others. SQL provides a standardized way of interacting with databases, allowing users to perform various operations such as querying, inserting, updating, and deleting data.

Here's a detailed explanation of some key aspects of SQL:

Data Definition Language (DDL):

• DDL statements are used to define, modify, and delete database objects such as tables, indexes, views, and schemas.

• Common DDL commands include CREATE, ALTER, DROP, and TRUNCATE.

Data Manipulation Language (DML):

• DML statements are used to manipulate data within database objects.

• Common DML commands include SELECT, INSERT, UPDATE, and DELETE.

Data Control Language (DCL):

• DCL statements are used to control access to data within the database.

• Common DCL commands include GRANT and REVOKE, which assign and revoke privileges respectively.

Data Query Language (DQL):

• DQL is a subset of SQL that specifically deals with querying data from databases.

• The primary DQL command is SELECT, which is used to retrieve data from one or more tables based on specified criteria.

Data Definition Statements:

• CREATE TABLE: Used to create a new table in the database.

• ALTER TABLE: Used to modify the structure of an existing table.

• DROP TABLE: Used to delete a table from the database.

• TRUNCATE TABLE: Used to delete all records from a table without removing the table structure.

Data Manipulation Statements:

• INSERT INTO: Used to add new records into a table.

• UPDATE: Used to modify existing records in a table.

• DELETE FROM: Used to remove records from a table.

• SELECT: Used to retrieve data from one or more tables. It can be combined with various clauses such as WHERE, GROUP BY, HAVING, ORDER BY, etc., to filter, group, and sort the results.

Constraints:

• Constraints are rules enforced on data columns to maintain the integrity and accuracy of the data.

• Common constraints include PRIMARY KEY, FOREIGN KEY, UNIQUE, NOT NULL, and CHECK.

Transactions:

• SQL supports transaction management, allowing multiple SQL statements to be grouped together into a single unit of work.

• Transactions ensure the atomicity, consistency, isolation, and durability (ACID properties) of database operations.

•Common transaction control commands include STARTTRANSACTION, COMMIT, ROLLBACK, and SAVEPOINT.

Joins:

• Joins are used to combine rows from two or more tables based on a related column between them.

• Common types of joins include INNER JOIN, LEFT JOIN, RIGHT JOIN, and FULL JOIN.

SQL is a powerful tool for managing and querying data in relational databases, and proficiency in SQL is essential for anyone working with databases or data-driven applications.

5.1 Characteristics of SQL

SQL, or Structured Query Language, possesses several characteristics that make it a widely used and effective tool for managing relational databases. Here are some of the key characteristics:

Declarative Language: SQL is a declarative language, meaning users specify what data they want to retrieve or manipulate rather than specifying how to do it. Users define the desired results, and the database management system (DBMS) determines the most efficient way to execute the query.

Standardization: SQL is an industry-standard language that is maintained and developed by various standards organizations such as ANSI (American National Standards Institute) and ISO (International Organization for Standardization). This standardization ensures consistency across different database platforms, making SQL portable and allowing users to transfer their skills between different database systems.

Comprehensive Data Manipulation: SQL provides a wide range of commands for manipulating data within relational databases. Users can perform tasks such as querying data (SELECT), inserting new records (INSERT INTO), updating existing records (UPDATE), and deleting records (DELETE FROM).

Data Definition Capabilities: SQL includes commands for defining the structure of a database, such as creating tables (CREATE TABLE), modifying table structure (ALTER TABLE), and dropping tables (DROP TABLE). These data definition language (DDL) commands allow users to define the schema of their database and specify constraints to enforce data integrity.

Transaction Control: SQL supports transactions, which are units of work consisting of one or more SQL statements that are executed together as a single logical operation. Users can start, commit, or rollback transactions to ensure data consistency and integrity, following the principles of ACID (Atomicity, Consistency, Isolation, Durability).

Data Integrity Enforcement: SQL allows users to define various constraints on database tables to enforce data integrity rules. Constraints such as primary keys, foreign keys, unique constraints, and check constraints help maintain the accuracy and consistency of data stored in the database.

Powerful Query Capabilities: SQL provides powerful querying capabilities, allowing users to retrieve data from one or more tables using complex criteria and conditions. SQL supports various clauses such as WHERE, GROUP BY, HAVING, ORDER BY, and JOIN operations, enabling users to filter, group, sort, and combine data to meet their specific requirements.

Client-Server Architecture: SQL operates on a client-server architecture, where client applications interact with a database server to send SQL queries and receive results. This architecture allows for centralized management of data, scalability, and concurrent access by multiple users.

Data Security: SQL provides features for implementing data security and access control mechanisms. Users can grant or revoke privileges to specific database objects, limiting access to sensitive data and ensuring that only authorized users can perform certain operations.

5.2 Advantages of SQL

SQL, or Structured Query Language, offers several advantages that make it a preferred choice for managing relational databases:

Ease of Use: SQL is a user-friendly language with a simple and intuitive syntax. Its declarative nature allows users to focus on what data they want to retrieve or manipulate rather than on how to perform the operations. This simplicity makes SQL accessible to both experienced database administrators and novice users.

Standardization: SQL is an industry-standard language governed by various standards organizations such as ANSI (American National Standards Institute) and ISO (International Organization for Standardization). This standardization ensures consistency across different database platforms, allowing users to transfer their skills and knowledge between different systems.

Scalability: SQL databases are highly scalable, allowing organizations to handle growing amounts of data efficiently. SQL databases can scale vertically by adding more resources (such as CPU and memory) to a single server or horizontally by distributing data across multiple servers in a clustered or distributed architecture.

Flexibility: SQL databases offer flexibility in terms of data modeling and schema design. Users can easily define relationships between tables, enforce data integrity constraints, and modify the database schema as requirements evolve. This flexibility enables organizations to adapt their databases to changing business needs without significant disruption.

Data Integrity: SQL databases enforce data integrity through various constraints such as primary keys, foreign keys, unique constraints, and check constraints. These constraints ensure the accuracy and consistency of data stored in the database, preventing data corruption and maintaining data quality over time.

Transaction Support: SQL databases support transactions, which are units of work consisting of one or more SQL statements that are executed together as a single logical operation. Transactions ensure the ACID properties (Atomicity, Consistency, Isolation and Durability), providing reliability and data consistency in multi-user environments.

Security: SQL databases offer robust security features to protect sensitive data from unauthorized access and malicious attacks. Users can implement access control mechanisms to grant or revoke privileges to specific database objects, ensuring that only authorized users can perform certain operations.

High Performance: SQL databases are optimized for performance, offering efficient storage, indexing, and retrieval of data. With features such as query optimization, caching, and indexing, SQL databases can handle complex queries and large datasets with low latency and high throughput.

Wide Range of Applications: SQL databases are widely used across various industries and applications, including e-commerce, finance, healthcare, telecommunications, and more. SQL's versatility and reliability make it suitable for a wide range of use cases, from small-scale applications to enterprise-level systems.

5.3 Limitations of SQL

While SQL offers numerous advantages for managing relational databases, it also has some disadvantages and limitations:

Complexity in Managing Large Datasets: SQL databases can face performance issues when handling large volumes of data. Queries may become slow and inefficient, especially if proper indexing and optimization techniques are not implemented. Managing and optimizing databases for scalability and performance can require advanced skills and expertise.

Lack of Support for Complex Data Types: SQL is primarily designed for managing structured data in a tabular format. While it supports basic data types such as integers, strings, and dates, it lacks native support for complex data types like JSON, XML, or arrays. Handling semi-structured or unstructured data can be challenging and may require additional processing or third-party tools.

Vendor Lock-In: Although SQL is a standardized language, different database vendors may implement their own proprietary extensions and optimizations. Switching between database platforms can be difficult and may require significant modifications to existing SQL code, leading to vendor lock-in and dependency on specific database technologies.

Limited Support for Real-Time Analytics: SQL databases are optimized for transactional workloads and may not perform well for real-time analytics or complex analytical queries. While SQL supports basic aggregation functions like SUM, AVG, and COUNT, performing advanced analytics or machine learning tasks may require integrating with specialized tools or platforms.

Concurrency and Scalability Challenges: SQL databases may face concurrency issues when multiple users or applications access the database simultaneously. Locking mechanisms are used to manage concurrent access to data, but they can lead to contention and performance bottlenecks, especially in high-traffic environments. Scaling SQL databases horizontally can also be challenging compared to NoSQL databases, which are designed for distributed architectures.

Cost of Licensing and Maintenance: Enterprise-grade SQL databases often come with licensing fees and ongoing maintenance costs. These costs can be significant, especially for large organizations with complex database requirements. Open-source alternatives like MySQL and PostgreSQL offer cost-effective solutions, but they may lack some features or support compared to commercial offerings.

Security Vulnerabilities: SQL databases are susceptible to various security threats, including SQL injection attacks, data breaches, and unauthorized access. Developers must follow best practices for secure coding and implement proper security measures such as encryption, authentication, and access controls to mitigate these risks. Failure to do so can expose sensitive data and compromise the integrity of the database.

Learning Curve for Complex Queries: While SQL is relatively easy to learn for basic queries, mastering complex SQL queries and optimization techniques can require considerable time and effort. Writing efficient queries that leverage indexes, joins, and aggregations effectively requires a deep understanding of database internals and query execution plans.

Limited Support for NoSQL Features: SQL databases are designed for relational data models and may not fully support NoSQL features such as schema flexibility, horizontal scaling, and eventual consistency. Organizations with evolving data requirements or complex data structures may find NoSQL databases like MongoDB or Cassandra more suitable for their needs.

5.4 Processing Capabilities of SQL

The processing capabilities of SQL, or Structured Query Language, primarily revolve around its ability to interact with relational databases efficiently. Here are some key processing capabilities of SQL:

Data Retrieval: SQL enables users to retrieve data from one or more tables in a database using the SELECT statement. Users can specify criteria, conditions, and sorting options to filter and sort the retrieved data. SQL also supports various aggregate functions such as SUM, AVG, COUNT, MIN, and MAX for performing calculations on grouped data.

Data Manipulation: SQL provides commands for manipulating data within a database. Users can insert new records into a table using the INSERT INTO statement, update existing records using the UPDATE statement, and delete records using the DELETE FROM statement. These data manipulation language (DML) commands allow users to modify the contents of a database according to their requirements.

Transaction Management: SQL supports transactions, which are units of work consisting of one or more SQL statements that are executed together as a single logical operation. Users can start a transaction using the BEGIN TRANSACTION statement, commit the transaction using the COMMIT statement to make the changes permanent, or rollback the transaction using the ROLLBACK statement to undo the changes.

Query Optimization: SQL databases employ query optimization techniques to improve the performance of SQL queries. The database management system (DBMS) analyzes SQL queries and generates an optimal execution plan to retrieve or manipulate data efficiently. Techniques such as index usage, join strategies, and query caching are employed to minimize query execution time and resource utilization.

Indexing: SQL databases use indexes to accelerate data retrieval operations, especially for frequently queried columns. Indexes are data structures that store a sorted copy of selected columns from a table, allowing the DBMS to quickly locate rows that match specific criteria. Users can create indexes using the CREATE INDEX statement and specify the columns to index to improve query performance.

Concurrency Control: SQL databases implement concurrency control mechanisms to manage concurrent access to data by multiple users or applications. Locking mechanisms such as row-level locks, table-level locks, and transaction isolation levels are used to ensure data consistency and prevent conflicts between concurrent transactions.

Stored Procedures and Functions: SQL allows users to define stored procedures and functions, which are precompiled SQL code blocks that can be executed repeatedly with different parameters. Stored procedures and functions improve code modularity, encapsulation, and reusability, reducing the need to duplicate SQL code across applications.

Error Handling: SQL provides mechanisms for error handling and exception management. Users can use try-catch blocks to handle errors gracefully and provide custom error messages or perform specific actions in case of exceptions. Error handling in SQL helps improve application robustness and reliability.

Analytical Capabilities: SQL supports analytical functions and window functions for performing advanced analytical and statistical calculations on data. Analytical functions such as RANK, DENSE_RANK, ROW_NUMBER, LEAD, and LAG allow users to perform ranking, windowing, and trend analysis on data partitions within a dataset.

5.5 Data Types used in SQL

SQL (Structured Query Language) supports various data types to define the type of data that can be stored in each column of a database table. These data types ensure data integrity, efficiency, and consistency. Here's an overview of some common SQL data types:

1. **Numeric Types:**

• INTEGER: A whole number without a decimal point. Example: INT, INTEGER.

• FLOAT: A floating-point number with decimal precision. Example: FLOAT, REAL, DOUBLE.

• DECIMAL: A fixed-point number with decimal precision. Example: DECIMAL (precision, scale), NUMERIC (precision, scale).

2. **Character String Types:**

• CHAR: Fixed-length character string. Example: CHAR (n).

• VARCHAR: Variable-length character string with a maximum length. Example:

VARCHAR (n).

• TEXT: Variable-length character string with no specified maximum length.

3. **Date and Time Types:**

• DATE: A date value in the format 'YYYY-MM-DD'.

• TIME: A time value in the format 'HH:MM:SS'.

• DATETIME: A combination of date and time values.

• TIMESTAMP: A date and time value representing a specific point in time, often used for recording the creation or modification of records.

4. Boolean Types:

• BOOLEAN: Represents true or false values.

5. Binary Types:

• BLOB (Binary Large Object): Stores large binary data like images, videos, etc.

• BYTEA: Similar to BLOB, used in PostgreSQL databases.

6. Other Types:

• ENUM: An enumeration type, allowing for a predefined list of values.

• ARRAY: Holds an array of values of the same data type.

• JSON: Stores JSON (JavaScript Object Notation) data.

7. Custom Types:

• Some databases allow defining custom data types to meet specific requirements.

Each database management system (DBMS) may have its own variations and additional data types beyond these standard ones. For instance, PostgreSQL provides several advanced data types like UUID, XML, JSONB, etc., while Oracle SQL may have CLOB for large text data.

It's important to choose appropriate data types based on the nature of the data being stored, considering factors like storage space, performance, and data integrity requirements.

5.6 Comparison between CHAR and VARCHAR data types

The main difference between CHAR and VARCHAR data types in SQL lies in how they store and handle character strings:

1. CHAR (Fixed-Length Character Strings):

•CHAR data type stores fixed-length character strings.

•It requires padding with spaces to reach the specified length if the actual data is shorter.

•The length is defined when creating the column and remains constant for all rows.

•It's useful when the data length is consistent, such as storing codes, identifiers, or fixed-length strings.

•CHAR is more efficient for columns that have a consistent length.

•Retrieval of CHAR data may be faster due to its fixed length.

Example:

CREATE TABLE Employees (

   EmployeeID CHAR(8),

   LastName VARCHAR(50),

   ...

     );

2. VARCHAR (Variable-Length Character Strings):

• VARCHAR data type stores variable-length character strings.

• It only consumes the necessary amount of storage space for the actual data length plus a small overhead.

• The length can vary for each row, depending on the length of the stored data.

• It's suitable for storing text data where the length varies significantly, such as names, addresses, or descriptions.

• VARCHAR is more flexible in terms of storage space and is generally preferred when the length of the data varies widely.

Example:

CREATE TABLE Customers (

   CustomerID INT,

   FirstName VARCHAR(50),

   LastName VARCHAR(50),

   Email VARCHAR(100),

   ...

      );

Usage Comparison:

• Use CHAR when the data length is fixed and known in advance, or when performance gains from fixed-length storage are desired.

• Use VARCHAR when the data length varies greatly or when storage efficiency is a concern, as it only uses the necessary amount of storage space.

5.7 Syntax for usage of various data types in SQL

CREATE TABLE Employees (

   EmployeeID INT,

   ...

      );

CREATE TABLE Products (

   Price FLOAT,

   ...

      );

CREATE TABLE Orders (

   TotalAmount DECIMAL(10, 2),

```
...

    );

CREATE TABLE Students (

  StudentID CHAR(8),

    ...

    );

CREATE TABLE Customers (

  FirstName VARCHAR(50),

    ...

    );

CREATE TABLE Comments (

  CommentText TEXT,

    ...

    );

CREATE TABLE Orders (

  OrderDate DATE,

    ...

    );

CREATE TABLE Appointments (

  StartTime TIME,

    ...

    );

CREATE TABLE Events (
```

```
EventDateTime TIMESTAMP,

...

    );

CREATE TABLE Permissions (

IsAdmin BOOLEAN,

...

    );

CREATE TABLE Images (

ImageData BLOB,

...

    );

CREATE TABLE DaysOfWeek (

Day ENUM('Monday', 'Tuesday', 'Wednesday', 'Thursday', 'Friday', 'Saturday',
'Sunday'),

...

    );

CREATE TABLE Scores (

TestScores INTEGER ARRAY,

...

    );

CREATE TABLE UserProfile (

UserData JSON,

...
```

```
);
```

5.8 NULL in SQL

In SQL, a NULL value represents the absence of a value in a column of a database table. It's not the same as a zero, an empty string, or a space. NULL indicates that the value for that particular column in a specific row is unknown, undefined, or not applicable. Understanding NULL values is crucial for database management and querying, as they can affect data retrieval and manipulation in various ways. Here are some key points about NULL values in SQL:

1. Meaning of NULL:

• NULL signifies the absence of a value or the lack of information for a particular attribute in a record.

• It does not represent "zero," "empty," or any other specific value.

2. Treatment of NULL:

• NULL values are treated differently than other values in SQL operations.

• Mathematical operations involving NULL typically yield NULL results.

• Comparison operations with NULL often result in unknown (or NULL) outcomes.

• Aggregate functions (such as COUNT, SUM, AVG) usually ignore NULL values unless explicitly specified otherwise.

3. Handling NULL Values:

• SQL provides functions like IS NULL and IS NOT NULL to check for NULL values in columns.

• COALESCE function can be used to replace NULL values with a specified default value.

• Use CASE statements to conditionally handle NULL values in queries.

4. Storage Considerations:

• NULL values generally do not consume any storage space beyond a single bit to indicate their presence.

• Columns allowing NULLs can store NULL values without requiring storage space for a default value.

5. Behavior in Indexes:

• Indexes usually do not include NULL values, although some database systems might allow indexing of NULLs.

• Queries using indexed columns might perform differently when NULLs are involved, depending on the database system and the query optimization strategy.

6. Joining Tables with NULL Values:

• When joining tables, NULL values might not match with non-NULL values unless explicitly handled in the query using appropriate join conditions.

7. Constraints and NULL:

• NULL values are generally allowed unless a column is explicitly defined as NOT NULL using constraints.

• NOT NULL constraints ensure that a column cannot contain NULL values, enforcing data integrity.

Understanding how NULL values behave and how they are handled is essential for writing accurate and efficient SQL queries and ensuring data integrity within a database.

5.9 Comments in SQL

In SQL, comments are non-executable pieces of text within SQL code that are ignored by the database engine during query execution. Comments are used to document the SQL code, providing explanations, descriptions, or reminders for developers and database administrators. They are useful for enhancing code readability, understanding, and maintenance. There are two common types of comments in SQL:

1. **Single-Line Comments:** Single-line comments start with two consecutive hyphens (--) and extend to the end of the line. Everything after -- on the same line is treated as a comment and ignored by the database engine.

Example:

-- This is a single-line comment

SELECT * FROM Employees; -- Retrieve all records from the Employees table

2. **Multi-Line Comments:** Multi-line comments can span across multiple lines and are enclosed between /* and */. All text between these delimiters, including line breaks, is treated as comments.

Example:

/*

This is a multi-line comment.

It can span across multiple lines.

*/

SELECT * FROM Orders;

Comments can be used for various purposes, including:

•Documenting the purpose and functionality of SQL statements.

•Providing explanations for complex queries or business logic.

•Temporarily disabling portions of SQL code during debugging or development.

•Adding reminders or to-do notes for future modifications or optimizations.

It's good practice to include comments regularly within SQL code to facilitate collaboration, troubleshooting, and maintenance. However, it's essential to avoid excessive or redundant comments that clutter the code unnecessarily. Well-placed comments that provide valuable insights into the logic and functionality of the SQL code can greatly enhance its readability and maintainability.

6 INTRODUCTION TO MySQL RDBMS

MySQL is one of the most popular and widely used open-source relational database management systems (RDBMS). It forms the backbone of many software applications, from simple websites to complex enterprise systems, due to its scalability, reliability, and ease of use. MySQL is primarily designed to handle large amounts of structured data efficiently, ensuring fast retrieval, storage, and manipulation of data. It supports the structured query language (SQL), which is the standard language used to interact with relational databases.

6.1 What is MySQL?

MySQL is a relational database management system that organizes data into tables, with rows and columns. It follows the relational model, where data is structured in a series of related tables, each identified by a unique key. This structure allows for efficient querying, updating, and managing large volumes of data.

As an RDBMS, MySQL provides the foundation for businesses and applications to store, retrieve, update, and manage data securely and efficiently. MySQL supports the ANSI SQL standard, ensuring compatibility across various platforms, tools, and applications.

6.2 Key Features of MySQL

Open Source: MySQL is free to use, making it accessible for a wide range of users, from individual developers to large organizations.

Cross-Platform Compatibility: MySQL runs on various operating systems, including Windows, Linux, macOS, and others, making it highly versatile.

Data Integrity: MySQL enforces data integrity through constraints like primary keys, foreign keys, and unique constraints, ensuring that data remains accurate and consistent.

ACID Compliance: MySQL supports ACID (Atomicity, Consistency, Isolation, and Durability) properties, which guarantee reliable and consistent transactions, making it suitable for critical applications like financial systems.

Scalability: MySQL supports both vertical (scaling up) and horizontal (scaling out) scaling, which is essential for applications that need to handle large amounts of data and concurrent users.

Replication and Clustering: MySQL offers replication (master-slave) and clustering (master-master) for high availability, fault tolerance, and load balancing.

Support for Stored Procedures and Triggers: MySQL allows developers to write complex queries, logic, and automation inside the database through stored procedures and triggers.

6.3 Basic Concepts in MySQL

Database: A container that holds tables, views, indexes, and other database objects. It is where data is stored and organized.

Table: The fundamental unit of data storage in MySQL, consisting of rows and columns. Each table has a specific structure that defines the types of data it can hold (e.g., integers, strings, dates).

Row: A single record in a table. Each row represents a unique entity, with values for each column defined in the table structure.

Column: A specific attribute or field in a table. Each column has a defined data type (e.g., integer, varchar, date).

Primary Key: A column or combination of columns that uniquely identifies a record in a table. Every table must have a primary key to ensure each record is distinct.

Foreign Key: A column or set of columns in one table that refers to the primary key in another table, establishing a relationship between the two tables.

Index: A data structure that speeds up data retrieval operations by allowing quick searches, sorting, and filtering based on column values.

6.4 SQL in MySQL

SQL (Structured Query Language) is the language used to interact with MySQL. It allows users to create, read, update, and delete data (commonly referred to as CRUD operations). Some of the key SQL operations in MySQL include:

CREATE DATABASE: Used to create a new database.

CREATE TABLE: Defines the structure of a table, including the columns and their data types.

INSERT INTO: Adds new rows of data to a table.

SELECT: Retrieves data from one or more tables.

UPDATE: Modifies existing data in a table.

DELETE: Removes data from a table.

ALTER TABLE: Alters the structure of a table (e.g., adding or removing columns).

DROP: Removes databases, tables, or indexes.

6.5 How MySQL Works

MySQL works by storing data in tables, which are logically grouped within databases. When an application needs to interact with data, it sends SQL queries to the MySQL server. The server processes the queries and interacts with the data stored in the databases.

The **Query Processor** translates SQL commands into internal MySQL commands.

The **Optimizer** selects the most efficient way to execute the queries.

The **Storage Engine** is responsible for physically storing and retrieving the data from disk. MySQL supports several storage engines, including InnoDB (the default), MyISAM, and MEMORY, each with its characteristics suited for different types of applications.

6.6 Popular Use Cases for MySQL

Web Applications: MySQL is a go-to choice for websites and web applications, often used in combination with technologies like PHP, Python, and Ruby on Rails.

Content Management Systems (CMS): Many popular CMS platforms like WordPress, Joomla, and Drupal use MySQL as their database backend.

E-Commerce: Online retail websites use MySQL for inventory management, order processing, and customer data management.

Data Warehousing: MySQL can be used to store large volumes of historical data for reporting and analytics, especially when coupled with tools like Apache Hadoop.

6.7 Advantages of Using MySQL

Cost-Effective: As an open-source platform, MySQL is free to use, offering significant cost savings, especially for startups and small businesses.

Strong Community Support: The MySQL community is vast, offering resources like documentation, forums, and tutorials. Additionally, Oracle (which owns MySQL) provides professional support for enterprises.

Performance and Efficiency: MySQL is designed for high performance, capable of handling millions of queries per second while maintaining data integrity and reliability.

Security Features: MySQL includes robust security features such as data encryption, SSL connections, and user privileges to control access to sensitive data.

6.8 MySQL Ecosystem

In addition to the core MySQL database, several tools and technologies complement and extend its capabilities:

MySQL Workbench: A graphical user interface (GUI) for database management, design, and administration.

MySQL Shell: A command-line interface for advanced users and developers, providing an interactive environment for running queries and managing the database.

MySQL Cluster: A distributed database solution for high availability, with data replication and automatic failover capabilities.

MySQL is an essential tool for developers and organizations that need an efficient, scalable, and reliable relational database system. Its open-source nature, robust feature set, and wide range of use cases make it a go-to choice for many applications. Understanding MySQL's key features, architecture, and SQL operations is the first step toward harnessing its full potential in building data-driven applications.

6.9 Architecture of MySQL

The architecture of MySQL is designed to provide a high-performance, scalable, and secure platform for managing relational data. It is built to handle complex database operations efficiently, making it suitable for applications ranging from small websites to large enterprise systems. Below is an in-depth explanation of MySQL's architecture, breaking it down into its key components.

MySQL Server Overview

MySQL's architecture is composed of several layers that work together to provide a seamless database management experience. At the core is the MySQL Server, which interacts with clients through a structured query language (SQL). The server is responsible for managing database operations such as query processing, transaction management, storage, and security.

The main components of the MySQL architecture are:

- **Client Layer**
- **MySQL Server Layer**
- **Storage Engine Layer**

Each of these layers performs a specific function that helps optimize MySQL's performance, scalability, and reliability.

Client Layer

The **client layer** is the topmost layer in the MySQL architecture, where users interact with the database. This layer includes applications, tools, and users that issue SQL queries to the MySQL server. Clients connect to MySQL through a variety of interfaces, including:

- **Command-Line Interface (CLI)**: MySQL's command-line client provides a simple interface for executing SQL queries.
- **Graphical User Interfaces (GUIs)**: Tools like MySQL Workbench, phpMyAdmin, or third-party applications provide more user-friendly ways to interact with the MySQL server.
- **Programming Languages**: Clients can connect to MySQL via programming languages like PHP, Python, Java, C++, and Ruby, using MySQL connectors or APIs.

Clients send SQL statements to the MySQL Server for processing, which are parsed and executed by the server.

MySQL Server Layer

The **MySQL Server Layer** is the heart of the MySQL architecture. It processes SQL queries, manages database transactions, and ensures the efficient execution of commands. The key components within this layer include:

a) Query Processor

The **Query Processor** is responsible for interpreting and optimizing SQL queries. It performs the following steps:

1. **Parser**: The SQL query is parsed to check for syntax errors. The query is converted into a parse tree, which is a hierarchical structure representing the SQL query's logical operations.
2. **Optimizer**: Once the query is parsed, the optimizer selects the most efficient execution plan. This process involves analyzing the available indexes, data distribution, and other factors to minimize query execution time.
3. **Query Cache**: If query caching is enabled, the MySQL server checks if the result of the query is already stored in the query cache. If found, the cached result is returned without executing the query again, enhancing performance.

51

b) Execution Engine

After the query is optimized, the **Execution Engine** carries out the actual operations, such as retrieving data, updating records, or deleting rows. It interacts directly with the Storage Engine to perform these operations.

The Execution Engine works alongside the **Transaction Manager** to ensure that queries are executed in a way that guarantees consistency and isolation, as per ACID (Atomicity, Consistency, Isolation, Durability) properties.

c) Transaction Management

MySQL uses transactions to group multiple operations into a single logical unit of work. The **Transaction Manager** is responsible for managing the lifecycle of transactions, including:

- **Commit**: Ensuring that all operations within a transaction are saved permanently to the database.
- **Rollback**: Undoing the changes made by a transaction if an error occurs or if the transaction is explicitly rolled back.
- **Locking**: Ensuring data consistency by locking rows or tables during transactions to prevent conflicts between concurrent operations.

Transactions in MySQL are typically handled by the InnoDB storage engine, which supports full ACID compliance.

d) Buffer Pool

The **Buffer Pool** is a memory area where MySQL caches frequently accessed data (such as table rows and indexes). This helps reduce disk I/O and improves query performance by reducing the need to read from disk repeatedly.

Storage Engine Layer

The **Storage Engine Layer** is the bottom-most layer in MySQL's architecture. It is responsible for how data is physically stored and retrieved from the disk. MySQL supports multiple storage engines, and each engine has its own features and performance characteristics. The most common storage engines are:

a) InnoDB

InnoDB is the default and most widely used storage engine in MySQL. It is known for its support for:

- **ACID Transactions**: InnoDB ensures data integrity by supporting transactions with full commit, rollback, and crash recovery capabilities.
- **Foreign Keys**: InnoDB supports referential integrity through foreign key constraints, ensuring that data relationships between tables are maintained.
- **Row-Level Locking**: InnoDB uses row-level locking, which enables better concurrency by allowing multiple transactions to update different rows of the same table without blocking each other.

b) MyISAM

MyISAM was the default storage engine before InnoDB. It is optimized for read-heavy workloads and supports:

- **Table-Level Locking**: MyISAM uses table-level locking, which can reduce performance in write-heavy applications due to contention.
- **Full-Text Indexing**: MyISAM supports full-text indexing, making it suitable for applications that require searching large text fields.
- **No Support for Transactions**: Unlike InnoDB, MyISAM does not support ACID transactions or foreign key constraints.

c) MEMORY (HEAP)

The **MEMORY** engine stores all data in memory (RAM), making it extremely fast for temporary tables or caching purposes. However, data is lost if the server crashes or shuts down, as it is not persistent.

d) NDB (Cluster)

The **NDB** storage engine is used in MySQL Cluster setups. It provides distributed, high-availability, and fault-tolerant storage. NDB ensures that data is replicated across multiple nodes, providing failover and load balancing capabilities.

Pluggable Storage Engines

One of MySQL's strengths is its support for pluggable storage engines, allowing users to choose the most appropriate engine based on their application's needs. When a client sends a query to the MySQL Server, the server interacts with the storage engine to handle the actual data operations. Each storage engine may implement its own method for indexing, locking, transactions, and crash recovery.

- **Storage Engine Interface**: The MySQL server communicates with the storage engine via a standard interface. This allows different engines to coexist within the same server.

Data Dictionary

The **Data Dictionary** is a system database that stores metadata about the database objects such as tables, columns, indexes, and constraints. The Data Dictionary is responsible for maintaining information about the structure of all databases and tables, as well as the relationships between them.

Replication and Clustering

MySQL supports replication and clustering features to ensure high availability, fault tolerance, and load balancing.

- **Replication**: In a typical replication setup, the MySQL server operates in a master-slave configuration where data written to the master server is replicated to one or more slave servers. This enables data redundancy and load balancing.
- **Clustering**: MySQL Cluster is a distributed database architecture that ensures data is automatically replicated across multiple nodes in the cluster. MySQL Cluster provides high availability and performance for large-scale, mission-critical applications.

The architecture of MySQL is built for efficiency, scalability, and reliability. By separating the system into distinct layers — the client layer, server layer, and storage engine layer — MySQL allows for flexible performance tuning and optimizations. Whether you are building small-scale applications or large enterprise systems, understanding MySQL's architecture helps you make informed decisions about design, optimization, and scaling. The ability to choose different storage engines and leverage replication and clustering makes MySQL a powerful solution for a wide range of database needs.

6.10 Why Choose MySQL for Learning Databases?

Choosing **MySQL** as a database management system (DBMS) for learning databases offers numerous benefits that make it an excellent choice for both beginners and more advanced learners. Here are several reasons why MySQL is ideal for studying database concepts:

Open Source and Free

MySQL is open-source software, meaning it is **free to download and use**, which makes it accessible for anyone who wants to learn without worrying about licensing costs. The open-source nature also provides access to the source code, allowing students to understand the internal workings of the database management system and customize it if needed.

Widely Used and Industry-Standard

MySQL is one of the most widely used relational database management systems in the world. It is employed by many organizations, from small startups to large enterprises. By learning MySQL, students acquire skills that are directly transferable to real-world applications. Understanding MySQL is often a requirement for various job roles, including database administrators, developers, and data analysts.

- **Popular in Web Development**: MySQL is frequently used in combination with programming languages such as PHP, Python, and JavaScript, especially in web development frameworks like LAMP (Linux, Apache, MySQL, PHP/Python/Perl).
- **Ecosystem**: Many widely used platforms and content management systems (CMS), such as WordPress, Joomla, and Drupal, rely on MySQL, which means learners can easily implement real-world database solutions.

Comprehensive Documentation and Community Support

MySQL has extensive documentation and a large, active community that can provide assistance, resources, and troubleshooting help. When learning, students can easily find answers to questions, explore tutorials, and discuss best practices through forums, blogs, and online communities. Some learning resources include:

- **Official Documentation**: MySQL's official website offers in-depth and detailed documentation on installation, configuration, SQL syntax, optimization, and advanced features.
- **Community Support**: Websites like Stack Overflow, MySQL forums, and other developer communities offer practical support when learning and debugging.
- **Tutorials and Courses**: There are numerous free and paid tutorials, courses, and video lectures available on platforms like YouTube, Udemy, and Coursera, making it easy for students to learn at their own pace.

Cross-Platform and Easy to Install

MySQL runs on all major operating systems, including Windows, macOS, and Linux, which makes it versatile for learners using different platforms. The installation process is relatively straightforward, and various tools like **MySQL Workbench** provide graphical interfaces for easier interaction with the database.

- **Environment Flexibility**: Students can easily install MySQL locally on their computer or use cloud-based platforms (such as AWS or Google Cloud) to practice.

Structured Query Language (SQL) Learning

SQL (Structured Query Language) is the standard language used to interact with relational databases, and **MySQL provides a clear, comprehensive platform for learning and mastering SQL**. Learning SQL through MySQL helps students:

- **Write Basic Queries**: Understand and execute basic SQL commands like SELECT, INSERT, UPDATE, DELETE, and WHERE.
- **Learn Advanced Concepts**: Dive into more advanced SQL topics like joins, Sub queries, transactions, indexing, and optimization.
- **Understand Database Design**: Gain practical knowledge in creating databases, tables, relationships, and constraints such as primary keys, foreign keys, and indexes.
- **Practice Data Manipulation**: MySQL allows learners to practice working with real data, learning how to structure, manipulate, and analyze data effectively.

Scalability and Flexibility

As learners progress from basic concepts to more complex applications, MySQL offers a level of **scalability** and **flexibility** that allows them to experiment with both small and large datasets.

- **Small to Large Applications**: MySQL can handle everything from simple, small-scale databases (e.g., for a class project) to large-scale enterprise-level applications.
- **NoSQL Features**: While primarily an RDBMS, MySQL supports features that allow for flexible data storage, such as JSON fields for semi-structured data, allowing students to experiment with hybrid database designs.

Support for Advanced Topics

MySQL is not just for beginners — it provides robust support for advanced database concepts. Once students are familiar with the basics, they can dive deeper into more complex topics, such as:

- **Normalization and Denormalization**: Learn how to design efficient database schemas by eliminating redundancy (normalization) or improving performance by combining tables (denormalization).
- **Transactions and ACID Compliance**: MySQL supports transaction management and adheres to ACID properties (Atomicity, Consistency, Isolation, Durability), providing an excellent foundation for learning about data consistency, recovery, and isolation levels.
- **Indexing and Optimization**: Students can explore query optimization by creating and using indexes to speed up data retrieval.
- **Replication and Backup**: Learn how to set up database replication for redundancy and high availability, which is essential for large-scale applications.

Real-Time Data and Practical Application

MySQL allows learners to work with **real-time data** and see the immediate results of their queries. By working with actual datasets, students get hands-on experience in database management, ensuring that theoretical concepts are tied to real-world applications. They can:

- Create and manage databases for different use cases like e-commerce, inventory management, customer relationship management (CRM), and more.

- Test and debug queries, improving their problem-solving skills in a practical context.

Support for Modern Web Development Practices

MySQL is deeply integrated into modern web development practices, especially in the context of the **LAMP stack** (Linux, Apache, MySQL, PHP/Python/Perl). This stack is a widely used combination for building dynamic websites and web applications. Learning MySQL gives students the foundation to build data-driven web applications and allows them to explore:

- **Integration with Web Frameworks**: MySQL works seamlessly with web frameworks like Laravel (PHP), Django (Python), Ruby on Rails (Ruby), and Express (Node.js), providing students with opportunities to develop full-stack applications.
- **Building REST APIs**: MySQL enables learners to create databases for backend systems that power REST APIs, which are commonly used in modern software architectures.

Security and User Management

MySQL has a robust security framework that allows students to learn about user access control, permissions, and database security best practices. Learners can practice creating user accounts, assigning roles, and managing access rights, which is essential for database administration.

- **Encryption**: MySQL supports data encryption, allowing learners to explore secure database practices.
- **Backup and Recovery**: MySQL offers tools for creating database backups, restoring data, and handling failures, which is crucial for learning data protection and disaster recovery.

MySQL is an ideal choice for learning databases due to its wide usage, open-source nature, comprehensive documentation, and scalability. It provides an excellent platform for mastering core database concepts such as SQL, database design, transactions, and optimization. Whether you're a beginner looking to understand relational databases or an advanced learner aiming to explore complex features, MySQL offers the resources and flexibility needed to build a strong foundation in database management.

7 INSTALLING AND SETTING UP MySQL

7.1 System Requirements for MySQL

System requirements for MySQL are essential to ensure that the database management system (DBMS) functions efficiently and securely. Here is a detailed breakdown of the system requirements for installing MySQL:

7.1.1 Hardware Requirements

Processor (CPU)

- MySQL requires a modern processor with a minimum of 1 GHz, but performance will be significantly better with multi-core processors, especially for large databases or heavy workloads.
- For production environments, 2 or more cores are recommended, as MySQL can take advantage of multi-core processors for better concurrency and faster query execution.

Memory (RAM)

- **Minimum:** 512 MB of RAM is the bare minimum for MySQL to run, but this will severely limit performance, especially with larger databases or multiple concurrent connections.
- **Recommended:** 2 GB or more of RAM is recommended for moderate to heavy use cases. The more RAM available, the better MySQL can cache data in memory, resulting in faster query performance and fewer disk I/O operations.
- For larger deployments, 4 GB or more may be necessary depending on the size of the database and traffic volume.

Disk Space

- **Minimum:** 1 GB of free disk space is required to install MySQL, but this doesn't account for the size of your actual databases, logs, and backups.
- **Recommended:** Depending on the size of your database and its growth over time, you should plan for much more disk space. A few hundred GB of space is typical for medium to large-scale databases.
  - o If using InnoDB (the default storage engine), disk space usage will depend on the size of your data, indexes, and transaction logs.

o   For backup purposes and logs (which are vital for recovery and auditing), additional disk space will be required.

Storage Type

- Solid State Drives (SSDs) are highly recommended for production MySQL deployments due to their faster read/write speeds, which can significantly improve performance compared to traditional Hard Disk Drives (HDDs).
- If SSDs are not available, ensure that your storage is fast enough to avoid I/O bottlenecks, especially with large databases.

7.1.2 Operating System Requirements

MySQL supports a variety of operating systems, including:

- **Linux:**
  - o   Distributions: MySQL works well with most major Linux distributions like Ubuntu, CentOS, Debian, Red Hat, Fedora, and others.
  - o   Recommended: 64-bit Linux distributions are typically preferred for better scalability and memory handling.
- **Windows:**
  - o   MySQL works with Windows versions 7, 8, 10, 11, and Windows Server 2012 and later.
  - o   On Windows, MySQL can be installed using a native Windows installer (MSI) or a ZIP archive.
- **macOS:**
  - o   MySQL works on macOS versions 10.15 (Catalina) and later, with native installers available for macOS.
- **Other Platforms:**
  - o   MySQL also supports Solaris, FreeBSD, and others, but these are less common for typical use cases.

7.1.3 Software Requirements

MySQL Version

The MySQL server version should be up-to-date to ensure compatibility with the latest features, security patches, and optimizations.

o **Recommended:** The latest stable version of MySQL (currently MySQL 8.0) is recommended for most users.
o Older versions like MySQL 5.7 are still supported but might not receive feature updates and security patches in the long term.

Web Server (If using with web applications)

If you're using MySQL as part of a web-based application (e.g., with PHP, Python, or Node.js), you'll need a compatible web server:

o Apache, Nginx, or IIS are common web servers that work well with MySQL.

Database Clients

MySQL also requires client software to interact with the database, such as:

o **MySQL Workbench** (a GUI tool for MySQL)
o **Command-line client** (a terminal-based interface)
o **Other third-party database management tools** (e.g., DBeaver, Navicat)

Libraries and Dependencies

MySQL requires certain libraries and dependencies to be installed for full functionality, such as:

o CMake or Make for compiling from source.
o SSL libraries (if using encrypted connections).
o Other libraries required for specific functionalities like replication, backups, or clustering.

7.1.4 Networking Requirements

TCP/IP Connection: MySQL typically communicates over TCP/IP, so ensure that the network is properly configured to allow access to the MySQL server from clients.

o Default port: 3306 (can be changed during setup if needed) o   If your MySQL server is intended to be accessed remotely, open the appropriate port in any firewall and configure MySQL to accept remote connections.

Hostname Resolution: MySQL depends on proper hostname resolution (either via /etc/hosts or DNS) for identifying clients or remote servers. It's important to have this configured correctly, especially for replication or clustering.

7.1.5 Security Requirements

Encryption: If data encryption is necessary (e.g., for sensitive data), make sure that SSL/TLS is configured properly. MySQL supports encrypted connections, ensuring that data transferred between the client and server is secure.

Backup and Recovery Tools: MySQL supports various backup strategies like:

o   Full backups (via mysqldump, mysqlbackup, or file-based methods).
o   Incremental backups and point-in-time recovery.
o   You should also consider having external backup solutions or replication systems in place for disaster recovery.

7.1.6 Other Considerations

Database Configuration: MySQL has several configuration parameters (e.g., buffer pool size, query cache, connection limits) that can be adjusted to optimize performance based on the hardware available and workload type.

o   The my.cnf or my.ini file is used for configuring various MySQL settings, such as memory buffers, connection limits, and storage engines.

Monitoring and Maintenance: Ongoing monitoring and maintenance tasks are critical to ensuring MySQL's optimal performance:

o   Use monitoring tools like **MySQL Enterprise Monitor, Prometheus**, or **Percona Monitoring and Management (PMM)**.

  o Regularly review slow queries, database indexes, and overall health metrics to identify performance bottlenecks.

By ensuring your system meets these hardware and software requirements, you'll set up a more robust MySQL database that can handle both current workloads and future growth efficiently.

7.2 Installing MySQL on Windows

Installing MySQL on Windows is a straightforward process, but it requires careful steps to ensure proper setup. Below is a detailed guide on how to install MySQL on a Windows operating system:

7.2.1 Prerequisites

- A Windows machine running Windows 7 or later (Windows 10, 11, or Server versions work best).
- Internet access to download MySQL installation packages.
- Administrative privileges on the computer.

7.2.2 Steps to Install MySQL on Windows

Step 1: Download MySQL Installer

1. **Visit the MySQL Website:**
   - o Go to the official MySQL website: https://dev.mysql.com/downloads/installer/
   - o MySQL provides two types of installers:
     - **MySQL Installer (Web Community):** A smaller file that downloads additional components during installation (recommended for most users).
     - **MySQL Installer (Community):** A larger file that includes all components for offline installation.
   - o Choose the version you prefer. The web installer is often sufficient, but the offline version is ideal if you want to install MySQL without an active internet connection.
2. **Download the Installer:**
   - o Click on the download link for the version you need (make sure you select **Windows** as the platform).
   - o After the download is complete, run the installer.

Step 2: Run the MySQL Installer

1. **Start the Installer:**
    o   Double-click the downloaded installer to run it.
    o   If prompted by Windows User Account Control (UAC), click **Yes** to allow the installer to make changes to your system.
2. **Choose Setup Type:** The installer provides several options for setting up MySQL. You'll need to choose one based on your needs:
    o   **Developer Default:** Installs MySQL Server, MySQL Workbench, MySQL Shell, and other development tools.
    o   **Server Only:** Installs only the MySQL server.
    o   **Client Only:** Installs MySQL client programs like MySQL Workbench and MySQL Command Line Client.
    o   **Full:** Installs all available MySQL components.
    o   **Custom:** Allows you to select specific components to install (useful if you want to install only certain parts of MySQL).
    o   Choose **Developer Default** (for most users) or **Custom** (if you have specific needs), then click **Next**.

Step 3: Install MySQL

1. **Check Dependencies:**
    o   The installer will check if required software dependencies are installed on your system (such as Visual C++ Redistributable packages).
    o   If any dependencies are missing, the installer will prompt you to install them. Follow the on-screen instructions to install any missing components and click **Next**.
2. **Select Features:**
    o   If you selected **Custom** during the previous step, you can choose which components you want to install, such as:
        ▪   **MySQL Server**
        ▪   **MySQL Workbench** (a GUI tool for managing your MySQL databases)
        ▪   **MySQL Shell** (an advanced command-line client)
        ▪   **MySQL Router** (for MySQL clustering and high availability)
        ▪   **MySQL Samples and Examples** (optional examples for learning)
        ▪   **MySQL Connector** for Python, Java, etc. (if you plan to use MySQL with programming languages)
    o   After selecting your desired components, click **Next**.

3. **Install:**
   o The installer will begin downloading and installing MySQL. This process may take several minutes, depending on your internet speed and the selected features.
   o Once completed, click **Next**.

Step 4: Configure MySQL Server

1. **Choose Configuration Type:**
   o The installer will prompt you to choose a MySQL configuration. The options are:
      ▪ **Development Computer:** The default option, optimized for a development environment.
      ▪ **Server Computer:** For a production server.
      ▪ **Dedicated MySQL Server Machine:** For systems with dedicated resources to MySQL.
   o Select **Development Computer** for most users and click **Next**.
2. **Configure MySQL Server:**
   o **Root Password:** The installer will ask you to set the **root password** (administrator password for MySQL). Enter a strong password that you will remember, as you will need it to log in to the MySQL server.
      ▪ Optionally, you can also enable **Validate Password Plugin** to enforce stronger passwords for MySQL users.
   o **Create an Account:** Optionally, you can create additional MySQL user accounts (e.g., for remote connections).
   o **Windows Service:** The installer will set up MySQL as a Windows service. Ensure that "Start MySQL Server at System Startup" is checked, so MySQL will automatically start when Windows boots.
      ▪ You can also choose to run MySQL as a **Standard System Account** or a **Local System Account**.
   o After configuring these options, click **Next**.
3. **Apply Configuration:**
   o The installer will now apply the configuration settings and initialize MySQL. It may take a few moments for the configuration to complete.
4. **Complete the Configuration:**

o Once MySQL has been configured, you will see a summary of your settings. Click **Finish** to complete the installation process.

Step 5: Start MySQL Server

1. **Start MySQL Server:**
   o If the installer hasn't already started MySQL automatically, you can start it manually:
      - Open the **Services** application in Windows (search for "Services" in the Start menu).
      - Find **MySQL** in the list of services, right-click it, and select **Start**.
2. **Test the MySQL Installation:**
   o To test the installation, open **Command Prompt** and type the following command:

   mysql -u root -p

   o Enter the root password you set earlier when prompted.
   o If successful, you'll see the MySQL command-line interface, and you can start executing MySQL queries.

Step 6: Install MySQL Workbench (Optional)

1. **Launch MySQL Workbench:**
   o If you installed MySQL Workbench during the setup process, you can now use it for managing your databases through a graphical user interface (GUI).
   o Launch **MySQL Workbench** from the Start menu and connect to your MySQL server by entering:
      - **Hostname:** localhost (or the IP address of the server if it's remote)
      - **Port:** 3306 (default MySQL port)
      - **Username:** root (unless you created other users)
      - **Password:** the root password you set earlier.
   o Click **Test Connection** to verify that MySQL Workbench can successfully connect to your MySQL server.

Step 7: Finalizing the Installation

Firewall Configuration (If necessary): If you plan to connect to MySQL from other computers on a network, you may need to allow the MySQL port (default is 3306) through the Windows firewall.

Backup Configuration: Consider configuring backup routines using mysqldump, MySQL Workbench, or another backup tool for your data.

MySQL Server Monitoring: Use MySQL Workbench or another monitoring tool to regularly check the health and performance of your server.

Troubleshooting Tips

- **Installation Errors:** If the installation fails, check for any errors in the installer log and verify that your system meets all the prerequisites (e.g., necessary software versions, system resources).
- **Access Issues:** If MySQL Workbench or the command-line client cannot connect to the server, verify that the MySQL service is running and that the firewall isn't blocking connections.
- **MySQL Errors:** If you encounter issues with specific MySQL commands or settings, refer to the MySQL error logs (located in the data directory of MySQL's installation folder).

By following these steps, MySQL should be successfully installed and configured on your Windows machine, allowing you to start using it for development or production environments.

7.3 Installing MySQL on Mac

Installing MySQL on macOS is a relatively simple process, and there are multiple ways to do it depending on your preference and needs. Here's a step-by-step guide to installing MySQL on macOS, covering both the official package and Homebrew installation methods.

7.3.1 Prerequisites

- A macOS machine (preferably macOS 10.15 or later).
- Administrative privileges (you must be able to install software on the system).
- Internet access to download MySQL.

The official MySQL macOS package is provided as a disk image file (DMG), which contains the installer.

Step 1: Download MySQL for macOS

1. **Visit the MySQL website:**
   o Open your web browser and go to the MySQL download page: https://dev.mysql.com/downloads/mysql/.
2. **Download the macOS DMG file:**
   o Under **"MySQL Community Server"**, select **macOS** as the operating system.
   o You will be prompted to select the version of MySQL you want to install. Choose the latest version (recommended).
   o Click **Download** to download the .dmg package.
3. **Login or Sign up (optional):**
   o You can sign up for a free Oracle account, but you can also skip this step and click **No thanks, just start my download**.

Step 2: Install MySQL from the DMG Package

1. **Open the DMG file:**
   o Once the download is complete, open the .dmg file. This will mount the disk image and display its contents.
2. **Start the installation:**
   o Inside the disk image, you will see an installer package named something like **mysql-<version>-macos10.x-x86_64.dmg**. Double-click this to start the MySQL installer.
3. **Follow the installation steps:**
   o The installer will guide you through the installation process. Click **Continue** on each screen, and accept the license agreement.
   o When prompted, choose the installation location (the default location is usually fine) and click **Install**.
4. **Authenticate the installation:**
   o You may be asked to enter your macOS administrator password to authorize the installation.
5. **Complete the installation:**
   o The installer will now install MySQL and its components, including MySQL Server, MySQL Workbench (if selected), and the MySQL preference pane (for system settings).
   o Once the installation finishes, click **Close**.

Step 3: Start MySQL Server

1. **System Preferences:**
   - Go to **System Preferences** on your Mac (via the Apple menu).
   - You should now see a new **MySQL** icon in the System Preferences window.
2. **Start MySQL:**
   - Click on the **MySQL** icon, and in the MySQL preferences pane, click **Start MySQL Server**.
   - This will start the MySQL server in the background.

Step 4: Set the MySQL Root Password

1. **Configure root password:**
   - Once MySQL is installed, it is highly recommended that you set a root password for MySQL.
   - Open **Terminal** (you can find it in Applications > Utilities).
   - Type the following command to set the root password (replace your_password with a password of your choice):

   sudo /usr/local/mysql/bin/mysql_secure_installation

   - This will prompt you to enter a root password. It will ask if you want to configure other security settings like removing the test database or disallowing root login remotely. You can choose the options that best fit your needs.

Step 5: Test the MySQL Installation

1. **Open Terminal:**
   - Type the following command to log into MySQL:

   /usr/local/mysql/bin/mysql -u root -p

   - Enter the root password you set during the mysql_secure_installation process.
   - You should now see the MySQL command-line interface, and you can start running SQL queries.
2. **Exit MySQL:**
   - To exit MySQL, type:

   exit

Step 6: Optional MySQL Workbench Installation

If you opted to install **MySQL Workbench** during the installation process, you can open it from your **Applications** folder and use it to manage MySQL visually.

If you didn't install it or want to install it separately, you can download MySQL Workbench from the MySQL website and follow the installation process for the GUI tool.

7.3.3 Method 2: Installing MySQL Using Homebrew (Alternative)

If you prefer using the command line and a package manager, **Homebrew** is an excellent alternative for installing MySQL. Homebrew is a popular package manager for macOS, and it makes installing MySQL easy.

Step 1: Install Homebrew (If Not Already Installed)

1. **Install Homebrew:**
   o Open **Terminal** and run the following command to install Homebrew if you don't have it already:

/bin/ -c "$(curl -fsSL https://raw.githubusercontent.com/Homebrew/install/HEAD/install.sh)"

This will install Homebrew. Follow the instructions in the Terminal to complete the installation.

Step 2: Install MySQL Using Homebrew

1. **Install MySQL:**
   o Once Homebrew is installed, you can easily install MySQL by running the following command in Terminal:

   brew install mysql

2. **Start MySQL Service:**
   o. Once MySQL is installed, you can start the MySQL server by running:

   brew services start mysql

Step 3: Set the MySQL Root Password

1. **Run the secure installation script:**
    o   Similar to the method above, you should set the root password and secure your MySQL installation. Run:

    mysql_secure_installation

    o   Follow the prompts to configure your MySQL installation.

Step 4: Test MySQL Installation

1. **Login to MySQL:**
    o   After completing the secure installation process, you can log into MySQL using the following command:

    mysql -u root -p

    o   Enter the password you set for the root user, and you should be able to access the MySQL prompt.

Step 5: Stop MySQL (When Finished)

1. **Stop MySQL Service:**
    o   If you need to stop the MySQL service, run the following command:

    brew services stop mysql

7.3.4 Managing MySQL on macOS

After installation, you can manage MySQL using several methods:

*   **Starting and Stopping MySQL:** If you need to start or stop MySQL manually, you can do so by using brew services start mysql and brew services stop mysql (Homebrew method) or by using the **MySQL** preferences pane in **System Preferences** (official package method).
*   **Auto-starting MySQL:** To have MySQL start automatically when your system boots up (recommended for production use), use:

    brew services start mysql

By following the steps outlined in this guide, you should now have MySQL installed and running on your macOS system. Whether you use the official DMG package or Homebrew depends on your personal preference. The official package is an easy option with a GUI for managing MySQL, while Homebrew offers a command-line method favored by developers. Either way, MySQL is now ready for use on your Mac for development, testing, or even production applications.

7.4 Installing MySQL on Linux

To install MySQL on a Linux system, the steps can vary slightly depending on the distribution (e.g., Ubuntu, CentOS, Fedora, etc.). Below, I'll cover a detailed guide for installing MySQL on a few common Linux distributions, particularly focusing on the most popular ones: Ubuntu (and other Debian-based distros) and CentOS (and other RHEL-based distros).

7.4.1 Installing MySQL on Ubuntu (Debian-based systems)

Update Your Package Index Start by updating the list of available packages:

sudo apt update

Install MySQL Server Next, install MySQL from the official Ubuntu repositories:

sudo apt install mysql-server

This will install the MySQL server, client, and other essential packages.

Check MySQL Installation After the installation, the MySQL service should start automatically. You can confirm this by checking its status:

sudo systemctl status mysql

The output should indicate that MySQL is active (running).

Run the MySQL Secure Installation Script It's a good practice to run the mysql_secure_installation script to configure MySQL's security settings (such as setting the root password and removing insecure default settings):

sudo mysql_secure_installation

This will prompt you to:

o Set the root password (if not already done).

o Remove insecure default settings like anonymous users, remote root login, and the test database.

o Reload privilege tables to apply changes.

Log into MySQL You can now log into the MySQL server using the mysql command:

sudo mysql -u root -p

After entering the root password, you should have access to the MySQL command-line interface.

Allow Remote Connections (Optional) If you want to allow MySQL to be accessed from other machines, you need to edit the MySQL configuration file and allow connections from remote IPs:

     o   Open the MySQL configuration file:

        sudo nano /etc/mysql/mysql.conf.d/mysqld.cnf

     o   Find the line starting with bind-address and change it from 127.0.0.1 (localhost) to 0.0.0.0 or the specific IP address you want to allow remote access from.

        bind-address = 0.0.0.0

     o   Restart MySQL for changes to take effect:

        sudo systemctl restart mysql

Check MySQL Version To verify your MySQL installation and check its version:

mysql --version

7.5 Installing MySQL on CentOS (RHEL-based systems)

Update Your System Start by ensuring your system is up-to-date:

sudo yum update

Install MySQL Repository MySQL is not included in the default CentOS repositories, so you need to install the MySQL repository package. For MySQL 8.0, use:

sudo yum localinstall https://dev.mysql.com/get/mysql80-community-release-el7-3.noarch.rpm

Install MySQL Server After adding the repository, install MySQL:

sudo yum install mysql-server

Start MySQL Service Once the installation is complete, start the MySQL service:

sudo systemctl start mysqld

Check MySQL Status To confirm that MySQL is running:

sudo systemctl status mysqld

Find the Temporary Root Password During installation, MySQL generates a temporary root password. You can find it by checking the MySQL log file:

sudo grep 'temporary password' /var/log/mysqld.log

The output will show the temporary password.

Run the MySQL Secure Installation Script Run the mysql_secure_installation script to set up a root password and improve security:

sudo mysql_secure_installation

This will ask you to:

- o   Set a new root password (use the temporary password from the log file if prompted).
- o   Remove insecure default settings like anonymous users, remote root login, and the test database.
- o   Reload privilege tables.

Log into MySQL Log into MySQL using the new root password:

mysql -u root -p

Enable MySQL to Start on Boot To make sure MySQL starts automatically after a reboot:

sudo systemctl enable mysqld

Allow Remote Connections (Optional) If you need to allow remote access, follow similar steps as for Ubuntu:

Edit the MySQL configuration file:

sudo nano /etc/my.cnf

Find the bind-address directive and change it to 0.0.0.0 or the IP address of the server.

Restart MySQL:

sudo systemctl restart mysqld

7.6 Verifying Installation

Once MySQL is installed and running, here are a few things to verify:

- •   **Check MySQL service status** (for both Ubuntu and CentOS):

  sudo systemctl status mysql   # On Ubuntu
  sudo systemctl status mysqld   # On CentOS

- •   **Check MySQL version:**

  mysql --version

- **Check MySQL running processes:**

ps aux | grep mysqld

- **Log into MySQL:**

mysql -u root -p

7.7 Post-Installation Configuration

Configure Firewall (if applicable): If you are using a firewall, you may need to open port 3306 for MySQL. On Ubuntu with ufw:

sudo ufw allow 3306

On CentOS, use firewalld:

sudo firewall-cmd --permanent --zone=public --add-port=3306/tcp
sudo firewall-cmd --reload

Create MySQL Users and Databases: After installation, you can create new MySQL users and databases:

```
CREATE DATABASE my_database;
CREATE USER 'my_user'@'localhost' IDENTIFIED BY 'my_password';
GRANT ALL PRIVILEGES ON my_database.* TO 'my_user'@'localhost';
FLUSH PRIVILEGES;
```

By following these steps, you should have a fully functional MySQL installation on your Linux system

7.8 MySQL Workbench Overview

MySQL Workbench is a powerful, integrated development environment (IDE) used to manage and interact with MySQL databases. It is a unified visual tool that streamlines a variety of database management tasks, including database design, query building, server configuration, and data modeling. MySQL Workbench is available for Windows, macOS, and Linux and is widely used by database administrators (DBAs), developers, and data analysts. Below is a detailed explanation of its core features and functionality.

User Interface

The MySQL Workbench UI is divided into several key sections to help manage databases efficiently:

- **Navigator Pane**: Located on the left, this pane allows you to navigate between various objects and schemas in the connected database. It lists all your connections, schemas (databases), tables, views, stored procedures, and more.
- **SQL Editor**: This is where you can write and execute SQL queries. It features syntax highlighting, autocompletion, and error checking, making it easier to write complex SQL queries.
- **Result Grid**: When a query is executed, the results are shown in a grid format. You can view tables, data, and perform basic operations like sorting and filtering.
- **Action/Toolbar**: At the top of the interface, you'll find quick access to common functions like opening a new SQL file, running queries, refreshing the database, and more.

Database Management

MySQL Workbench provides several tools to manage and interact with databases:

- **Connection Management**: You can create and manage multiple connections to different MySQL servers. Each connection can store details like the hostname, port, user credentials, and SSL settings. This allows you to connect to local or remote MySQL servers without manually entering credentials every time.
- **Schema/Database Navigation**: After establishing a connection, the "Navigator" panel displays a list of schemas (databases) and their objects (tables, views, etc.). You can browse, create, delete, or modify schemas and objects.
- **SQL Query Execution**: The SQL editor allows you to run ad-hoc queries to manipulate data, create, alter, and delete database objects. The SQL Workbench offers real-time error checking and syntax highlighting for better code quality.

Visual Database Design

MySQL Workbench has an excellent tool for visual database design known as the **Modeling** tool:

- **EER Diagrams**: Workbench lets you create Enhanced Entity-Relationship (EER) diagrams. These diagrams provide a visual representation of your database schema, showing how tables relate to each other using foreign keys and indexes. You can generate these diagrams from an existing database or create them from scratch.
- **Forward and Reverse Engineering**: Workbench supports both forward and reverse engineering. Forward engineering involves creating SQL scripts based on the visual model, while reverse engineering allows you to generate a model from an existing database schema.

Data Import and Export

MySQL Workbench supports both importing and exporting data from various formats:

- **Data Import**: You can import data from CSV, TSV, and SQL dump files into your tables. The "Data Import/Restore" option allows you to upload large datasets directly into your MySQL database. It also supports importing data from other MySQL databases or even other database types (e.g., PostgreSQL, SQLite).
- **Data Export**: Workbench allows you to export databases, tables, or query results into various formats such as SQL, CSV, or JSON. This is useful for backup purposes or migrating data between different servers.

Server Administration and Configuration

MySQL Workbench has built-in tools for server administration:

- **User and Privilege Management**: You can manage MySQL server users and define their privileges (GRANT, REVOKE). This allows you to control access to your database and enforce security policies.
- **Server Status Monitoring**: Workbench provides a dashboard to monitor the server's health, including metrics like CPU usage, memory, disk I/O, and query performance.
- **Backup and Restore**: You can back up your MySQL server using Workbench's backup tools. The "Data Export" and "Data Import/Restore" features can be used to schedule regular backups or restore backups to new instances.
- **Configuration Management**: You can view and modify server configuration settings, such as buffer sizes, log locations, and more,

via the Workbench interface. These settings can help optimize performance.

Stored Procedures and Triggers

MySQL Workbench allows you to create and manage stored procedures, functions, and triggers:

- **Stored Procedures**: These are precompiled SQL statements that can be executed multiple times, which can encapsulate complex logic or repetitive tasks. Workbench provides an interface to write, edit, and execute stored procedures.
- **Triggers**: Triggers are SQL statements that are automatically executed in response to certain events (INSERT, UPDATE, DELETE) on a table. MySQL Workbench lets you create, modify, and delete triggers.

Performance Tuning and Query Optimization

MySQL Workbench has features that help improve query performance and optimize databases:

- **Query Profiler**: You can profile your queries to understand their execution plans and see if indexes are being used efficiently. This tool helps identify performance bottlenecks and provides suggestions for optimization.
- **Explain Plan**: The "EXPLAIN" feature allows you to analyze how MySQL executes a query. By understanding the query execution plan, you can improve indexing strategies and optimize queries for better performance.

Advanced Features

In addition to the basic functionalities, MySQL Workbench includes some advanced tools:

- **Version Control Integration**: Workbench supports integration with version control systems like Git, so you can manage your SQL scripts and database models with versioning.
- **MySQL Query Profiler**: This tool helps identify slow-running queries and provides insights into their performance.

- **Database Migration**: The database migration tool helps transfer data from other relational databases (e.g., SQL Server, PostgreSQL) to MySQL.

Cross-Platform Support

MySQL Workbench is cross-platform, meaning it works on Windows, macOS, and Linux. This allows users to work with MySQL databases regardless of their operating system, and it's often used in development environments where multiple developers might be working on different platforms.

Security Features

Security is a major consideration for MySQL Workbench. It includes features to help with:

- **SSL Connections**: MySQL Workbench supports Secure Sockets Layer (SSL) connections, which encrypt data as it travels between the client and the server, providing enhanced security.
- **Authentication Plugins**: You can configure various authentication plugins (e.g., SHA-256, PAM) for more secure logins.
- **Access Control**: The built-in user and privilege management tools ensure that only authorized users can access specific databases and perform certain operations.

Plugins and Extensions

MySQL Workbench supports a variety of plugins that extend its functionality. Some plugins include options for backup automation, enhanced performance analytics, and additional data connectors.

MySQL Workbench is an all-in-one tool that simplifies database administration, development, and design. It supports everything from basic query execution to advanced server management, offering a streamlined, integrated environment for MySQL developers and DBAs. Whether you're managing a small project or a large production environment, MySQL Workbench provides the necessary features to ensure efficient and secure database operations.

7.9 Configuring MySQL Server

Configuring a MySQL server involves setting up various parameters and options to ensure the server operates optimally, securely, and efficiently based on your environment and use case. Whether you're configuring MySQL for development, testing, or production, the configuration process covers a wide range of tasks, from basic installation to fine-tuning server settings. Below is a comprehensive explanation of how to configure a MySQL server, including key aspects like system requirements, installation, configuration files, and tuning.

Installing MySQL Server

Before configuring the MySQL server, you must first install it on your system. MySQL is available on various platforms, including Linux, macOS, and Windows. Here's a basic overview of the installation process:

On Linux (Ubuntu/Debian example):

sudo apt update
sudo apt install mysql-server
sudo systemctl start mysql
sudo systemctl enable mysql

On Windows:

1. Download the MySQL installer from the official MySQL website.
2. Run the installer and follow the steps to install MySQL Server, MySQL Workbench, and other optional tools.
3. Set the root password and configure the server.

On macOS (using Homebrew):

brew install mysql
brew services start mysql

Once the MySQL server is installed, you can start configuring it.

MySQL Configuration Files

MySQL's configuration is controlled primarily through a file called my.cnf or my.ini (depending on the operating system). This configuration file contains various options that dictate how the MySQL server operates. It is usually located in one of these places:

- **Linux/Unix**: /etc/my.cnf, /etc/mysql/my.cnf, or /etc/mysql/mysql.conf.d/mysqld.cnf
- **Windows**: C:\Program Files\MySQL\MySQL Server 8.0\my.ini or C:\ProgramData\MySQL\MySQL Server 8.0\my.ini
- **macOS**: /usr/local/etc/my.cnf

You can configure the MySQL server by editing these files. Typically, you need to modify sections like [mysqld] (for the server daemon) and [client] (for the MySQL client).

Example my.cnf Configuration Section:

```
user = mysql
pid-file = /var/run/mysqld/mysqld.pid
socket = /var/run/mysqld/mysqld.sock
port = 3306
bind-address = 0.0.0.0
max_connections = 200
key_buffer_size = 256M
innodb_buffer_pool_size = 1G
innodb_log_file_size = 256M

[client]
port = 3306
socket = /var/run/mysqld/mysqld.sock
```

Basic Server Configuration

A. Network Configuration

- **Port**: The port option specifies the TCP/IP port that MySQL listens on. By default, it is set to 3306. If you need to run multiple MySQL instances on the same machine, you can change this port.

  ```
  port = 3306
  ```

- **Bind Address**: The bind-address option specifies which IP addresses the server listens to for incoming connections. The default is 127.0.0.1 (localhost), which restricts access to the local machine. For remote connections, you can use 0.0.0.0 (all available network interfaces) or a specific IP address.

bind-address = 0.0.0.0 # Allows connections from any IP

B. Memory and Buffer Settings

These settings influence how MySQL uses memory to cache data and indexes, which can have a significant impact on performance.

- **key_buffer_size**: This controls the memory allocated for caching index blocks for MyISAM tables. If you're using InnoDB (which is the default), this parameter may not have much effect, but it's important if you're working with MyISAM.

  key_buffer_size = 256M # Adjust based on available RAM

- **innodb_buffer_pool_size**: For InnoDB tables, this is one of the most important parameters. It defines how much memory InnoDB uses to cache table and index data. Typically, you want to allocate around 70-80% of your server's available RAM to this buffer (depending on the system load and other services running).

  innodb_buffer_pool_size = 1G # Adjust based on available RAM

- **innodb_log_file_size**: This controls the size of InnoDB's log files. Larger log files help with performance for write-heavy workloads but require more disk space.

  innodb_log_file_size = 256M

C. Connection Limits

- **max_connections**: This option sets the maximum number of simultaneous client connections allowed. Increasing it can be useful if you expect a high volume of concurrent connections.

  max_connections = 200 # Default is usually 151

- **wait_timeout** and **interactive_timeout**: These settings define how long MySQL will wait before closing idle connections. The wait_timeout is for non-interactive sessions, and interactive_timeout is for interactive sessions (e.g., using the MySQL client).

wait_timeout = 28800
interactive_timeout = 28800

Security Configuration

A. Root Password and Authentication

- **root password**: One of the first steps in configuring MySQL is setting the root user's password. This ensures only authorized users can administer the server.

  mysql_secure_installation

  The mysql_secure_installation script can help set the root password, remove insecure default settings, and secure the server.

B. SSL Configuration

For securing client-server communication, you can configure SSL (Secure Sockets Layer) connections:

- **ssl-ca**, **ssl-cert**, and **ssl-key**: These options define the paths to your certificate authority file, SSL certificate file, and SSL key file.

  ssl-ca = /etc/ssl/certs/ca-certificates.crt
  ssl-cert = /etc/ssl/certs/server-cert.pem
  ssl-key = /etc/ssl/private/server-key.pem

C. User Privileges

You can manage user access and privileges using SQL commands. The following command grants a user full access to a database:

GRANT ALL PRIVILEGES ON database_name.* TO 'username'@'localhost' IDENTIFIED BY 'password';

To apply changes after modifying user privileges, run:

FLUSH PRIVILEGES;

Performance Optimization

MySQL provides various options to optimize performance. Below are some common performance-related settings:

query_cache_size: Enables query caching to speed up repetitive SELECT queries. However, on heavily concurrent servers, it's often better to disable it.

query_cache_size = 0 # Disable query cache for better concurrency

tmp_table_size and **max_heap_table_size**: These settings define the maximum size of in-memory temporary tables. If a temporary table exceeds this size, it is written to disk, which can slow down queries.

tmp_table_size = 64M
max_heap_table_size = 64M

slow_query_log: Enabling the slow query log helps identify queries that take longer than a certain threshold to execute. This can be useful for performance tuning.

slow_query_log = 1
low_query_log_file = /var/log/mysql/mysql-slow.log
long_query_time = 2 # Log queries that take longer than 2 seconds

Backup Configuration

Backing up your data is crucial. You can use the mysqldump utility or configure MySQL's **Enterprise Backup** tool. For automated backups, you can use cron jobs (Linux) or Task Scheduler (Windows) to run periodic backups.

To perform a basic backup using mysqldump:

mysqldump -u root -p --all-databases > backup.sql

To restore a backup:

mysql -u root -p < backup.sql

Restart MySQL Server

After making changes to the configuration file (my.cnf or my.ini), you need to restart the MySQL server for the changes to take effect.

On Linux:

sudo systemctl restart mysql

On Windows:

Open **Services** from the Control Panel, locate **MySQL**, and restart the service.

Configuring MySQL involves adjusting settings related to performance, security, networking, and user management. By properly tuning MySQL for your specific use case and workload, you can ensure better performance, security, and reliability. Always back up your data regularly and monitor the system for any signs of performance bottlenecks or security vulnerabilities.

7.10 Connecting to MySQL via Command Line and Workbench

Connecting to MySQL through both the command line and MySQL Workbench is a common practice for database administrators, developers, and data analysts. Below is a detailed explanation of how to connect to MySQL via both methods, outlining the necessary steps, configurations, and considerations.

Connecting to MySQL via Command Line

The MySQL command-line client is a simple tool for connecting to and interacting with a MySQL database. It can be used to run queries, manage databases, and perform various administrative tasks.

A. Prerequisites

- **MySQL Server**: Ensure MySQL is installed and running on your system.
- **MySQL Client**: The MySQL command-line client comes bundled with MySQL server. If MySQL is installed, you should have access to the command-line client.

- **Credentials**: You need the MySQL username (usually root for administrative tasks) and the password associated with it.
- **Host**: By default, MySQL listens on localhost (127.0.0.1). If connecting to a remote server, you'll need the IP address or domain name of the MySQL server.

B. Connecting to MySQL (Local Connection)

1. Open a terminal or command prompt.
2. Use the mysql command followed by the -u flag for the username and -p for the password prompt.

Syntax:

mysql -u username -p

Example for connecting as root:

mysql -u root -p

3. After pressing Enter, you will be prompted for the password. Enter the password associated with the MySQL user (the root password in this example).

Enter password: *******

4. If the credentials are correct, you will be connected to the MySQL server, and you will see the MySQL prompt (mysql>), indicating that the MySQL client is ready to accept SQL commands.

Example output:

Welcome to the MySQL monitor. Commands end with ; or \g.
Your MySQL connection id is 10
Server version: 8.0.23 MySQL Community Server - GPL

Type 'help;' or '\h' for help. Type '\c' to clear the current input statement.

mysql>

C. Connecting to MySQL (Remote Connection)

To connect to a remote MySQL server, you need to specify the **host** using the -h flag followed by the IP address or domain name of the MySQL server.

Syntax:

mysql -u username -p -h remote_host

Example:

mysql -u root -p -h 192.168.1.100

After entering the password, you will be connected to the remote MySQL server.

D. Specifying a Database to Connect To

To connect directly to a specific database, you can specify the database name after the username and password:

Syntax:

mysql -u username -p database_name

Example:

mysql -u root -p my_database

This command connects to the my_database immediately after login.

E. Command Line Options and Flags

You can use additional flags to configure the connection:

--port: Specify the port number if MySQL is running on a port other than the default (3306).

mysql -u root -p -h localhost --port=3307

--socket: Specify the socket file when connecting to a local MySQL instance, especially on Unix-based systems.

mysql -u root -p --socket=/var/run/mysqld/mysqld.sock

--ssl: If your connection requires SSL encryption, you can specify SSL options.

mysql -u root -p -h remote_host --ssl-ca=/path/to/ca.pem --ssl-cert=/path/to/client-cert.pem --ssl-key=/path/to/client-key.pem

Connecting to MySQL via MySQL Workbench

MySQL Workbench is a popular GUI-based tool that simplifies the process of interacting with MySQL servers. It provides an intuitive interface for managing databases, running queries, and configuring server settings. Below is a detailed guide for connecting to MySQL using Workbench.

A. Prerequisites

- **MySQL Server**: Ensure MySQL is installed and running on your system (or remotely).
- **MySQL Workbench**: Download and install MySQL Workbench from the official MySQL website. It's available for Windows, macOS, and Linux.

B. Launching MySQL Workbench

1. Open **MySQL Workbench** from your applications or programs menu.
2. When you open Workbench, you will see the "MySQL Connections" window, which lists any saved connections. If this is your first time using Workbench, you need to create a new connection.

C. Creating a New MySQL Connection

1. In the "MySQL Connections" window, click the **+** button next to "MySQL Connections" to create a new connection.
2. **Connection Settings**: Enter the necessary information in the connection settings window:
   - ○ **Connection Name**: This can be any name you choose for the connection (e.g., "Local MySQL" or "Remote Server").
   - ○ **Connection Method**: Choose the appropriate method for connecting:
     - ▪ **Standard (TCP/IP)**: For connecting to a remote or local MySQL server using TCP/IP.

- **Socket/Pipe**: For Unix-based systems, connecting via a Unix socket.
  - o **Hostname**: Enter the IP address or hostname of the MySQL server (e.g., localhost for local, or an IP address for remote).
  - o **Port**: Enter the port number if it's different from the default (3306).
  - o **Username**: Enter the MySQL username (e.g., root).
  - o **Password**: Click **Store in Vault** (or **Keychain** on macOS) to save the password securely, or enter it manually each time.

Example settings for connecting to a local MySQL server:

  - o **Hostname**: localhost
  - o **Port**: 3306
  - o **Username**: root

3. Once all settings are entered, click **Test Connection** to ensure that the connection works. If everything is correct, you should see a "Successfully made the MySQL connection" message.
4. Click **OK** to save the connection. The new connection will now appear in the "MySQL Connections" window.

D. Connecting to MySQL

1. Click on the newly created connection in the "MySQL Connections" window.
2. You will be prompted to enter the password (if not saved). Enter the password for the MySQL user and click **OK.**
3. Once connected, you will see the Workbench interface, where you can interact with your MySQL databases, run SQL queries, and manage server settings.

E. Working with Databases in Workbench

After connecting, you can:

- **Manage Databases**: In the left-hand panel, you can expand the connection and see all available schemas (databases). You can right-click on schemas to create, drop, or modify them.
- **Run SQL Queries**: In the SQL editor, you can write and execute queries against the connected database. The results will appear in the result grid at the bottom of the screen.

- **Server Administration**: Workbench also allows you to perform administrative tasks, such as managing users, configuring the server, and monitoring performance.

Troubleshooting MySQL Connections

- **Incorrect Credentials**: If you're unable to connect, double-check your username, password, and host. Ensure the credentials are correct and the user has sufficient privileges.
- **Firewall Issues**: If you're connecting to a remote server, ensure that the MySQL port (3306 by default) is open in the firewall on both the server and your local machine.
- **Binding Issues**: Ensure that MySQL is configured to accept remote connections (check the bind-address in the my.cnf file). It should not be set to 127.0.0.1 for remote connections.
- **SSL Issues**: If using SSL to connect, verify the SSL certificates and ensure they are correctly configured in both the client and server.
- **Timeouts**: If the connection times out, increase the connect_timeout and wait_timeout values in the MySQL configuration file (my.cnf).

Both the MySQL command line and MySQL Workbench provide essential tools for connecting to MySQL servers, with the command line offering a lightweight and powerful interface for advanced users and Workbench providing a more user-friendly, visual approach for managing MySQL databases. Whether you're administering a local or remote MySQL instance, both methods allow you to interact with your databases efficiently and perform a wide range of tasks from running queries to managing users and server settings.

7.11 Troubleshooting Installation Issues

Troubleshooting MySQL installation issues can be a complex process because the problem might arise from several factors, including system configurations, permission issues, network settings, or even MySQL-specific problems. Here's a comprehensive guide to help diagnose and resolve common issues that occur during MySQL installation and configuration.

Prerequisites for MySQL Installation

Before diving into troubleshooting, ensure that the system meets the necessary prerequisites for MySQL:

- **Operating System**: Ensure that your OS is compatible with the MySQL version you are installing (Linux, macOS, Windows).
- **Disk Space**: Make sure your machine has sufficient disk space for both MySQL binaries and databases.
- **RAM**: Ensure your system has enough memory to run MySQL, especially if you plan to handle large databases.
- **Dependencies**: Make sure that any required libraries or dependencies (like libaio for Linux systems) are installed.

Common Installation Problems and Solutions

A. Problem: MySQL Installation Package Not Found (Linux)

Cause:

- The installation package may not be available in the default package manager repositories for your system.

Solution:

1. **Check the repository**: Make sure that your package manager's repository list is up to date. Run:

   sudo apt update   # For Ubuntu/Debian-based systems
   sudo yum update   # For CentOS/Red Hat-based systems

2. **Use the correct repository**: If the package isn't available, add the official MySQL repository to your package manager:
   o   For Ubuntu/Debian:

      wget   https://dev.mysql.com/get/mysql-apt-config_0.8.17-1_all.deb
      sudo dpkg -i mysql-apt-config_0.8.17-1_all.deb
      sudo apt update
      sudo apt install mysql-server

3. **Install MySQL manually**: Download the MySQL installation package from the official MySQL website, then install it manually.

B.   Problem: MySQL   Service   Not   Starting   After   Installation (Linux/Windows)

Cause:

- MySQL may fail to start due to missing configuration files, permission issues, or conflicting services.

Solution:

1. **Check MySQL logs**: Look for error messages in the MySQL log files to diagnose the problem. Log files are typically found in:
   o Linux: /var/log/mysql/error.log or /var/log/mysqld.log
   o Windows: C:\ProgramData\MySQL\MySQL Server X.X\data\

   Look for any entries that provide clues, such as InnoDB errors, permissions issues, or missing directories.

2. **Start MySQL manually**:
   o On Linux, you can try to start the service manually:

   sudo systemctl start mysql
   sudo systemctl status mysql

   On Windows, go to **Control Panel** → **Administrative Tools** → **Services**, then locate **MySQL**, and start it manually.

3. **Permissions issue**: Ensure that the mysql user has appropriate permissions to access the MySQL data directory.

   sudo chown -R mysql:mysql /var/lib/mysql
   sudo chmod -R 755 /var/lib/mysql

4. **MySQL configuration errors**: Check the configuration file (my.cnf or my.ini) for syntax or incorrect settings. It's common to encounter issues with bind-address (which should be 0.0.0.0 for remote connections) or innodb_buffer_pool_size (if set too high for available RAM).

5. **Check for conflicting processes**: Ensure there is no other MySQL or MariaDB instance running that could conflict with your MySQL installation.

C. Problem: "Access Denied" Error During Login (Root or Other User)

Cause:

- MySQL might not have the appropriate user permissions or the root password may not be set correctly during installation.

Solution:

1. **Reset the root password**: If you can't access MySQL with the root user, you may need to reset the root password.
    o Stop MySQL server:

       sudo systemctl stop mysql

    o Start MySQL in safe mode (without loading the grant tables):

       sudo mysqld_safe --skip-grant-tables &

    o Log in as root without a password.

       mysql -u root

    o Update the root password:

       ```
       USE mysql;
       UPDATE user SET
       authentication_string=PASSWORD('new_password')
       WHERE User='root';
       FLUSH PRIVILEGES;
       ```

    o Exit MySQL and restart the service:

       sudo systemctl restart mysql

2. **Check the MySQL user permissions**: Ensure the MySQL user has the appropriate privileges to access databases:

    SHOW GRANTS FOR 'username'@'localhost';

3. **Check MySQL authentication plugin**: Sometimes, MySQL may be configured to use auth_socket plugin for authentication, which only allows login through the system user.

SELECT user, host, plugin FROM mysql.user;

If auth_socket is used, you may either need to change it to mysql_native_password or log in using the system user.

ALTER USER 'root'@'localhost' IDENTIFIED WITH mysql_native_password BY 'new_password';

D. Problem: MySQL Fails to Install Due to Incompatible Version

Cause:

- Version incompatibility could arise from an older version of MySQL being installed, or there may be dependencies on certain versions of libraries.

Solution:

1. **Check for old MySQL versions**: If an old MySQL version is present, remove it before attempting to install a new version. Use the following commands to uninstall:
   o On Ubuntu/Debian:

     sudo apt-get remove --purge mysql-server mysql-client mysql-common mysql-libs mysql-*
     sudo apt-get autoremove
     sudo apt-get autoclean

   o On CentOS/RHEL:

     sudo yum remove mysql mysql-server

2. **Use specific MySQL version**: Download and install the required version of MySQL from the official website if your system is incompatible with the latest version.

E. Problem: MySQL Crashes or Stops Unexpectedly

Cause:

- MySQL may crash due to resource limitations (memory, disk space), corrupted databases, or hardware failure.

Solution:

1. **Check system resources**: Ensure your system has sufficient memory and CPU to run MySQL. Use top, htop, or free -m to monitor system resources.
2. **Check the error logs**: The error logs will typically provide insights into the cause of the crash. Look for memory or disk-related errors.
3. **Repair corrupted tables**: If MySQL crashes due to corrupted tables, you can attempt to repair them:

   mysqlcheck -u root -p --auto-repair --all-databases

4. **Increase system limits**: If you are hitting system limits on file descriptors or connections, increase these limits in /etc/security/limits.conf (Linux systems):

   mysql soft nofile 4096
   mysql hard nofile 65535

5. **Update MySQL**: Ensure you are running the latest stable version of MySQL, as bug fixes and stability improvements are included in newer versions.

7.12 Troubleshooting MySQL on Windows

If you're facing issues on Windows, here are some additional common problems and solutions:

A. Problem: MySQL Service Not Starting (Windows)

Solution:

1. **Check Event Viewer**: Use the Event Viewer to check MySQL-specific logs (located under **Windows Logs → Application**) for any error messages.

2. **Check port availability**: Ensure that no other service is occupying the default MySQL port (3306). If needed, change the port in the my.ini file.
3. **Check for permissions**: Make sure that the MySQL service has the appropriate permissions to access the necessary directories.

B. Problem: MySQL Workbench Can't Connect to Local MySQL Server

Solution:

1. **Check the server**: Ensure that the MySQL server is running. If it's not, start the MySQL service from the **Services** application in Windows.
2. **Check the bind address**: If you're unable to connect, ensure that the bind-address in my.ini is set to 127.0.0.1 for local connections, or 0.0.0.0 for remote connections.

7.13 General Troubleshooting Steps

Regardless of the platform, here are some general troubleshooting tips:

- **Verify MySQL version**: Ensure the MySQL version you're using is compatible with your operating system and hardware.
- **Check the firewall**: Ensure your firewall or security software is not blocking MySQL's port (3306 by default).
- **Test the connection**: If you're trying to connect remotely, use the telnet command or equivalent to verify that the MySQL port is open and reachable.
- **Reinstall MySQL**: As a last resort, uninstall and reinstall MySQL to ensure a fresh installation, ensuring all settings are configured properly.

Troubleshooting MySQL installation issues requires systematic checking of system configurations, logs, and permissions. By identifying common problems like service startup failures, authentication issues, version conflicts, and system resource limitations, you can usually pinpoint and resolve the underlying issues. Always consult MySQL logs and error messages for more specific guidance, and don't hesitate to search for known issues in MySQL's official documentation or community forums.

8 CATEGORIES OF SQL COMMANDS

8.1 Data Definition Language (DDL) commands like CREATE DATABASE, CREATE TABLE, ALTER and DROP

These commands helps user in creating a database, table, changing structure of the table and dropping database or table from the database management system software. The syntax and examples of these commands are given below.

CREATE DATABASE dbname;

Example:
CREATE DATABASE company;

To enter into database the user needs to open database before creating tables. The syntax for opening a database can vary depending on the database management system (DBMS) you are using. Below are examples for some common database systems:

MySQL/MariaDB:

mysql -u username -p

USE dbname;

PostgreSQL:

psql -U username -d dbname

SQL Server:

USE dbname;

SQLite:

sqlite3 dbname.db

Remember to replace username with your actual username, dbname with the name of the database you want to open/connect to, and dbname.db with the path to your SQLite database file.

```
CREATE TABLE table_name (
    column1 datatype [constraint],
    column2 datatype [constraint],
    ...
    columnN datatype [constraint]
        );
```

Example:
```
CREATE TABLE employees (
    emp_id INT PRIMARY KEY,
    emp_name VARCHAR(100),
    emp_salary DECIMAL(10,2),
    emp_department VARCHAR(50)
        );
```
In the above example:

• employees is the name of the table being created.

• emp_id, emp_name, emp_salary, and emp_department are column names.

• INT, VARCHAR, and DECIMAL are data types for the respective columns.

• PRIMARY KEY is a constraint applied to the emp_id column, making it a primary key.

Constraints are optional and can be used to enforce rules on data in the table, such as uniqueness, not null, etc.

8.2 Database Constraints

Constraints in SQL are rules applied to columns in a table to enforce data integrity. Here are some common constraints along with examples:

The syntax to apply table constraints are as given in the examples below

1. PRIMARY KEY: Ensures that each row in a table has a unique identifier and cannot be NULL.

Example:

```
CREATE TABLE students (

   student_id INT PRIMARY KEY,

   student_name VARCHAR(100),

   age INT

        );
```

2. **FOREIGN KEY:** Enforces referential integrity by defining a relationship between two tables. The foreign key column in one table refers to the primary key column in another table.

Example:

```
CREATE TABLE orders (

   order_id INT PRIMARY KEY,

   product_id INT,

   quantity INT,

   FOREIGN KEY (product_id) REFERENCES products(product_id)

        );
```

3. **UNIQUE:** Ensures that all values in a column are unique (except for NULL values).

Example:

```
CREATE TABLE employees (

   emp_id INT PRIMARY KEY,

   emp_email VARCHAR(255) UNIQUE,

   emp_name VARCHAR(100)

        );
```

4. **CHECK:** Defines a condition that must be met for the data to be valid.

Example:

CREATE TABLE students (

   student_id INT PRIMARY KEY,

   student_name VARCHAR(100),

   age INT CHECK (age >= 18)

      );

5. **NOT NULL:** Ensures that a column cannot contain NULL values.

Example:

CREATE TABLE customers (

   customer_id INT PRIMARY KEY,

   customer_name VARCHAR(100) NOT NULL,

   email VARCHAR(255) NOT NULL

      );

6. **DEFAULT:** Specifies a default value for a column when no value is specified during insertion.

Example:

CREATE TABLE employees (

   emp_id INT PRIMARY KEY,

   emp_name VARCHAR(100),

   emp_salary DECIMAL(10,2) DEFAULT 0.00);

These constraints help maintain the integrity and consistency of data in a database by enforcing rules and relationships between tables. When creating constraints, you can assign custom names to them. This can be useful for better understanding and managing the constraints within your database. Here's how you can assign names to constraints:

```
CREATE TABLE table_name (

    column1 datatype,

    column2 datatype,

    ...

    CONSTRAINT    constraint_name1    constraint_type    (column1)
    [constraint_options],

    CONSTRAINT    constraint_name2    constraint_type    (column2)
    [constraint_options],

    ...

        );
```

In this syntax:

• constraint_name1, constraint_name2, etc., are the custom names you assign to the constraints.

• constraint_type refers to the type of constraint such as PRIMARY KEY, FOREIGN KEY, UNIQUE, CHECK, etc.

• column1, column2, etc., are the columns on which the constraint is being applied.

• constraint_options are additional options specific to the constraint type.

Here's an example illustrating how to assign names to constraints:

```
CREATE TABLE employees (

    emp_id INT,

    emp_name VARCHAR(100),

    emp_department VARCHAR(50),

    CONSTRAINT pk_emp_id PRIMARY KEY (emp_id),

    CONSTRAINT fk_emp_department FOREIGNKEY(emp_department)
```

REFERENCES departments(dept_id)

);

In this example:

• pk_emp_id is the custom name for the primary key constraint on the emp_id column.

• fk_emp_department is the custom name for the foreign key constraint on the emp_department column.

Assigning custom names to constraints can make it easier to manage and reference them, especially in larger databases with multiple tables and complex relationships. It also helps in understanding the purpose of each constraint when reviewing the database schema.

8.3 Role of Foreign Key

The role of foreign key constraints in a relational database is to enforce referential integrity, which ensures that relationships between tables remain valid. Foreign key constraints establish a link between two tables based on the values of a column or columns in one table referencing the primary key or unique key in another table. Here's a breakdown of the role and importance of foreign key constraints:

1. **Maintaining Data Integrity:** Foreign key constraints ensure that data remains consistent and accurate by enforcing relationships between tables. They prevent actions that would violate these relationships, such as deleting a parent record when child records still exist.

2. **Enforcing Referential Integrity:** Foreign key constraints ensure referential integrity by requiring that values in the foreign key column of one table must match values in the primary key or unique key column of another table.

3. **Preventing Orphaned Records:** Foreign key constraints prevent the creation of orphaned records, which are records in a child table that reference non-existent records in the parent table. This ensures that data remains meaningful and usable.

4. **Maintaining Consistency:** By enforcing relationships between tables,

foreign key constraints help maintain consistency across the database. They prevent inconsistent or invalid data from being introduced, improving the overall quality and reliability of the database.

5. **Supporting Joins and Queries:** Foreign key constraints facilitate the use of joins in SQL queries, allowing for efficient retrieval of related data from multiple tables. This simplifies data retrieval and analysis tasks.

8.4 Viewing a table structure

To view the structure of a table in SQL, you typically use the DESCRIBE or DESC statement in most database systems. However, the exact method can vary depending on the database management system you are using. Below are examples for some common database systems:

MySQL / MariaDB:

DESCRIBE table_name;

-- OR

SHOW COLUMNS FROM table_name;

PostgreSQL:

\d table_name;

-- OR

DESCRIBE table_name;

SQL Server:

sp_help table_name;

-- OR

EXEC sp_columns table_name;

SQLite:

SELECT * FROM sqlite_master WHERE type='table' AND name='table_name';

-- OR

PRAGMA table_info(table_name);

Replace table_name with the name of the table whose structure you want to view. This will provide information about the columns in the table, including their names, data types, and any constraints applied to them.

8.5 Creating a new table from existing table

To create a new table from an existing table in SQL, you can use the CREATE TABLE statement with a SELECT query that retrieves data from the existing table. This is commonly known as creating a table with the results of a query. Here's the syntax:

Syntax

CREATE TABLE new_table_name AS

SELECT column1, column2, ...

FROM existing_table_name

[WHERE condition];

This syntax creates a new table named new_table_name with columns and data derived from existing_table_name. You can also apply conditions using the WHERE clause to filter the data from the existing table.

Example: Suppose we have an existing table called employees and we want to create a new table new_employees with only the employees who belong to the IT department:

CREATE TABLE new_employees AS

SELECT emp_id, emp_name, emp_salary, emp_department

FROM employees

WHERE emp_department = 'IT';

This will create a new table new_employees containing only the employees from the IT department, with columns emp_id, emp_name, emp_salary, and emp_department. The data will be copied from the employees table based on the specified condition.

8.6 To see list of databases in Data Base Management System

To see the list of databases in a relational database management system (RDBMS), you typically use a specific command or query depending on the database system you are using. Below are examples for some common database systems:

MySQL / MariaDB:

You can use the SHOW DATABASES;

Command:

SHOW DATABASES;

PostgreSQL:

PostgreSQL does not have a direct command to show databases like MySQL. Instead, you can use the \l command in psql:

\l

SQL Server:

You can query the sys.databases system view:

SELECT name FROM sys.databases;

SQLite:

SQLite does not have a concept of multiple databases in the same way as other RDBMS. Instead, you connect directly to a specific SQLite database file.

Note: Make sure you have appropriate permissions to view the list of databases in the RDBMS you are working with.

To see list of tables in a particular database

The syntax for seeing a list of tables in a database management system (DBMS) varies depending on the specific DBMS you're using. Below are examples for some of the most common database systems: MySQL, PostgreSQL, and SQL Server.

MySQL:

Syntax:

SHOW TABLES;

Example:

SHOW TABLES;

PostgreSQL:

Syntax:

\dt

Example:

\dt

SQL Server (using SQLCMD):

Syntax:

SELECT * FROM INFORMATION_SCHEMA.TABLES WHERE TABLE_TYPE = 'BASE TABLE';

Example:

SELECT * FROM INFORMATION_SCHEMA.TABLES WHERE TABLE_TYPE = 'BASE TABLE';

These commands will provide you with a list of tables in the currently selected database for the respective DBMS. Note that you need appropriate permissions to execute these commands, and the specific syntax may vary depending on the version of the DBMS you're using.

8.7 ALTERcommand

Consider the Employee table given below

EmployeeID	Name	Department	Position	Salary	HireDate
1001	John Doe	IT	Developer	$85,000	2022-03-15
1002	Jane Smith	HR	Manager	$95,000	2021-07-20
1003	Alex Johnson	Finance	Accountant	$80,000	2023-01-10
1004	Emily Brown	Marketing	Marketing	$75,000	2022-11-30
1005	Michael Clark	IT	System Admin	$90,000	2023-05-05

The example queries to alter the structure of Employee table are as given below.

a. To add a new column Hobby to the Employee table

Example:

ALTER TABLE Employee ADD Hobby VARCHAR(30);

b. To remove column Hobby from the Employee table

Example:

ALTER TABLE Employee DROP Hobby;

c. To remove primary key constraint from the column EmployeeID

Example:

ALTER TABLE Employee DROP PRIMARY KEY;

d. To declare EmployeeID Primary Key in already existing table

Example:

ALTER TABLE Employee ADD PRIMARY KEY(EmployeeID);

e. To change the size of the Name column to 30.

Example:

ALTER TABLE Employee MODIFY Name VARCHAR (30);

f. To change the data type of Position column to CHAR (20)

Example:

ALTER TABLE Employee MODIFY Position CHAR (20);

g. To give Name column NOT NULL constraint

Example:

ALTER TABLE Employee MODIFY Name VARCHAR (30) NOT NULL;

h. To give Name column NULL constraint

Example:

ALTER TABLE Employee MODIFY Name VARCHAR(30) NULL;

i. To reorder the column position by bringing HireDate column to first position

Example:

ALTER TABLE Employee MODIFY HireDate DATE FIRST;

j. To reorder the column position by bringing Name column after Department column

Example:

ALTER TABLE Employee MODIFY Name VARCHAR(30) AFTER Department;

k. To rename the Name column to EmpName

ALTER TABLE Employee CHANGE Name EmpName VARCHAR(30);

l. To rename the Employee table to Emp

Example:

RENAME TABLE Employee TO Emp;

m. To give UNIQUE constraint to existing column Name

Example:

ALTER TABLE Employe ADD CONSTRAINT unique_name UNIQUE(Name);

DROP command to remove a table from database

To remove a table from a database in SQL, you use the DROP TABLE statement. Here's the syntax:

Syntax

DROP TABLE table_name;

Where table_name is the name of the table you want to remove.

Example:

DROP TABLE employees;

This SQL statement will drop the table named employees from the database, permanently removing it along with all its data and associated objects such as indexes, triggers, and constraints. Use this statement with caution as it cannot be undone, and all data within the table will be lost.

8.8 Removing database from DBMS

The syntax to remove a database varies depending on the database management system (DBMS) you are using. Here are examples for some common database systems:

MySQL / MariaDB:

To drop a database in MySQL or MariaDB, you use the DROP DATABASE statement:

Syntax

DROP DATABASE database_name;

Example:

DROP DATABASE mydatabase;

PostgreSQL:

To drop a database in PostgreSQL, you use the DROP DATABASE statement:

Syntax

DROP DATABASE database_name;

Example:

DROP DATABASE mydatabase;

SQL Server:

To drop a database in SQL Server, you use the DROP DATABASE statement:

Syntax

DROP DATABASE database_name;

Example:

DROP DATABASE mydatabase;

SQLite:

SQLite does not have a built-in command to drop a database like other DBMS. Instead, you simply delete the SQLite database file from the file system.

8.9 Operators used in SQL Queries

SQL (Structured Query Language) provides various operators to perform operations like arithmetic, comparison, logical, and string operations. Here's an explanation of some common operators in SQL with examples:

Arithmetic Operators:

+ (Addition)

- (Subtraction)

* (Multiplication)

/ (Division)

% (Modulo - returns the remainder of a division)

Example:

SELECT 10 + 5; -- Result: 15

SELECT 10 - 5; -- Result: 5

SELECT 10 * 5; -- Result: 50

SELECT 10 / 5; -- Result: 2

SELECT 10 % 3; -- Result: 1

Comparison Operators:

= (Equal to)

<> or != (Not equal to)

< (Less than)

> (Greater than)

<= (Less than or equal to)

>= (Greater than or equal to)

Example:

SELECT * FROM users WHERE age > 25;

SELECT * FROM products WHERE price <= 100;

Logical Operators:

AND (Both conditions must be true)

OR (At least one condition must be true)

NOT (Negates a condition)

Example:

SELECT * FROM employees WHERE department = 'IT' AND salary > 50000;

SELECT * FROM customers WHERE age < 18 OR age > 60;

SELECT * FROM products WHERE NOT category = 'Electronics';

Concatenation Operator:

|| (Used to concatenate strings)

Example:

SELECT first_name || ' ' || last_name AS full_name FROM employees;

IN Operator:

Used to specify multiple values in a WHERE clause.

Example:

SELECT * FROM products WHERE category IN ('Electronics', 'Clothing', 'Books');

8.10 Data Manipulation Language (DML) commands like INSERT, SELECT,UPDATE and DELETE

DML stands for Data Manipulation Language, which is a subset of SQL (Structured Query Language) used for managing data within a database. There are four primary DML commands: INSERT, SELECT, UPDATE, and DELETE. Here's an explanation of each with examples:

Consider the Employee table given below

EmployeeID	Name	Department	Position	Salary$	HireDate
1001	John Doe	IT	Developer	85000	2022-03-15
1002	Jane Smith	NULL	Manager	NULL	2021-07-20
1003	Alex Johnson	Finance	Accountant	80000	2023-01-10
1004	Emily Brown	Marketing	Marketing	75000	2022-11-30

INSERT: This command is used to insert records in the table.

Examples

a.To insert record with values for all the columns.

Example:

INSERT INTO Employee VALUES (1001,"John Doe","IT","Developer",85000,"2022-03-15);

b.To insert record with NULL values

Example:

INSERT INTO Employee VALUES(1002,"Jane Smith",NULL,"Manager",NULL,"2021-07-20");

Remember that NULL should not be given in quotation marks.

c.To insert values in selected columns.

Example:

INSERT INTO Employee(EmployeeID,Name,Position,HireDate) VALUES(1002,"Jane Smith","Manager","2021-07-20");

In this query the columns for which values are to be given need to be qualified by giving with table name. Failing to qualify column names will result into error of column count does not match the values count. For all other columns whose values are not passed are automatically set as NULL.

d. To insert data in Emp table from Employee table.

Example:

INSERT INTO Emp SELECT * FROM Employee;

UPDATE: This command is used to update /change data in the table cell.

a. change salary of EmployeeID 1001 to 90000$

Example:

UPDATE Employee SET Salary$=90000 WHERE EmployeeID=1001;

WHERE clause is given as condition in the above statement. Failing to give condition will set salary of all the records to 90000.

b. To change salary from NULL to 92000 in the table.

Example:

UPDATE Employee SET Salary$=92000 WHERE Salary$ IS NULL;

This statement will update all the records whose salary was NULL to 92000

c. To change department and salary of EmployeeID 1004 to Sales and 76000 respectively.

Example:

UPDATE Employee SET Department="Sales",Salary$=76000 WHERE EmployeeID=1004;

Two columns values can be updated simultaneously by giving one statement.

DELETE: The DELETE command can delete one, more than one or all the records from the table.

a. Delete record of EmployeeID 1004

Example:

DELETE FROM Employee WHERE EmployeeID=1004;

b.Delete records from EmployeeID 1001 to 1003

Example:

DELETE FROM Employee WHERE EmployeeID BETWEEN 1001 AND 1003;

c. Delete all the records from Employee table

Example:

DELETE FROM Employee;

This statement deletes all the records from the table and makes table empty. However, the table structure still exist in the database.

SELECT: SELECT statement is a data retrieval command. It extracts the required data from the table based on the query statement and displays on the screen.

a. Display all the records of Employee table

Example:

SELECT * FROM Employee;

b. Display EmployeeID, Name, and Salary of all the employees.

Example:

SELECT EmployeeID,Name,Salary$ FROM Employee;

Output:

EmployeeID	Name	Salary$
1001	John Doe	85000
1002	Jane Smith	NULL
1003	Alex Johnson	80000
1004	Emily Brown	75000

c .Display records of Employee table with alias name of column Name as EmpName

Example:

SELECT EmployeeID, Name as "EmpName",Department, Position,Salary$,HireDate FROM Employee;

Output

EmployeeID	EmpName	Department	Position	Salary$	HireDate
1001	John Doe	IT	Developer	85000	2022-03-15
1002	Jane Smith	NULL	Manager	NULL	2021-07-20
1003	Alex Johnson	Finance	Accountant	80000	2023-01-10
1004	Emily Brown	Marketing	Marketing	75000	2022-11-30

The alias name does not change the column name permanently in the table.

d. Display names of employee and salary multiplied by 2

Example:

SELECT Name, Salary$*2 FROM Employee;

Output

Name	Salary$
--------------- ---	---------
John Doe	170000
Jane Smith	NULL
Alex Johnson	160000
Emily Brown	150000

Selecting Specific Rows by giving WHERE clause

e. Display records of Employees whose salary is greater than 75000

Example:

SELECT * FROM Employee WHERE Salary$>75000

Output

EmployeeID	Name	Department	Position	Salary$	HireDate
1001	John Doe	IT	Developer	85000	2022-03-15
1003	Alex Johnson	Finance	Accountant	80000	2023-01-10

In the above example WHERE clause is given to give condition. Records satisfyingthe given condition are only displayed in the output.

f. Display records of Employees whose position is Accountant

Example:

SELECT * FROM Employee WHERE Position="Accountant;

Output

EmployeeID	Name	Department	Position	Salary$	HireDate
1003	Alex Johnson	Finance	Accountant	80000	2023-01-10

g. Display records of Employees whose position is not Developer.

Example:

SELECT * FROM Employee WHERE Position<> "Developer";

Output

EmployeeID	Name	Department	Position	Salary$	HireDate

| 1002 | Jane Smith | NULL | Manager | NULL | 2021-07-20 |

| 1003 | Alex Johnson | Finance | Accountant | 80000 | 2023-01-10 |

| 1004 | Emily Brown | Marketing | Marketing | 75000 | 2022-11-30 |

h. Display records of Employee whose salary is NULL

Example:

SELECT * FROM Employee WHERE Salary$ IS NULL;

Output

EmployeeID	Name	Department	Position	Salary$	HireDate
1002	Jane Smith	NULL	Manager	NULL	2021-07-20

i. Display records of Employees whose salary is not NULL

Example:

SELECT * FROM Employee WHERE Salary$ IS NOT NULL;

Output

EmployeeID	Name	Department	Position	Salary$	HireDate
1001	John Doe	IT	Developer	85000	2022-03-15
1003	Alex Johnson	Finance	Accountant	80000	2023-01-10
1004	Emily Brown	Marketing	Marketing	75000	2022-11-30

j.Display records of Employees whose position is Accountant and salary is 80000 using logical AND operator.

Example:

SELECT * FROM Employee WHERE Salary$=80000 AND

Positon="Accountant;

Output

EmployeeID	Name	Department	Position	Salary$	HireDate
1003	Alex Johnson	Finance	Accountant	80000	2023-01-10

k .Display records of Employees whose position is Manager or salary is more than 80000 using logical OR operator.

Example:

SELECT * FROM Employee WHERE Position="Manager" OR Salary$>80000;

Output

EmployeeID	Name	Department	Position	Salary$	HireDate
1001	John Doe	IT	Developer	85000	2022-03-15
1002	Jane Smith	NULL	Manager	NULL	2021-07-20

l. Display records of Employee who are not Manager using logical NOT operator.

Example:

SELECT * FROM Employee WHERE NOT(Position="Manager");

Output

EmployeeID	Name	Department	Position	Salary$	HireDate
1001	John Doe	IT	Developer	85000	2022-03-15

| 1003 | Alex Johnson | Finance | Accountant | 80000 | 2023-01-10 |
| 1004 | Emily Brown | Marketing | Marketing | 75000 | 2022-11-30 |

The symbolic notation for AND logical operator is (&&), form OR is (||) and for NOT is (!). Symbolic notation can also be used for connecting search condition in WHERE clause instead of AND, OR NOT.

m. Display records of Employees whose salary is in the range 75000 to 80000 using BETWEEN clause.

Example:

SELECT * FROM Employee WHERE Salary$ BETWEEN 75000 AND 80000;

Output

EmployeeID	Name	Department	Position	Salary	HireDate
1003	Alex Johnson	Finance	Accountant	80000	2023-01-10
1004	Emily Brown	Marketing	Marketing	75000	2022-11-30

The BETWEEN clause includes the range values in output. In above example all the records where salary lies in the range from 75000 to 80000 including these range values are displayed.

n. Display records of Employees whose salary does not lie in the range 75000 to 80000 using BETWEEN clauses.

Example:

SELECT * FROM Employee WHERE Salary$ NOT BETWEEN 75000 AND 80000;

Output

EmployeeID	Name	Department	Position	Salary$	HireDate

| 1001 | John Doe | IT | Developer | 85000 | 2022-03-15 |

o. Display records of Employees who are either developer or manager using membership operator

Example:

SELECT * FROM Employee WHERE Position IN ("Developer","Manager");

Output

EmployeeID	EmpName	Department	Position	Salary$	HireDate
1001	John Doe	IT	Developer	85000	2022-03-15
1002	Jane Smith	NULL	Manager	NULL	2021-07-20

p.Display records of Employees who are neither developer nor manager using membership operator.

Example:

SELECT * FROM Employee WHERE Position NOT IN ("Developer","Manager");

Output

EmployeeID	EmpName	Department	Position	Salary$	HireDate
1003	Alex Johnson	Finance	Accountant	80000	2023-01-10
1004	Emily Brown	Marketing	Marketing	75000	2022-11-30

q. Display distinct positions of employees.

Example:

SELECT DISTINCT(Position) FROM Employee;

Output

| DISTINCT (Position)|

|-----------------------------|

| Developer |

| Manager |

| Accountant |

| Marketing |

The DISTINCT clause retrieves non duplicate values from the specified column. The ALL clause may be used instead of DISTINCT clause to display all the values from the specified column including repeating values.

r. Display records of employees whose name contains alphabet 'a'.

Example:

SELECT * FROM Employee WHERE Name LIKE "%a%";

Output

EmployeeID	Name	Department	Position	Salary$	HireDate
1002	Jane Smith	NULL	Manager	NULL	2021-07-20
1003	Alex Johnson	Finance	Accountant	80000	2023-01-10

s. Display records of employees whose name does not contain alphabet 'a'.

Example:

SELECT * FROM Employee WHERE Name NOT LIKE "%a%";

Output

EmployeeID	Name	Department	Position	Salary$	HireDate

--|

| 1001 | John Doe | IT | Developer | 85000 | 2022-03-15 |

| 1004 | Emily Brown | Marketing | Marketing | 75000 | 2022-11-30 |

t. Display records of employees whose name starts with "John."

Example:

SELECT * FROM Employee WHERE Name LIKE "John%";

Output

EmployeeID	Name	Department	Position	Salary$	HireDate
1001	John Doe	IT	Developer	85000	2022-03-15

u. Display records of employees whose name ends with "Brown".

Example:

SELECT * FROM Employee WHERE Name LIKE "%Brown";

Output

EmployeeID	Name	Department	Position	Salary$	HireDate
1004	Emily Brown	Marketing	Marketing	75000	2022-11-30

v. Display records of employees whose name has "h" as third alphabet in the Name column.

Example:

SELECT * FROM Employee WHERE Name LIKE "_ _h%";

EmployeeID	Name	Department	Position	Salary$	HireDate
1001	John Doe	IT	Developer	85000	2022-03-15

LIKE and NOT LIKE clauses are used to extract records from the table by giving pattern using wild card characters like ' % ' and ' _ '. The '%' symbol represents zero, one or more characters in the pattern and '_' represents exactly one character. The LIKE clause returns records matching with the given pattern and NOT LIKE clause returns records not matching the given pattern.

w.Insert a text "Joined on" between Name and HireDate columns and display.

Example:

SELECT Name, "Joined on", HireDate from Employee;

Output

Name	Joined on	HireDate
John Doe	Joined on	2022-03-15
Jane Smith	Joined on	2021-07-20
Alex Johnson	Joined on	2023-01-10
Emily Brown	Joined on	2022-11-30

x. To display the name of current / active database in which the user is working.

Example:

SELECT DATABASE();

8.11 Data Control Language (DCL) commands like GRANT and REVOKE

DCL (Data Control Language) is a subset of SQL (Structured Query Language) that deals with permissions, security, and other access controls within a database management system. DCL commands primarily include GRANT and REVOKE. Here are examples of how these commands are used:

GRANT: This command is used to give specific privileges to database users.

Example:

GRANT SELECT, INSERT ON employees TO user1;

This grants the user named user1 the privileges to select data from and insert data into the employees table.

REVOKE: This command is used to take away previously granted privileges from database users.

Example:

REVOKE INSERT ON employees FROM user1;

This revokes the privilege of inserting data into the employees table from the user user1.

8.12 Transaction Control Language (TCL) commands like COMMIT, ROLLBACK, BEGIN TRANSACTION, START TRANSACTION, AUTOCOMMIT and SAVEPOINT.

Transaction Control Language (TCL) commands are essential for managing transactions within a database management system. Transactions are sequences of database operations (such as inserts, updates, or deletes) that are treated as a single unit of work. TCL commands allow you to control the beginning, ending, and rollback of transactions, ensuring data consistency, integrity, and reliability. Here's a detailed explanation of each TCL command along with examples:

COMMIT:

The COMMIT command is used to permanently save the changes made during the current transaction to the database. Once committed, the changes become permanent and visible to other users.

Syntax:

COMMIT;

Example:

BEGIN TRANSACTION;

UPDATE employees SET salary = salary * 1.1 WHERE department = 'Engineering';

INSERT INTO audit_log (user_id, action, timestamp) VALUES (123, 'Salary increase for Engineering department', NOW());

COMMIT;

In this example, the changes made to the salaries of employees in the Engineering department are updated and logged in an audit log. The COMMIT command commits these changes, making them permanent in the database.

ROLLBACK:

The ROLLBACK command is used to undo the changes made during the current transaction. It allows you to revert the database to its state before the transaction began.

Syntax:

ROLLBACK;

Example:

BEGIN TRANSACTION;

UPDATE employees SET salary = salary * 1.1 WHERE department =

'Engineering';

-- An error occurs before COMMIT

ROLLBACK;

In this example, if an error occurs after updating the salaries but before committing the transaction, the ROLLBACK command can be used to undo the changes made to the salaries, ensuring data consistency.

SAVEPOINT:

The SAVEPOINT command is used to set a savepoint within a transaction. Savepoints allow you to roll back part of a transaction rather than the entire transaction.

Syntax:

SAVEPOINT savepoint_name;

Example:

BEGIN TRANSACTION;

UPDATE employees SET salary = salary * 1.1 WHERE department = 'Engineering';

SAVEPOINT before_audit;

INSERT INTO audit_log (user_id, action, timestamp) VALUES (123, 'Salary increase for Engineering department', NOW());

-- An error occurs after logging to the audit log

ROLLBACK TO SAVEPOINT before_audit;

COMMIT;

In this example, a savepoint named before_audit is set before logging the action in the audit log. If an error occurs after logging but before committing the transaction, the ROLLBACK TO SAVEPOINT command can be used to roll back to the savepoint, undoing the changes made after it.

AUTO-COMMIT

Auto-commit is a feature in database management systems where each SQL statement is automatically committed as a separate transaction. In other words, with auto-commit enabled, each individual SQL statement (such as INSERT, UPDATE, DELETE, etc.) is treated as a transaction that is automatically committed upon completion. This means that changes made by each SQL statement are immediately made permanent in the database.

When auto-commit is disabled, SQL statements are grouped together into transactions, and changes are not automatically committed. Instead, you have to explicitly issue a COMMIT command to make the changes permanent or a ROLLBACK command to discard them.

Advantages of Auto-commit:

• Simplifies transaction management, as you don't need to explicitly manage transaction boundaries.

• Reduces the risk of accidentally leaving transactions open and causing locks or concurrency issues.

• Provides a consistent and predictable behavior for each SQL statement.

Disadvantages of Auto-commit:

• May result in performance overhead, especially for large numbers of transactions.

• Limits the ability to group related operations into a single transaction.

Enabling/Disabling Auto-commit:

In many database systems, auto-commit is enabled by default. However, you can disable it if needed.

Enabling Auto-commit:

SET autocommit = 1; -- Enables auto-commit mode

Disabling Auto-commit:

SET autocommit = 0; -- Disables auto-commit mode

Example:

-- Enable auto-commit

SET autocommit = 1;

-- Insert a new record into a table

INSERT INTO users (username, email) VALUES ('john_doe', 'john@example.com');

-- With auto-commit enabled, the INSERT statement is automatically committed.

-- Disable auto-commit

SET autocommit = 0;

-- Begin a transaction explicitly

START TRANSACTION;

-- Update a record

UPDATE users SET email = 'new_email@example.com' WHERE username = 'john_doe';

-- With auto-commit disabled, the UPDATE statement is not automatically committed.

-- Commit the transaction explicitly

COMMIT;

-- The changes made by the UPDATE statement are now committed.

In this example:
• With auto-commit enabled, each SQL statement (INSERT) is automatically committed upon completion.
• With auto-commit disabled, you need to explicitly begin a transaction, execute SQL statements, and then commit the transaction.

9. SUB QUERIES IN MySQL

9.1 What is a Sub query?

A **Sub query** in MySQL is a query nested inside another SQL query. It is also known as an **inner query** or **nested query**, and it provides results that are used by an **outer query**. Sub queries are used to perform complex queries by breaking them down into smaller parts.

9.2 Types of Sub queries

Sub queries in MySQL can be classified based on their placement and functionality:

1. Single-row Sub query
2. Multi-row Sub query
3. Correlated Sub query
4. Sub query in **SELECT** clause
5. Sub query in **FROM** clause

Single-row Sub query

A **single-row sub query** returns **only one row** as a result. It is often used with comparison operators such as =, >, <, >=, and <=.

Example: Find the employee with the highest salary

SELECT * FROM employees
WHERE salary = (SELECT MAX(salary) FROM employees);

Explanation:

- The inner query:

  SELECT MAX(salary) FROM employees;

  This finds the highest salary from the employees table.

- The outer query:

```
SELECT * FROM employees WHERE salary =
(result_of_inner_query);
```

Retrieves the employee(s) who have this maximum salary.

Multi-row Sub query

A **multi-row Sub query** returns multiple rows as a result. It is used with operators like IN, ANY, and ALL.

Example 1: Find employees who have the same salary as at least one of the sales employees

```
SELECT name, salary FROM employees
WHERE salary IN (SELECT salary FROM employees WHERE department = 'Sales');
```

Explanation:

- The inner query:

  ```
  SELECT salary FROM employees WHERE department = 'Sales';
  ```

  This retrieves the salaries of all employees in the Sales department.

- The outer query:

  ```
  SELECT name, salary FROM employees WHERE salary IN
  (result_of_inner_query);
  ```

  Finds all employees who have a salary matching any of the salaries retrieved by the Sub query.

Correlated Sub query

A **correlated Sub query** is a Sub query that refers to columns in the outer query. It is evaluated **once for each row** processed by the outer query.

Example: Find employees who earn more than the average salary of their own department

SELECT e1.name, e1.salary, e1.department
FROM employees e1
WHERE e1.salary > (SELECT AVG(e2.salary) FROM employees e2
WHERE e1.department = e2.department);

Explanation:

- The sub query:

    SELECT AVG(e2.salary) FROM employees e2 WHERE
    e1.department = e2.department;

    Computes the average salary **per department.**

- The outer query:

    SELECT e1.name, e1.salary, e1.department FROM employees e1
    WHERE e1.salary > (result_of_inner_query);

    Filters employees who earn more than their department's average
    salary.

Sub query in the SELECT Clause

A sub query can be used inside the SELECT clause to retrieve a value for
each row.

Example: Show each employee's salary along with the company's average
salary

SELECT name, salary, (SELECT AVG(salary) FROM employees) AS
company_avg_salary
FROM employees;
Explanation:

- The Sub query:

    SELECT AVG(salary) FROM employees;

    Calculates the average salary of all employees.

- The outer query:

  SELECT name, salary, (result_of_inner_query) AS company_avg_salary FROM employees;

  Retrieves each employee's salary and adds the company-wide average salary in each row.

Sub query in the FROM Clause (Derived Table)

A sub query can act as a temporary table within the FROM clause.

Example: Find the highest salary in each department using a derived table

SELECT department, MAX(salary) AS highest_salary
FROM (SELECT department, salary FROM employees) AS dept_salaries
GROUP BY department;

Explanation:

- The inner query:

  SELECT department, salary FROM employees;

  Creates a temporary table (dept_salaries) with department and salary columns.

- The outer query:

  SELECT department, MAX(salary) FROM dept_salaries GROUP BY department;

  Finds the maximum salary in each department.

Using EXISTS with Sub queries

The EXISTS keyword checks if a Sub query returns **any** rows.

Example: Find departments that have employees earning more than $50,000

```
SELECT DISTINCT department
FROM employees e1
WHERE EXISTS (SELECT 1 FROM employees e2 WHERE e2.department
= e1.department AND e2.salary > 50000);
```
Explanation:

- The inner query:

  ```
  SELECT 1 FROM employees e2 WHERE e2.department =
  e1.department AND e2.salary > 50000;
  ```

  Checks if there is at least one employee in the same department earning more than $50,000.

- The outer query:

  ```
  SELECT DISTINCT department FROM employees e1 WHERE
  EXISTS (result_of_inner_query);
  ```

  Retrieves departments where the condition is met.

Performance Considerations

1. **Avoid Correlated Sub queries**
   - Correlated Sub queries run **once per row**, making them slow for large datasets.
   - Consider using **JOINs** instead.
2. **Indexing Helps**
   - Ensure that columns used in Sub queries have indexes for faster execution.
3. **Use EXISTS Instead of IN When Possible**
   - EXISTS is generally faster than IN, especially for large datasets.
4. **Use Derived Tables When Necessary**
   - Sometimes, breaking down Sub queries into **temporary tables** improves performance.

- **Sub queries** are powerful tools for performing complex queries in MySQL.

- They can be used in various places (WHERE, SELECT, FROM) to retrieve specific data.
- **Single-row, multi-row, and correlated Sub queries** each serve different purposes.
- Using Sub queries efficiently requires understanding **performance implications** and choosing the right approach (EXISTS, JOIN, etc.).

Let's work with a sample **employees** table and a **departments** table.

Sample Tables

employees Table

emp_id	name	department_id	salary
1	Alice	1	60000
2	Bob	2	55000
3	Charlie	1	70000
4	David	3	50000
5	Emma	2	65000
6	Frank	3	48000
7	Grace	1	62000

departments Table

department_id	department_name
1	HR
2	IT
3	Finance

Single-Row Sub query Example

Find the employee who has the highest salary.

SELECT * FROM employees
WHERE salary = (SELECT MAX(salary) FROM employees);

Result:

emp_id	name	department_id	salary
3	Charlie	1	70000

Explanation

- The Sub query (SELECT MAX(salary) FROM employees) returns **70000**.
- The outer query selects the employee with that salary.

Multi-Row Sub query Example

Find employees who have the same salary as someone in the IT department.

SELECT name, salary FROM employees
WHERE salary IN (SELECT salary FROM employees WHERE department_id = 2);

Result:

name	salary
Alice	60000
Bob	55000
Emma	65000
Grace	62000

Explanation

- The Sub query SELECT salary FROM employees WHERE department_id = 2 returns: **55000, 65000**.
- The outer query finds all employees with those salaries.

Correlated Sub query Example

Find employees who earn more than the average salary of their own department.

```
SELECT e1.name, e1.salary, e1.department_id
FROM employees e1
WHERE e1.salary > (SELECT AVG(e2.salary) FROM employees e2
WHERE e2.department_id = e1.department_id);
```

Result:

name	salary	department_id
Charlie	70000	1
Emma	65000	2

Explanation

- The Sub query (SELECT AVG(e2.salary) FROM employees e2 WHERE e2.department_id = e1.department_id) calculates **the average salary per department**.
- The outer query finds employees earning **above their department's average**.

Sub query in the SELECT Clause

Show each employee's salary along with the company's average salary.

```
SELECT name, salary, (SELECT AVG(salary) FROM employees) AS
company_avg_salary
FROM employees;
```

Result:

name salary company_avg_salary

Alice	60000	59285.71
Bob	55000	59285.71
Charlie	70000	59285.71

Explanation

- The Sub query (SELECT AVG(salary) FROM employees) calculates the **overall average salary.**
- The outer query retrieves each employee's salary and adds the **same company-wide average salary.**

Sub query in the FROM Clause (Derived Table)

Find the highest salary in each department.

```
SELECT department_id, MAX(salary) AS highest_salary
FROM (SELECT department_id, salary FROM employees) AS dept_salaries
GROUP BY department_id;
```

Result:

department_id highest_salary

1	70000
2	65000
3	50000

Explanation

- The Sub query creates a **temporary table (dept_salaries)** with department and salary columns.
- The outer query finds **the highest salary per department.**

Using EXISTS with a Sub query

Find departments that have at least one employee earning more than 60,000.

SELECT DISTINCT department_id
FROM employees e1
WHERE EXISTS (SELECT 1 FROM employees e2 WHERE e2.department_id = e1.department_id AND e2.salary > 60000);

Result:

department_id

    1

    2

Explanation

- The sub query checks if any **employee in the same department** earns more than 60000.
- The outer query **selects those departments.**

Using NOT EXISTS

Find departments that do not have any employee earning more than 60000.

SELECT department_id FROM departments d
WHERE NOT EXISTS (SELECT 1 FROM employees e
   WHERE e.department_id = d.department_id AND e.salary > 60000
);

Result:

department_id

    3

Explanation

- The Sub query checks if a department has **any employee earning above 60000.**
- The outer query **filters out those departments.**

Performance Tip: Use JOIN Instead of Sub queries When Possible

Some sub queries can be rewritten using JOIN for better performance.

Example: Find the highest salary in each department (Using JOIN)

SELECT e.department_id, e.name, e.salary
FROM employees e
JOIN (SELECT department_id, MAX(salary) AS max_salary FROM employees GROUP BY department_id) AS max_salaries
ON e.department_id = max_salaries.department_id AND e.salary = max_salaries.max_salary;

Result:
department_id name   salary

department_id	name	salary
1	Charlie	70000
2	Emma	65000
3	David	50000

Conclusion

- **Single-Row Sub queries** → Use with comparison operators (=, >, <).
- **Multi-Row Sub queries** → Use with IN, ANY, ALL.
- **Correlated Sub queries** → Run **for each row** in the outer query.
- **Sub queries in SELECT** → Useful for calculations like averages.
- **Sub queries in FROM** → Used for derived tables.

EXISTS/NOT EXISTS → Check for the existence of rows

10 VIEWS IN DATABASES

In SQL, a view is a virtual table derived from one or more tables or other views. Unlike a base table, which stores data physically, a view does not store data directly; instead, it is defined by a query that retrieves data from one or more underlying tables. Views provide several benefits, including simplifying complex queries, providing security by restricting access to specific columns or rows, and abstracting the underlying schema to simplify application development. Here's a detailed explanation of the concept of views in SQL with suitable examples:

10.1 Creating a View

You can create a view using the CREATE VIEW statement, specifying the view name and the query that defines the view.

Syntax:

CREATE VIEW view_name AS

SELECT column1, column2, ...

FROM table_name

WHERE condition;

Example:

CREATE VIEW employee_details AS

SELECT emp_id, emp_name, salary

FROM employees

WHERE department = 'IT';

In this example, a view named employee_details is created, which retrieves the emp_id, emp_name, and salary columns from the employees table where the department is 'IT'.

10.2 Querying a View

Once a view is created, you can query it like a regular table using the SELECT statement.

Example:

SELECT * FROM employee_details;

10.3 Updating Views

In some database systems, you can update the data through a view, provided that certain conditions are met. These conditions typically include ensuring that the view represents a single table and does not contain any complex expressions.

Example:

-- Assuming employee_details view represents a single table

UPDATE employee_details

SET salary = salary * 1.05

WHERE emp_id = 1001;

10.4 Dropping a View

You can drop a view using the DROP VIEW statement.

Syntax:

DROP VIEW view_name;

Example:

DROP VIEW employee_details;

10.5 Benefits of Views

1. **Data Abstraction:** Views allow you to abstract the underlying schema, providing a simplified and consistent interface to applications.

2. **Security:** Views can be used to restrict access to specific columns or rows, providing a level of security by hiding sensitive information.

3. **Simplified Queries:** Views can simplify complex queries by encapsulating logic and joining multiple tables.

4. **Performance Optimization:** Views can be precomputed or indexed to improve query performance.

10.6 Limitations of Views

1.**Performance Overhead:** Views may introduce performance overhead, especially if the underlying query is complex or involves large datasets.

2. **Read-only Nature:** Some views may be read-only, meaning you cannot update data through them.

3. **Complexity:** Views may become difficult to maintain if they encapsulate complex logic or depend on other views.

11 JOINS IN DATABASE

SQL joins are used to combine rows from two or more tables based on a related column between them. Joins are fundamental in SQL and are crucial for querying data from multiple tables in a relational database. There are several types of joins in SQL, including INNER JOIN, LEFT JOIN (or LEFT OUTER JOIN), RIGHT JOIN (or RIGHT OUTER JOIN), FULL JOIN (or FULL OUTER JOIN), and CROSS JOIN. Let's go through each type with examples:

Suppose we have two tables:

1. Employees table:

EmployeeID	Name	DepartmentID
1001	John Doe	1
1002	Jane Smith	2
1003	Alex Johnson	1
1004	Emily Brown	3
1005	Michael Clark	2

2.Departments table:

DepartmentID	DepartmentName
1	IT
2	HR
3	Marketing

11.1 INNER JOIN

An INNER JOIN returns rows from both tables where there is a match based on the specified condition.

Example:

SELECT Employees.Name, Departments.DepartmentName

FROM Employees

INNER JOIN Departments ON Employees.DepartmentID = Departments.DepartmentID;

Output:

Name	DepartmentName
John Doe	IT
Jane Smith	HR
Alex Johnson	IT
Emily Brown	Marketing
Michael Clark	HR

11.2 LEFT JOIN (or LEFT OUTER JOIN)

A LEFT JOIN returns all rows from the left table (Employees), and the matched rows from the right table (Departments). If there is no match, NULL values are returned for the right table.

Example:

SELECT Employees.Name, Departments.DepartmentName

FROM Employees

LEFT JOIN Departments ON Employees.DepartmentID = Departments.DepartmentID;

Output:

Name	DepartmentName
John Doe	IT
Jane Smith	HR

Alex Johnson	IT
Emily Brown	Marketing
Michael Clark	HR
NULL	NULL

11.3 RIGHT JOIN (or RIGHT OUTER JOIN):

A RIGHT JOIN returns all rows from the right table (Departments), and the matched rows from the left table (Employees). If there is no match, NULL values are returned for the left table.

Example:

SELECT Employees.Name, Departments.DepartmentName

FROM Employees

RIGHT JOIN Departments ON Employees.DepartmentID = Departments.DepartmentID;

Output:

Name	DepartmentName
John Doe	IT
Jane Smith	HR
Alex Johnson	IT
Emily Brown	Marketing
Michael Clark	HR
NULL	Operations

11.4 FULL JOIN (or FULL OUTER JOIN)

A FULL JOIN returns all rows when there is a match in either the left (Employees) or right (Departments) table. If there is no match, NULL values are returned for the missing side.

Example:

SELECT Employees.Name, Departments.DepartmentName

FROM Employees

FULL JOIN Departments ON Employees.DepartmentID = Departments.DepartmentID;

Output:

Name	DepartmentName
John Doe	IT
Jane Smith	HR
Alex Johnson	IT
Emily Brown	Marketing
Michael Clark	HR
NULL	Operations

11.5 CROSS JOIN

A CROSS JOIN returns the Cartesian product of rows from the joined tables, i.e., all possible combinations of rows.

Example:

SELECT Name, DepartmentName FROM Employees,Departments;

Output:

Name	DepartmentName
John Doe	IT
John Doe	HR
John Doe	Marketing
Jane Smith	IT

Jane Smith	HR
Jane Smith	Marketing
Alex Johnson	IT
Alex Johnson	HR
Alex Johnson	Marketing
Emily Brown	IT
Emily Brown	HR
Emily Brown	Marketing
Michael Clark	IT
Michael Clark	HR
Michael Clark	Marketing

These are the examples and outputs for each type of SQL join. Each type of join serves different purposes and understanding those helps in querying data effectively from relational databases.

12 QUERYING USING SQL

12.1 Viewing list of tables

The syntax for seeing a list of tables in a database management system (DBMS) varies depending on the specific DBMS you're using. Below are examples for some of the most common database systems: MySQL, PostgreSQL, and SQL Server.

MySQL:

Syntax:

SHOW TABLES;

Example:

SHOW TABLES;

PostgreSQL:

Syntax:

\dt

Example:

\dt

SQL Server (using SQLCMD):

Syntax:

SELECT * FROM INFORMATION_SCHEMA.TABLES WHERE TABLE_TYPE = 'BASE TABLE';

Example:

SELECT * FROM INFORMATION_SCHEMA.TABLES WHERE TABLE_TYPE = 'BASE TABLE';

These commands will provide you with a list of tables in the currently selected database for the respective DBMS. Note that you need appropriate permissions to execute these commands, and the specific syntax may vary depending on the version of the DBMS you're using.

12.2 GROUP BY Clause

The GROUP BY clause is used in SQL to group rows that have the same values into summary rows. It's commonly used with aggregate functions like COUNT(), SUM(), AVG(), etc., to perform operations on each group of rows.

Here's the syntax:

SELECT column1, aggregate_function(column2)

FROM table

GROUP BY column1;

Example:

Consider a table named sales that contains data about sales transactions:

product_id	category	sales_amount
1	Electronics	1000
2	Clothing	500
3	Electronics	800
4	Clothing	300
5	Electronics	1200

Let's say we want to calculate the total sales amount for each category:

SELECT category, SUM(sales_amount) AS total_sales

FROM sales

GROUP BY category;

Output:

category	total_sales
Electronics	3000
Clothing	800

12.3 HAVING Clause

The HAVING clause is used in combination with the GROUP BY clause to filter group rows based on specified conditions. It's similar to the WHERE clause but is used specifically with aggregated data.

Here's the syntax:

SELECT column1, aggregate_function(column2)

FROM table

GROUP BY column1

HAVING condition;

Example:

Building upon the previous example, let's say we want to find categories with total sales greater than 1000:

SELECT category, SUM(sales_amount) AS total_sales

FROM sales

GROUP BY category

HAVING SUM(sales_amount) > 1000;

Output:

| category | total_sales |

| ------------- | -------------- |

| Electronics | 3000 |

In this example, the HAVING clause filters out the groups where the total sales are not greater than 1000.

So, in summary:

• The GROUP BY clause is used to group rows that have the same values into summary rows.

• The HAVING clause is used to filter group rows based on specified conditions after the GROUP BY clause has been applied.

Here's one more example to illustrate how the GROUP BY clause works:

Suppose we have a table named orders that stores information about orders made by customers:

order_id	customer_id	order_date	total_amount
1	101	2023-01-01	50.00
2	102	2023-01-02	75.00
3	101	2023-01-03	100.00
4	103	2023-01-04	30.00
5	102	2023-01-05	25.00

Now, let's say we want to calculate the total amount of orders made by each customer. We can achieve this using the GROUP BY clause:

SELECT customer_id, SUM (total_amount) AS total_order_amount

FROM orders

GROUP BY customer_id;

Output:

customer_id	total_order_amount
101	150.00
102	100.00
103	30.00

In this query:

• We selected the customer_id column and applied the SUM () function to the total_amount column.

• We used GROUP BY customer_id to group the rows by customer_id.

• The result is the total order amount for each customer.

The GROUP BY clause is essential for performing aggregate operations on groups of data in SQL. It allows us to summarize data in a meaningful way, making it easier to analyze large datasets.

13 FUNCTIONS IN SQL-SINGLE ROW FUNCTIONS

Functions are very powerful features of SQL. These are used to carry out operations on data very quickly by using ready to use inbuilt functions. Functions in SQL are broadly classified into single row functions and aggregate/multi row functions.

Single row functions are numeric functions, string/text functions and date & time functions.

13.1 Numeric Functions

Numeric single row functions in SQL are functions that operate on individual rows of a table and return numeric values. These functions can perform various mathematical operations, conversions, and manipulations on numeric data types such as integers, decimals, and floating-point numbers. These functions can be applied to scalar data values or to column data of tables. Here are some commonly used numeric single row functions:

1. **ABS ():** Returns the absolute value of a number.

Example:

SELECT ABS (-10) AS absolute_value;

Output:

| absolute_value |

|--------------------|

| 10 |

2. **CEIL () or CEILING ():** Rounds a number up to the nearest integer.

Example:

SELECT CEIL (4.3) AS rounded_up;

Output:

| rounded_up |

```
|------------------ |

| 5              |
```

3. **FLOOR ():** Rounds a number down to the nearest integer.

Example:

SELECT FLOOR (4.7) AS rounded_down;

Output:

```
| rounded_down   |

|--------------------|

| 4              |
```

4. **ROUND ():** Rounds a number to a specified number of decimal places.

Example:

SELECT ROUND (4.567, 2) AS rounded_number;

Output:

```
| rounded_number  |

|-----------------------|

| 4.57           |
```

5. **SQRT ():** Returns the square root of a number.

Example:

SELECT SQRT (25) AS square_root;

Output:

```
| square_root   |

|-----------------|

| 5             |
```

6. **POWER () or POW():** Raises a number to a specified power.

Example:

SELECT POWER(2, 3) AS result;

Output:

| result |

|---------|

| 8 |

7. **MOD ():** Returns the remainder of a division operation.

Example:

SELECT MOD (10, 3) AS remainder;

Output:

| remainder |

|--------------|

| 1 |

8. **SIGN ():** Returns the sign of a number (-1 for negative, 0 for zero, 1 for positive).

Example:

SELECT SIGN(-5) AS sign_value;

Output:

| sign_value |

|--------------|

| -1 |

These functions are useful for performing various calculations and transformations on numeric data in SQL queries.

9. **TRUNCATE ()**: This function is used to truncate a number to a specified number of decimal places or digits. This function effectively removes the digits or decimal places beyond the specified precision.

TRUNCATE (number, precision);

• number: The number or expression to be truncated.

• precision: The number of decimal places to which the number should be truncated.

Example:

Suppose we have a table named sales with a column total_sales that contains sales amounts with several decimal places:

total_sales
123.456
789.123
456.789

Now, let's say we want to truncate these sales amounts to two decimal places.

Example:

SELECT TRUNCATE (total_sales, 2) AS truncated_sales

FROM sales;

Output:

truncated_sales
123.45
789.12

| 456.78 |

In this example:

• The TRUNCATE () function is used to truncate the total_sales values to two decimal places.

• The result is a new column named truncated_sales with the truncated values.

Keep in mind that the TRUNCATE () function doesn't round the number; it simply removes the digits or decimal places beyond the specified precision. If rounding is required, you may need to use the ROUND () function instead.

13.2 String or Text Functions

Single-row string functions in SQL operate on individual rows of string data and return modified string values. These functions are useful for manipulating string data in various ways, such as changing case, extracting substrings, searching for specific patterns, and performing conversions. These functions can be applied to scalar data values or to column data of tables. Here are some commonly used single-row string functions along with examples and outputs:

1. LOWER (): This function converts all characters in a string to lowercase.

Example:

SELECT LOWER ('Hello World') AS lower_case_string;

Output:

| lower_case_string |

| ------------------------- |

| hello world |

2. UPPER () or UCASE(): These functions converts all characters in a string to uppercase.

Example:

SELECT UPPER('Hello World') AS upper_case_string;

Output:

| upper_case_string |

|---------------------------|

| HELLO WORLD |

3. **SUBSTRING () or SUBSTR () or MID ():** These functions extracts a substring from a string.

Example:

SELECT SUBSTRING('Hello World', 1, 5) AS substring_result;

Output:

| substring_result |

|----------------------|

| Hello |

In this example "Hello Word" is the string. 1 is the starting index and 5 is the total number of characters to be extracted including starting index index character. Remember, the index of characters begins from 1 from extreme left of the string.

4. **CONCAT ():** This function concatenates two or more strings together.

Example:

SELECT CONCAT('Hello', ' ', 'World') AS concatenated_string;

Output:

| concatenated_string |

|---------------------------|

| Hello World |

5. LENGTH () or LEN(): This function returns the length of a string.

Example:

SELECT LENGTH ('Hello World') AS string_length;

Output:

| string_length |

|-----------------|

| 11 |

6. **TRIM():**This function removes leading and trailing spaces from a string.

Example:

SELECT TRIM(' Hello World ') AS trimmed_string;

Output:

| trimmed_string |

|--------------------|

| Hello World |

7. REPLACE(): This function replaces occurrences of a substring within a string with another substring.

Example:

SELECT REPLACE('Hello World', 'World', 'Universe') AS replaced_string;

Output:

| replaced_string |

|----------------------|

| Hello Universe |

In this example "Hello World" is the string. "World" is the substring. "Universe" is the new substring to be replaced with.

8. **LEFT() or RIGHT():**These functions returns a specified number of characters from the left or right side of a string.

Example:

SELECT LEFT('Hello World', 5) AS left_part, RIGHT('Hello World', 5) AS right_part;

Output:

left_part	right_part
Hello	World

In this example 5 is the number of characters to be extracted from left or right

9. **INSTR():**This function is used to find the starting position of a substring within a string. It returns the position of the first occurrence of the substring within the string. If the substring is not found, it returns 0.

Example:

SELECT INSTR('hello world', 'world') AS position;

Output:

position
7

Example:

SELECT INSTR('hello world', 'universe') AS position;

Output:

position

| 0 |

You can also specify a start position to begin the search from a specific position within the string.

Example:

SELECT INSTR('hello world, hello universe', 'hello', 7) AS position;

Output:

| position |

|-------------|

| 14 |

In this example, the substring "hello" is found starting at position 14 within the string "hello world, hello universe", starting the search from position 7.

10. **LOWER() or LCASE():** This function is used to convert all characters in a string to lowercase. It's a single-row string function, meaning it operates on individual rows of data and returns modified string values

Suppose we have a table named users with a column username containing usernames in various cases:

| username |

|-----------------|

| JohnDoe |

| JaneSmith |

| Johndoe |

| janeSmith |

Now, let's use the LOWER() function to convert all usernames to lowercase:

Example:

SELECT LOWER(username) AS lowercase_username

FROM users;

Output:

lowercase_username
johndoe
janesmith
johndoe
janesmith

11. **LTRIM():** This functionis used to remove leading (leftmost) characters or spaces from a string.

Suppose we have a table named employees with a column full_name containing employee names with leading spaces:

full_name
John Doe
Jane Smith
Alice Lee
Bob Johnson

Now, let's use the LTRIM() function to remove leading spaces from the full_name column:

Example:

SELECT LTRIM(full_name) AS trimmed_name

FROM employees;

Output:

| trimmed_name |

|--------------------|

| John Doe |

| Jane Smith |

| Alice Lee |

| Bob Johnson |

In this example, the LTRIM() function removes leading spaces from each value in the full_name column. As a result, all names are left-aligned in the output, with no leading spaces.

12. **RTRIM():** This function is used to remove trailing (rightmost) characters or spaces from a string.

Suppose we have a table named products with a column product_name containing product names with trailing spaces:

| product_name |

|------------------------|

| Laptop |

| Desktop |

| Tablet |

| Monitor |

Now, let's add trailing spaces to some product names and use the RTRIM() function to remove them:

Example:

SELECT RTRIM(product_name || ' ') AS trimmed_name

FROM products;

Output:

| trimmed_name |

|----------------------|

| Laptop |

| Desktop |

| Tablet |

| Monitor |

In this example, the RTRIM() function removes trailing spaces from each value in the product_name column. As a result, all product names are left-aligned in the output, with no trailing spaces.

ASCII String functions

ASCII():In SQL, ASCII functions are used to retrieve the ASCII (American Standard Code for Information Interchange) value of the first character of a given string. There are two main ASCII-related functions in SQL: ASCII() and CHAR(). Let me explain each with examples and their outputs.

13. **ASCII():**This function returns the ASCII value of the first character in a string.

Example:

SELECT ASCII('A');

Output:

|ASCII('A') |

|---------------|

| 65 |

In this example, the ASCII value of the character 'A' is returned, which is 65.

14. **CHAR():** This function returns the character associated with the ASCII code passed to it.

Example:

SELECT CHAR(65);

Output:

|CHAR(65) |

|---------------|

|A |

In this example, the character associated with the ASCII code 65 is returned, which is 'A'.

These functions are commonly used when dealing with character manipulation or when you need to work with ASCII values directly in SQL queries.

These functions provide powerful tools for manipulating string data within SQL queries, allowing for tasks such as formatting, cleaning, and transforming strings according to specific requirements.

13.3 Date and Time Functions

Date and time functions in SQL are used to perform operations on date and time values, such as extracting parts of dates, adding or subtracting time intervals, formatting dates and times, and more. These functions vary slightly between different database management systems, but they generally provide similar functionalities. The date format used is YYYY-MM-DD. These functions can be applied to scalar values or column data. Here are some commonly used date and time functions along with examples and outputs:

1. **CURRENT_DATE () or CURDATE ():** These functions returns the current date.

Example:

SELECT CURRENT_DATE AS current_date;

Output:

| current_date|

|---------------|

| 2024-02-22 |

2. **CURRENT_TIME:**This function returns the current time.

Example:

SELECT CURRENT_TIME AS current_time;

Output:

| current_time |

|------------------|

| 18:30:45 |

3. **CURRENT_TIMESTAMP:** This function returns the current timestamp (date and time).

Example:

SELECT CURRENT_TIMESTAMP AS current_timestamp;

Output:

| current_timestamp |

|------------------------------|

| 2024-02-22 18:30:45 |

4. **DATE_PART() / EXTRACT():**This function extracts a specific part of a date (e.g., year, month, day).

Example:

SELECT DATE_PART ('year', CURRENT_DATE) AS current_year,

   DATE_PART ('month', CURRENT_DATE) AS current_month,

   DATE_PART ('day', CURRENT_DATE) AS current_day;

Output:

current_year	current_month	current_day
2024	2	22

5. **DATE_ADD() / DATE_SUB():**These functions adds or subtracts a specified interval from a date.

Example:

SELECT DATE_ADD(CURRENT_DATE, INTERVAL 7 DAY) AS next_week,DATE_SUB(CURRENT_DATE, INTERVAL 1 MONTH) AS last_month;

Output:

next_week	last_month
2024-02-29	2024-01-22

6. **TO_CHAR():**This function formats a date or timestamp into a string using a specified format.

Example:

SELECT TO_CHAR(CURRENT_TIMESTAMP, 'YYYY-MM-DD HH24:MI:SS') AS formatted_timestamp;

Output:

formatted_timestamp
2024-02-22 18:30:45

7. **AGE():**This function calculates the difference between two dates.

Example:

SELECT AGE('2024-02-22', '2000-01-01') AS age_difference;

Output:

| age_difference |

|-------------------|

| 24 years |

8. **NOW():**This function is used to retrieve the current date and time from the system's clock. It returns a timestamp value representing the current date and time according to the system's time zone.

Example:

SELECT NOW() AS current_timestamp;

Output:

| current_timestamp |

|----------------------------|

| 2024-02-22 18:30:45 |

9. **SYSDATE():** This function is used to retrieve the current date and time from the system's clock. Similar to NOW(), it returns a timestamp value representing the current date and time according to the system's timezone.

Example:

SELECT SYSDATE() AS current_timestamp;

Output:

| current_timestamp |

|------------------------------|

| 2024-02-22 18:30:45 |

10. **DATE():**This function is used to extract the date part from a datetime or timestamp expression. It returns only the date portion of a datetime value,

discarding any time component.

Suppose we have a table named orders with a column order_date containing datetime values:

| order_date |

|---------------------------|

| 2024-02-22 12:30:45 |

| 2024-02-21 09:45:00 |

| 2024-02-20 16:20:30 |

Example:

SELECT DATE(order_date) AS order_date_only

FROM orders;

Output:

| order_date_only |

|--------------------|

| 2024-02-22 |

| 2024-02-21 |

| 2024-02-20 |

11. **MONTH():** This function is used to extract the month component from a date or datetime expression. It returns an integer representing the month portion of the given date or datetime value.

Suppose we have a table named orders with a column order_date containing datetime values:

| order_date |

|---------------------------|

| 2024-02-22 12:30:45 |

| 2024-04-21 09:45:00 |

| 2024-07-20 16:20:30 |

Example:

SELECT MONTH(order_date) AS order_month FROM orders;

Output:

| order_month |

|------------------|

| 2 |

| 4 |

| 7 |

12. **MONTHNAME():** This function is not a standard SQL function available in all database management systems. However, some database systems like MySQL do have a MONTHNAME() function. This function is used to retrieve the name of the month from a given date or datetime expression. It returns the full name of the month as a string.

Suppose we have a table named orders with a column order_date containing datetime values:

| order_date |

|----------------------------|

| 2024-02-22 12:30:45 |

| 2024-04-21 09:45:00 |

| 2024-07-20 16:20:30 |

Example:

SELECT MONTHNAME(order_date) AS order_month_name

FROM orders;

Output:

| order_month_name |

|----------------------------|

| February |

| April |

| July |

13. **YEAR():** This function in SQL is used to extract the year component from a date or datetime expression. It returns an integer representing the year portion of the given date or datetime value.

Suppose we have a table named orders with a column order_date containing datetime values:

| order_date |

|--------------------------|

| 2024-02-22 12:30:45 |

| 2025-04-21 09:45:00 |

| 2026-07-20 16:20:30 |

Example

SELECT YEAR(order_date) AS order_year

FROM orders;

Output:

| order_year |

|----------------|

| 2024 |

| 2025 |

| 2026 |

14.**DAY()**: This function is used to extract the day component from a date or datetime expression. It returns an integer representing the day portion of the given date or datetime value.

Suppose we have a table named orders with a column order_date containing datetime values:

| order_date |

|----------------------------|

| 2024-02-22 12:30:45 |

| 2025-04-21 09:45:00 |

| 2026-07-20 16:20:30 |

Example:

SELECT DAY(order_date) AS order_day

FROM orders;

Output:

| order_day |

|--------------|

| 22 |

| 21 |

| 20 |

15. **DAYNAME()**: This function is used to retrieve the name of the day of the week from a given date or datetime expression. It returns the full name of the day of the week as a string.

Suppose we have a table named orders with a column order_date containing datetime values:

| order_date |

| -------------------------- |

| 2024-02-22 12:30:45 |

| 2025-04-21 09:45:00 |

| 2026-07-20 16:20:30 |

Example:

SELECT DAYNAME(order_date) AS order_day_name

FROM orders;

Output:

| order_day_name |

| --------------------- |

| Sunday |

| Monday |

| Tuesday |

16. **DAYOFWEEK():** This function is used to retrieve the day of the week from a given date or datetime expression. It returns an integer representing the day of the week, where Sunday is 1, Monday is 2, Tuesday is 3, and so on.

Suppose we have a table named orders with a column order_date containing datetime values:

| order_date |

| -------------------------- |

| 2024-02-23 12:30:45 |

| 2025-04-21 09:45:00 |

| 2026-07-20 16:20:30 |

Example:

SELECT DAYOFWEEK(order_date) AS day_of_week

FROM orders;

Output:

| day_of_week|

|------------------|

| 2 |

| 3 |

| 3 |

17. **WEEKDAY ():**This function is used to retrieve the day of the week index from a given date or datetime expression. It returns an integer representing the day of the week index, where Monday is 0, Tuesday is 1, Wednesday is 2, and so on, up to Sunday being 6.

Suppose we have a table named orders with a column order_date containing datetime values:

| order_date |

|----------------------------|

| 2024-02-23 12:30:45 |

| 2025-04-21 09:45:00 |

| 2026-07-20 16:20:30 |

Example:

SELECT WEEKDAY(order_date) AS day_of_week_index

FROM orders;

Output:

```
| day_of_week_index |

|---------------------------|

| 1                 |

| 2                 |

| 2                 |
```

These are just a few examples of the many date and time functions available in SQL. They provide powerful tools for working with temporal data, enabling various types of date and time calculations and manipulations within SQL queries.

14 FUNCTIONS IN SQL-AGGREGATE FUNCTIONS

(Multi Row Functions)

Aggregate functions in SQL are used to perform calculations on groups of rows to return a single result. The aggregate functions ignores NULL value in the columns and returns the value as output. These functions summarize data from multiple rows into a single value. Some common aggregate functions include COUNT, SUM, AVG, MIN, and MAX. Let's delve into each with examples and their respective outputs.

Consider a simple table named "Orders" that tracks sales orders. It has the following columns:

• order_id: The unique identifier for each order.

• customer_id: The identifier for the customer who placed the order.

• order_date: The date when the order was placed.

• total_amount: The total amount of the order.

order_id	customer_id	order_date	total_amount
1	101	2024-02-01	100.00
2	102	NULL	150.00
3	101	2024-02-03	200.00
4	103	2024-02-04	120.00
5	102	2024-02-05	180.00

Aggregate Functions:

1. COUNT(): This function counts the number of rows that meet a specified condition or the total number of rows in a table.

Example 1: Count the total number of orders.

SELECT COUNT(*) AS total_orders FROM Orders;

Output:

total_orders
5

Example 2: Count the number of orders placed by customer 101.

SELECT COUNT(*) AS orders_by_customer_101 FROM Orders WHERE customer_id = 101;

Output:

orders_by_customer_101
2

Example 3: Count the number of order_date.

SELECT COUNT(order_date) FROM Orders;

Output:

order_date
4

In this example, the NULL values in the column order_date are ignored by COUNT() function and returns only the number of non NULL values.

2. SUM(): This function calculates the sum of values in a specified column.

Example: Calculate the total amount of all orders.

SELECT SUM(total_amount) AS total_sales FROM Orders;

Output:

| total_sales |

|----------------|

| 750.00 |

3. AVG(): This function calculates the average value of a numeric column.

Example: Calculate the average order amount.

SELECT AVG(total_amount) AS average_order_amount FROM Orders;

Output:

| average_order_amount |

|-----------------------------|

| 150.00 |

4. MIN(): This function returns the minimum value from a specified column.

Example: Find the smallest order amount.

SELECT MIN(total_amount) AS smallest_order_amount FROM Orders;

Output:

| smallest_order_amount |

|------------------------------|

| 100.00 |

5. MAX(): This function returns the maximum value from a specified column.

Example: Find the largest order amount.

SELECT MAX(total_amount) AS largest_order_amount FROM Orders;

Output:

| largest_order_amount |

|-----------------------------|

| 200.00 |

These are some basic examples of how aggregate functions can be used in SQL queries to perform calculations on groups of rows and return single values summarizing the data.

15 TRIGGERS IN SQL

Triggers are database objects that are automatically executed or fired in response to certain events on a particular table. These events may include INSERT, UPDATE, DELETE operations, or even database schema changes like CREATE, ALTER, or DROP statements.

SQL supports both row-level and statement-level triggers. Row-level triggers are executed once for each row affected by the triggering event, while statement-level triggers are executed once for each SQL statement.

Creating a Trigger

The syntax to create a trigger in MySQL is as follows:

CREATE TRIGGER trigger_name

{BEFORE | AFTER} {INSERT | UPDATE | DELETE} ON table_name

FOR EACH ROW

BEGIN

    -- Trigger body, which can include SQL statements

END;

Let's go through an example to illustrate this:

Suppose we have a table called orders with the following structure:

CREATE TABLE orders (

    order_id INT AUTO_INCREMENT PRIMARY KEY,

    order_date DATE,

    total_amount DECIMAL(10, 2)

        );

Now, let's say we want to create a trigger that automatically updates a separate order_logs table whenever a new order is inserted into the orders table. The order_logs table will store the order ID and the timestamp of when the order was placed.

Here's how we can create this trigger:

CREATE TRIGGER after_order_insert

AFTER INSERT ON orders

FOR EACH ROW

BEGIN

    INSERT INTO order_logs (order_id, timestamp)

    VALUES (NEW.order_id, NOW());

END;

In this trigger:

• after_order_insert is the name of the trigger.

• AFTER INSERT ON orders specifies that the trigger should be fired after an INSERT operation on the orders table.

• FOR EACH ROW indicates that this is a row-level trigger, meaning it will be executed once for each row affected by the INSERT operation.

• BEGIN ... END defines the body of the trigger, which contains the SQL statements to be executed when the trigger is fired.

• NEW.order_id refers to the order_id of the newly inserted row in the orders table.

• NOW() retrieves the current timestamp.

Now, whenever a new order is inserted into the orders table, the trigger will automatically insert a corresponding entry into the order_logs table with the order ID and the current timestamp.

This is just one example of how triggers can be used in SQL to automate certain tasks or maintain data integrity based on specific database events.

Triggers offer a powerful mechanism for enforcing business rules or implementing complex logic within the database itself.

16 INDEXES IN SQL

Indexes in SQL are database objects that improve the speed of data retrieval operations on a table by providing quick access to the rows based on key values. They work similarly to indexes in books, where you can quickly locate information by referring to the index at the back of the book.

In SQL databases, indexes are created on one or more columns of a table. When you perform a query that involves the indexed columns, the database engine can use the index to quickly locate the rows that satisfy the query conditions, rather than scanning the entire table.

16.1 Types of Indexes

1.Single-Column Index: An index created on a single column.

2.Composite Index: An index created on multiple columns.

Creating an Index:

In SQL, you can create an index using the CREATE INDEX statement. Here's the basic syntax:

CREATE INDEX index_name ON table_name (column1, column2, ...);

Now, let's illustrate indexes with an example:

Suppose we have a table called employees with the following structure:

CREATE TABLE employees (

    employee_id INT PRIMARY KEY,

    first_name VARCHAR(50),

    last_name VARCHAR(50),

    department_id INT,

    salary DECIMAL(10, 2)

      );

Now, let's say we frequently perform queries to retrieve employees based on their department_id. To improve the performance of these queries, we can create an index on the department_id column.

Here's how we can create the index:

CREATE INDEX idx_department_id ON employees (department_id);

Now, whenever we execute a query that filters or sorts by the department_id column, the database engine can use the idx_department_id index to quickly locate the relevant rows.

16.2 Benefits of Indexes

1. Faster Data Retrieval: Indexes allow the database engine to locate specific rows quickly, resulting in faster query execution times.

2. Improved Performance: Queries that involve indexed columns typically perform better, especially for large tables.

3. Enforcement of Uniqueness: Indexes can enforce uniqueness constraints on columns, preventing duplicate values from being inserted into the table.

Considerations:

1. Overhead: Indexes consume additional storage space and require maintenance overhead during data modification operations (such as INSERT, UPDATE, DELETE).

2. Choosing Columns: It's essential to carefully select the columns for indexing based on the queries frequently executed against the table.

3. Composite Indexes: Composite indexes can be beneficial for queries that involve multiple columns, but they should be used judiciously to avoid unnecessary overhead.

In summary, indexes play a crucial role in optimizing database performance by providing fast access to the data based on key values. They are an essential tool for improving query performance and should be carefully designed and maintained to maximize their benefits.

17 MANAGING DATABASES AND TABLES

17.1 Creating Relationships between Tables in MySQL

In MySQL, relationships between tables are established using **keys** to maintain data integrity and ensure efficient data retrieval. The most common types of relationships include:

1. **One-to-One (1:1)**
2. **One-to-Many (1:M)**
3. **Many-to-Many (M:N)**

Each relationship type is implemented using **Primary Keys (PK)** and **Foreign Keys (FK)**.

Understanding Primary and Foreign Keys

- **Primary Key (PK):** A unique identifier for each record in a table.
- **Foreign Key (FK):** A column that refers to the Primary Key of another table, creating a relationship between them.

Foreign keys help enforce referential integrity, preventing actions that would break the relationship.

One-to-One (1:1) Relationship

A **one-to-one** relationship means each record in Table A corresponds to one record in Table B.

Example: Users and Profiles

Each user has exactly **one** profile.

```
CREATE TABLE Users (
    user_id INT PRIMARY KEY,
    username VARCHAR(50) NOT NULL UNIQUE
);

CREATE TABLE Profiles (
    profile_id INT PRIMARY KEY,
    user_id INT UNIQUE,
```

```
bio TEXT,
FOREIGN KEY (user_id) REFERENCES Users(user_id) ON DELETE
CASCADE
);
```

Explanation:

- Users table has user_id as the primary key.
- Profiles table has user_id as a **foreign key** referencing Users(user_id).
- ON DELETE CASCADE: If a user is deleted, their profile is also deleted.

3. One-to-Many (1:M) Relationship

A **one-to-many** relationship means a record in Table A can have multiple corresponding records in Table B.

Example: Customers and Orders

Each customer can place multiple orders.

```
CREATE TABLE Customers (
    customer_id INT PRIMARY KEY,
    name VARCHAR(100) NOT NULL
);
```

```
CREATE TABLE Orders (
    order_id INT PRIMARY KEY,
    customer_id INT,
    order_date DATE,
    total_amount DECIMAL(10,2),
    FOREIGN KEY (customer_id) REFERENCES Customers(customer_id)
ON DELETE CASCADE
);
```

Explanation:

- A single customer can have multiple orders.
- The customer_id in Orders references the customer_id in Customers.
- ON DELETE CASCADE ensures all orders are deleted when the corresponding customer is removed.

Many-to-Many (M:N) Relationship

A **many-to-many** relationship occurs when multiple records in Table A relate to multiple records in Table B. This is implemented using a **junction table**.

Example: Students and Courses

A student can enroll in multiple courses, and each course can have multiple students.

```
CREATE TABLE Students (
    student_id INT PRIMARY KEY,
    name VARCHAR(100) NOT NULL
);

CREATE TABLE Courses (
    course_id INT PRIMARY KEY,
    course_name VARCHAR(100) NOT NULL
);

CREATE TABLE Enrollments (
    student_id INT,
    course_id INT,
    enrollment_date DATE,
    PRIMARY KEY (student_id, course_id),
    FOREIGN KEY (student_id) REFERENCES Students(student_id) ON DELETE CASCADE,
    FOREIGN KEY (course_id) REFERENCES Courses(course_id) ON DELETE CASCADE
);
```

Explanation:

- Students and Courses have a **many-to-many** relationship.
- Enrollments acts as a **junction table** with composite primary keys (student_id, course_id).
- Foreign keys reference Students(student_id) and Courses(course_id).
- ON DELETE CASCADE ensures enrollment records are removed if a student or course is deleted.

Using JOIN Queries to Retrieve Related Data

After establishing relationships, you can use JOIN queries to fetch related data.

Example Queries

Get all orders of a specific customer

```
SELECT Customers.name, Orders.order_id, Orders.total_amount
FROM Customers
JOIN Orders ON Customers.customer_id = Orders.customer_id
WHERE Customers.customer_id = 1;
```

Get students enrolled in a specific course

```
SELECT Students.name, Courses.course_name
FROM Enrollments
JOIN Students ON Enrollments.student_id = Students.student_id
JOIN Courses ON Enrollments.course_id = Courses.course_id
WHERE Courses.course_id = 101;
```

Relationship Constraints and Best Practices

- **Use appropriate ON DELETE rules:**
  - o CASCADE: Deletes related records automatically.
  - o SET NULL: Sets foreign key to NULL instead of deleting.
  - o RESTRICT: Prevents deletion if related records exist.
- **Index Foreign Keys** for better query performance.
- **Normalize data** to reduce redundancy and improve efficiency.

MySQL allows the creation of relationships using **Primary Keys** and **Foreign Keys** to enforce data integrity. By implementing **One-to-One**, **One-to-Many**, and **Many-to-Many** relationships, we can design efficient databases that prevent redundancy and ensure consistency.

17.2 Data Backup and Recovery in MySQL

Data backup and recovery are crucial processes in MySQL to ensure data integrity, prevent data loss, and recover from system failures, accidental deletions, or corruption. In this guide, we will cover the different types of backups, methods of performing backups, and various recovery strategies with practical examples.

Importance of Backup and Recovery in MySQL

- Protects data from accidental deletion, corruption, or hardware failure.
- Ensures business continuity in case of data loss.
- Helps recover historical data.
- Provides a mechanism for disaster recovery.

Types of MySQL Backups

MySQL supports different types of backups based on requirements:

1. **Logical Backup**
   - Uses SQL statements to export database structure and data.
   - Can be taken using mysqldump or MySQL Shell's dump utilities.
   - Example: Creates a .sql file containing CREATE TABLE and INSERT statements.
2. **Physical Backup**
   - Copies raw database files from the MySQL data directory.
   - Faster than logical backups but requires MySQL to be stopped.
   - Used for large datasets.
   - Can be performed using xtrabackup or direct filesystem copies.
3. **Incremental Backup**
   - Captures only changes made after the last backup.
   - Efficient for large databases as it minimizes storage usage and backup time.
   - Tools: xtrabackup, binary logs.
4. **Full Backup**
   - A complete snapshot of the database at a given time.
   - Used to restore the entire system.
   - Can be performed using both logical (mysqldump) and physical methods.
5. **Differential Backup**
   - Captures changes since the last full backup.
   - A balance between full and incremental backups.
6. **Binary Log Backup**
   - Stores all changes made to the database.

o   Useful for point-in-time recovery.
o   Stored in binary logs (binlog).

Performing Backups in MySQL

Logical Backup Using mysqldump

mysqldump is a command-line tool that generates SQL scripts for database export.

Full Backup Example

mysqldump -u root -p --all-databases > full_backup.sql

- -u root: Username.
- -p: Prompts for password.
- --all-databases: Dumps all databases.
- >: Redirects output to full_backup.sql.

Backup a Single Database

mysqldump -u root -p my_database > my_database_backup.sql

Backup a Specific Table

mysqldump -u root -p my_database my_table > my_table_backup.sql

Backup Without Data (Schema Only)

mysqldump -u root -p --no-data my_database > schema_backup.sql

Backup with Compression

mysqldump -u root -p my_database | gzip > my_database_backup.sql.gz

17.3 Physical Backup

Physical backups involve copying database files from the MySQL data directory.

Example Using tar

tar -czvf mysql_backup.tar.gz /var/lib/mysql/

- Requires MySQL to be stopped to ensure data consistency.

Using Percona XtraBackup (Hot Backup)

xtrabackup --backup --target-dir=/backup/

- Provides a non-blocking backup process.

17.4 Incremental Backup Using Binary Logs

Binary logs store all changes made to the database.

Enable Binary Logging

Edit MySQL configuration (my.cnf):

log-bin=mysql-bin

binlog-format=ROW

Restart MySQL:

systemctl restart mysql

Backup Binary Logs

mysqlbinlog --read-from-remote-server -u root -p mysql-bin.000001 > binlog_backup.sql

17.5 Data Recovery in MySQL

There are multiple ways to restore MySQL data depending on the backup type.

Restoring from mysqldump **Backup**

Restore Full Database

mysql -u root -p < full_backup.sql
Restore Single Database

mysql -u root -p my_database < my_database_backup.sql

Restore a Specific Table

mysql -u root -p my_database < my_table_backup.sql

Restoring from Physical Backup

Using tar to Restore

tar -xzvf mysql_backup.tar.gz -C /var/lib/mysql/

- Ensure MySQL is stopped before restoring:

systemctl stop mysql

- After restoring, restart MySQL:

systemctl start mysql

17.6 Point-in-Time Recovery Using Binary Logs

If accidental deletion occurs, binary logs can help restore data to a specific point.

Step 1: Identify the Binary Log Position

SHOW BINARY LOGS;

Step 2: Restore Using Binary Logs

mysqlbinlog --start-datetime="2025-02-20 10:00:00" \
--stop-datetime="2025-02-20 12:00:00" mysql-bin.000001 | mysql -u root -p

- This restores data between 10 AM and 12 PM.

17.7 Best Practices for MySQL Backup and Recovery

Automate Backups: Use cron jobs or scripts to automate backups.

crontab -e

Add:

0 2 * * * mysqldump -u root -p my_database | gzip > /backups/my_database_$(date +\%F).sql.gz

    o   Runs every day at 2 AM.

Use Multiple Backup Types: Combine logical, physical, and incremental backups.

Store Backups Securely: Use offsite storage (cloud or remote servers).

Test Backup Integrity: Regularly verify backups.

mysql -u root -p -e "SHOW TABLES;" my_database

Enable Binary Logging for Point-in-Time Recovery.

Monitor Storage Space: Ensure adequate disk space for backups.

Use Replication: MySQL replication can serve as a backup mechanism.

Backup Type	Method	Pros	Cons
Logical	mysqldump	Portable, easy to use	Slow for large databases
Physical	File copy, tar	Fast, efficient for large data	Requires MySQL to be stopped
Incremental	xtrabackup, binlog	Saves space, reduces backup time	Complex to restore
Full	mysqldump, tar	Complete snapshot, easy to restore	Requires more storage
Binary Logs	mysqlbinlog	Point-in-time recovery	Needs proper

Backup Type	Method	Pros	Cons
			configuration

By implementing proper backup strategies and recovery techniques, you can ensure data safety, minimize downtime, and quickly recover from data loss events in MySQL.

17.8 Introduction to Stored Procedures and Functions

Stored Procedures

Stored Procedures and Functions are essential database objects in MySQL that allow you to encapsulate SQL logic for reuse and modularity.

A **Stored Procedure** is a set of SQL statements that can be stored in the database and executed as a single unit. It allows procedural programming constructs like loops, conditionals, and error handling, making it useful for automating repetitive tasks and enforcing business logic.

Functions

A **Function** is similar to a Stored Procedure but differs in key ways:

- It **must** return a value.
- It can be used in **SELECT** statements.
- It is mainly used for calculations and transformations.

Creating and Using Stored Procedures

Basic Syntax of Stored Procedures

DELIMITER //

CREATE   PROCEDURE   procedure_name   ([IN|OUT|INOUT]
parameter_name DataType)
BEGIN
   -- SQL statements
END //

DELIMITER ;

- **DELIMITER**: Changes the statement delimiter to // to avoid conflicts with ; inside the procedure.
- **IN**: Input parameter (default).
- **OUT**: Output parameter.
- **INOUT**: Input and output parameter.

Example: Stored Procedure Without Parameters

DELIMITER //

```
CREATE PROCEDURE GetAllEmployees()
BEGIN
   SELECT * FROM employees;
END //
```

DELIMITER ;

Execution

CALL GetAllEmployees();

Example: Stored Procedure With Input Parameter

DELIMITER //

```
CREATE PROCEDURE GetEmployeeByID(IN emp_id INT)
BEGIN
   SELECT * FROM employees WHERE id = emp_id;
END //
```

DELIMITER ;

Execution

CALL GetEmployeeByID(101);

Here, 101 is passed as an argument to filter the employee with id = 101.

Example: Stored Procedure With Output Parameter

DELIMITER //

CREATE PROCEDURE GetEmployeeCount(OUT emp_count INT)
BEGIN
    SELECT COUNT(*) INTO emp_count FROM employees;
END //

DELIMITER ;

Execution

CALL GetEmployeeCount(@total);
SELECT @total; -- Displays the employee count

The **OUT** parameter stores the result in a session variable @total.

Example: Stored Procedure With INOUT Parameter

DELIMITER //

CREATE PROCEDURE DoubleNumber(INOUT num INT)
BEGIN
    SET num = num * 2;
END //

DELIMITER ;

Execution

SET @value = 5;
CALL DoubleNumber(@value);
SELECT @value; -- Output will be 10

Here, the value of @value is modified inside the procedure.

Creating and Using Functions in MySQL

Basic Syntax of Functions

DELIMITER //

```
CREATE    FUNCTION    function_name    (parameter_name    DataType)
RETURNS ReturnType
DETERMINISTIC
BEGIN
    -- Function body
    RETURN value;
END //

DELIMITER ;
```

- **RETURNS ReturnType**: Specifies the return type (e.g., INT, VARCHAR(255), etc.).
- **DETERMINISTIC**: Indicates that the function always returns the same result for the same inputs.

Example: Simple Function

```
DELIMITER //

CREATE    FUNCTION    SquareNumber(num    INT)    RETURNS    INT
DETERMINISTIC
BEGIN
    RETURN num * num;
END //

DELIMITER ;
```

Execution

```
SELECT SquareNumber(4); -- Returns 16
```

Unlike procedures, functions can be used in SQL queries.

Example: Function for Full Name Concatenation

```
DELIMITER //

CREATE FUNCTION GetFullName(first_name VARCHAR(50), last_name
VARCHAR(50)) RETURNS VARCHAR(100) DETERMINISTIC
BEGIN
    RETURN CONCAT(first_name, ' ', last_name);
END //
```

DELIMITER ;

Execution

SELECT GetFullName('John', 'Doe'); -- Returns 'John Doe'

Example: Function to Calculate Tax

```
DELIMITER //

CREATE FUNCTION CalculateTax(salary DECIMAL(10,2)) RETURNS
DECIMAL(10,2) DETERMINISTIC
BEGIN
   RETURN salary * 0.15;
END //

DELIMITER ;
```

Execution

SELECT CalculateTax(5000); -- Returns 750 (15% of 5000)

Differences Between Stored Procedures and Functions

Feature	Stored Procedure	Function
Returns a value?	Optional (via OUT parameter)	Yes (must return a value)
Can be used in SELECT?	No	Yes
Can execute DML statements?	Yes (INSERT, UPDATE, DELETE)	No (mostly used for calculations)
Supports transactions?	Yes	No

Feature	Stored Procedure	Function
Can call other procedures?	Yes	No

Using Stored Procedures with Cursors and Loops

Cursors are used in stored procedures when dealing with result sets row-by-row.

Example: Using Cursor in a Stored Procedure

```
DELIMITER //

CREATE PROCEDURE ListEmployees()
BEGIN
    DECLARE done INT DEFAULT 0;
    DECLARE emp_name VARCHAR(100);
    DECLARE emp_cursor CURSOR FOR SELECT name FROM
employees;
    DECLARE CONTINUE HANDLER FOR NOT FOUND SET done =
1;

    OPEN emp_cursor;

    read_loop: LOOP
        FETCH emp_cursor INTO emp_name;
        IF done THEN
            LEAVE read_loop;
        END IF;
        SELECT emp_name;
    END LOOP;

    CLOSE emp_cursor;
END //

DELIMITER ;
```

Execution

```
CALL ListEmployees();
```

This will iterate over all employee names and display them.

Managing Stored Procedures and Functions

Show All Stored Procedures

SHOW PROCEDURE STATUS WHERE Db = 'your_database';

Show All Functions

SHOW FUNCTION STATUS WHERE Db = 'your_database';

Drop a Stored Procedure

DROP PROCEDURE IF EXISTS GetEmployeeByID;

Drop a Function

DROP FUNCTION IF EXISTS SquareNumber;

Best Practices for Using Stored Procedures and Functions

- Use **Stored Procedures** for business logic and complex operations.
- Use **Functions** for calculations and transformations.
- Optimize **performance** by avoiding unnecessary queries inside procedures.
- Always **handle errors** using **DECLARE HANDLER**.
- Use **meaningful names** for procedures and functions.

Summary

- **Stored Procedures**: Useful for modularizing SQL logic, automating tasks, and improving performance.
- **Functions**: Best for calculations and transformations that return single values.
- **Key Differences**: Procedures are more powerful for operations, while functions are best for computation.
- Triggers
- Transactions and ACID Properties

17.9 Transactions and ACID Properties in MySQL

What is a Transaction in MySQL?

A **transaction** in MySQL is a sequence of one or more SQL statements that are executed as a single unit of work. The transaction ensures that the database remains consistent and reliable even in cases of system failures, power outages, or crashes.

A transaction typically involves **multiple SQL statements** that perform operations such as inserting, updating, or deleting data. If all operations within a transaction are successfully completed, the changes are **committed** to the database. However, if any part of the transaction fails, all operations should be **rolled back** to maintain database integrity.

ACID Properties in MySQL

MySQL transactions follow the **ACID properties** to ensure consistency and reliability. ACID stands for:

1. **Atomicity**
2. **Consistency**
3. **Isolation**
4. **Durability**

Let's discuss each property in detail with an example.

Atomicity

Atomicity ensures that a transaction is treated as a **single, indivisible unit of work**. Either **all** operations within the transaction are completed successfully, or **none** are executed (rollback).

Example of Atomicity

Consider a banking system where you transfer money from one account to another.

START TRANSACTION;

UPDATE accounts SET balance = balance - 500 WHERE account_id = 1; --
Deduct money from Account 1

UPDATE accounts SET balance = balance + 500 WHERE account_id = 2; -- Add money to Account 2

COMMIT;

- If both SQL statements execute successfully, the transaction is committed.
- If the second statement fails (e.g., due to a network failure), MySQL will **rollback** all changes, ensuring that money is not deducted from Account 1 without being credited to Account 2.

Consistency

Consistency ensures that the database remains in a **valid state** before and after a transaction. It guarantees that a transaction follows **all constraints, rules, and relationships** defined in the database schema.

Example of Consistency

Assume the accounts table has a **CHECK constraint** that does not allow balances to go below zero.

START TRANSACTION;

UPDATE accounts SET balance = balance - 1500 WHERE account_id = 1; -- Deducting 1500
UPDATE accounts SET balance = balance + 1500 WHERE account_id = 2; -- Adding 1500

COMMIT;

- If account_id = 1 has only $1,000, the first statement will **violate the CHECK constraint**.
- The transaction will be **rolled back**, ensuring that the database remains in a consistent state.

Isolation

Isolation ensures that concurrent transactions do not interfere with each other. MySQL provides different **isolation levels** to control how transactions interact.

Isolation Levels in MySQL

1. **READ UNCOMMITTED** – Allows reading uncommitted changes (dirty reads).
2. **READ COMMITTED** – Only committed changes are visible.
3. **REPEATABLE READ** (Default in MySQL) – Ensures the same result for a query in a transaction.
4. **SERIALIZABLE** – Highest level, transactions execute sequentially.

Example of Isolation

Consider two users trying to **withdraw money** from the same account at the same time.

SET TRANSACTION ISOLATION LEVEL READ COMMITTED;
START TRANSACTION;

SELECT balance FROM accounts WHERE account_id = 1; -- User A reads balance: $1000
UPDATE accounts SET balance = balance - 500 WHERE account_id = 1; -- Deduct $500

COMMIT;

- If **User B** also tries to withdraw money at the same time, **READ COMMITTED** ensures that User B will only see the updated balance after **User A's transaction is committed**.
- This prevents **dirty reads** where User B might see uncommitted changes.

Durability

Durability ensures that once a transaction is **committed**, the changes are **permanently stored** in the database, even in case of a system crash.

Example of Durability

When we commit a transaction:

START TRANSACTION;

UPDATE accounts SET balance = balance - 500 WHERE account_id = 1;

UPDATE accounts SET balance = balance + 500 WHERE account_id = 2;

COMMIT;

- MySQL ensures that committed changes are **written to disk** using logs (like the binary log).
- Even if the system crashes, MySQL can **recover** committed transactions when restarted.

Implementing Transactions in MySQL

Here's a complete MySQL transaction example:

```
-- Enable transactions
START TRANSACTION;

-- Deduct amount from sender
UPDATE accounts SET balance = balance - 1000 WHERE account_id = 1;

-- Add amount to receiver
UPDATE accounts SET balance = balance + 1000 WHERE account_id = 2;

-- Check if there is an error
IF (SELECT balance FROM accounts WHERE account_id = 1) >= 0
THEN
    COMMIT; -- Save changes
ELSE
    ROLLBACK; -- Undo changes if insufficient balance
END IF;
```

- If the **sender's account balance is negative**, the transaction **rolls back**.
- Otherwise, the transaction **commits successfully**.

Transactions in MySQL are crucial for maintaining **data integrity** and **reliability**. The **ACID properties** (Atomicity, Consistency, Isolation, and Durability) ensure that transactions work **correctly** even in concurrent environments or system failures.

17.10 Error Handling in MySQL

Error handling is a crucial aspect of database management and application development. In MySQL, error handling mechanisms allow you to detect, respond to, and recover from errors efficiently. This guide covers:

1. Understanding MySQL Errors
2. Types of Errors in MySQL
3. Using SQLSTATE and Error Codes
4. Handling Errors with **SHOW ERRORS** and **SHOW WARNINGS**
5. Error Handling in Stored Procedures and Triggers
6. Using **DECLARE, HANDLER,** and **EXIT** Handlers
7. Transaction Handling for Error Recovery (**ROLLBACK**)
8. Practical Examples of Error Handling

Understanding MySQL Errors

When an error occurs in MySQL, it typically provides:

- **Error Code** – A unique numeric identifier for the error.
- **SQLSTATE Code** – A five-character string representing the error category.
- **Error Message** – A human-readable description of the error.

For example, if you try to insert a duplicate primary key:

INSERT INTO users (id, name) VALUES (1, 'John Doe');
INSERT INTO users (id, name) VALUES (1, 'Jane Doe');

You might get an error like:

Error Code: 1062
SQLSTATE: 23000
Message: Duplicate entry '1' for key 'PRIMARY'

Types of Errors in MySQL

Errors in MySQL can be categorized as follows:

a) Syntax Errors

Errors due to incorrect SQL syntax.

SELCT * FROM users; -- Incorrect spelling of SELECT

Error:

Error Code: 1064
SQLSTATE: 42000
Message: You have an error in your SQL syntax...

b) Constraint Violations

Violating constraints like PRIMARY KEY, FOREIGN KEY, NOT NULL, etc.

INSERT INTO users (id, name) VALUES (NULL, 'Alice');

Error:

Error Code: 1048
SQLSTATE: 23000
Message: Column 'id' cannot be null

c) Connection Errors

Errors related to database connections, e.g., wrong credentials.

d) Locking Errors

When two transactions try to access the same resource.

Error Code: 1205
SQLSTATE: 40001
Message: Lock wait timeout exceeded; try restarting transaction

Using SQLSTATE and Error Codes

MySQL provides predefined SQLSTATE values to categorize errors. Some common ones:

SQLSTATE	Category	Example
23000	Integrity constraint	Duplicate key
42000	Syntax error	Misspelled SQL command
HY000	General error	Out of memory
08001	Connection failure	Database connection lost

To retrieve the last error:

SELECT LAST_INSERT_ID(), @@ERROR;

Handling Errors with SHOW ERRORS **and** SHOW WARNINGS

To display recent errors and warnings:

SHOW ERRORS;
SHOW WARNINGS;

To get the count of errors:

SELECT COUNT(*) FROM information_schema.INNODB_TRX WHERE state='ACTIVE';

Error Handling in Stored Procedures and Triggers

MySQL provides structured error handling using DECLARE HANDLER.

Using DECLARE HANDLER for Error Handling

You can use:

- **CONTINUE** – Ignore the error and continue execution.
- **EXIT** – Stop execution when an error occurs.

Example: Handling Duplicate Key Error

```
DELIMITER $$

CREATE    PROCEDURE    InsertUser(IN    uid    INT,    IN    uname
VARCHAR(50))
BEGIN
  DECLARE CONTINUE HANDLER FOR SQLSTATE '23000'
  BEGIN
    SELECT 'Duplicate Key Error: Skipping insert' AS Message;
  END;

  INSERT INTO users (id, name) VALUES (uid, uname);
END $$

DELIMITER ;
```

Now, calling the procedure with an existing id will not terminate execution.

```
CALL InsertUser(1, 'Alice');
```

Transaction Handling for Error Recovery (ROLLBACK)

MySQL transactions help recover from errors using ROLLBACK.

Example: Rollback on Error

```
DELIMITER $$

CREATE PROCEDURE TransferFunds(IN from_acc INT, IN to_acc INT,
IN amount DECIMAL(10,2))
BEGIN
  DECLARE EXIT HANDLER FOR SQLEXCEPTION
  BEGIN
    ROLLBACK;
    SELECT 'Transaction Failed. Rolled Back.' AS Message;
  END;

  START TRANSACTION;

  UPDATE accounts SET balance = balance - amount WHERE id =
from_acc;
```

```
UPDATE accounts SET balance = balance + amount WHERE id =
to_acc;

COMMIT;
END $$
```

DELIMITER ;

If any UPDATE fails, ROLLBACK prevents inconsistent balances.

Practical Examples of Error Handling

Example 1: Handling Division by Zero

DELIMITER $$

```
CREATE PROCEDURE SafeDivision(IN num1 INT, IN num2 INT)
BEGIN
   DECLARE EXIT HANDLER FOR SQLSTATE '22012'
   BEGIN
     SELECT 'Error: Division by zero is not allowed' AS Message;
   END;

   SELECT num1 / num2 AS Result;
END $$
```

DELIMITER ;

CALL SafeDivision(10, 0);

Output:

Error: Division by zero is not allowed

Example 2: Handling Table Not Found Error

DELIMITER $$

```
CREATE PROCEDURE CheckTable()
BEGIN
   DECLARE CONTINUE HANDLER FOR SQLSTATE '42S02'
   BEGIN
     SELECT 'Table does not exist' AS Message;
```

```
  END;

  SELECT * FROM non_existing_table;
END $$

DELIMITER ;
```

Calling CheckTable() gracefully handles the missing table.

MySQL error handling is essential for robust database operations. Key takeaways:

- Use **SQLSTATE and error codes** to diagnose issues.
- Use **DECLARE HANDLER** for structured error handling.
- Use **transactions (ROLLBACK)** to maintain data integrity.
- Use **SHOW ERRORS and SHOW WARNINGS** for debugging.
- Always handle **common issues like duplicate keys and division by zero** in stored procedures.

18 MySQL PERFORMANCE OPTIMIZATION

Optimizing MySQL performance is essential for ensuring efficient query execution, faster response times, and reduced resource consumption. Below is a comprehensive guide covering key areas of MySQL performance optimization.

Understanding Performance Bottlenecks

Before optimizing MySQL, it's crucial to identify where performance issues arise. The main bottlenecks typically occur in:

- **Slow Queries**: Poorly written SQL queries or unoptimized indexes.
- **Database Design**: Inefficient schema, redundant data, or missing normalization.
- **Hardware Constraints**: Insufficient RAM, slow disks, or CPU limitations.
- **Configuration Issues**: Incorrect buffer sizes, cache mismanagement, or suboptimal thread handling.

18.1 Query Optimization
Use the EXPLAIN Command

EXPLAIN helps analyze how MySQL executes a query, providing insight into:

- Table access methods (index scan, full table scan, etc.)
- Join strategies
- Use of indexes

Example:

EXPLAIN SELECT name FROM customers WHERE age > 30;

Check the type column in the output. **Avoid ALL (full table scan)** and aim for index or const.

Optimize SELECT Queries

- **Fetch only necessary columns**: Avoid SELECT *, fetch only required columns.
- **Use LIMIT**: If paginating, avoid pulling all data at once. Example:

  SELECT name FROM users LIMIT 10 OFFSET 50;

- **Avoid unnecessary joins**: Normalize data but ensure joins are minimal.

Use Proper Indexing

Indexes speed up read queries significantly. Types of indexes:

- **Primary Key**: Unique identifier for a row.
- **Unique Index**: Ensures uniqueness in a column.
- **Composite Index**: Speeds up queries involving multiple columns.
- **Full-Text Index**: Improves performance in text-based searches.

Example of an index:

CREATE INDEX idx_customer_age ON customers(age);

Use **covering indexes** where possible:

CREATE INDEX idx_orders_customer_id ON orders(customer_id, order_date);

Optimize Joins

- Use indexed columns for joins.
- Prefer INNER JOIN over OUTER JOIN where possible.
- Use STRAIGHT_JOIN to enforce join order if necessary.

Example:

SELECT c.name, o.amount FROM customers c
JOIN orders o ON c.id = o.customer_id
WHERE c.age > 30;

Use Query Caching

MySQL's query cache stores results of SELECT statements, reducing repeated execution time.

To enable:

SET GLOBAL query_cache_size = 268435456; -- 256MB

Optimize WHERE and ORDER BY Clauses

- Use indexed columns in WHERE clauses.
- Avoid using OR (use IN instead if possible).
- Optimize ORDER BY by indexing sorting columns. Example:

SELECT * FROM employees ORDER BY last_name ASC;

If last_name is indexed, sorting is much faster.

18.2 Database Schema Optimization

Normalize Data (But Not Excessively)

- First Normal Form (1NF): Eliminate duplicate columns.
- Second Normal Form (2NF): Ensure all non-key attributes are dependent on the primary key.
- Third Normal Form (3NF): Remove transitive dependencies.

Use Proper Data Types

- Use **INT** instead of **BIGINT** when possible.
- Use **VARCHAR** instead of **TEXT** if the data length is predictable.
- Use **ENUM** for fixed-value columns instead of VARCHAR.
- Store timestamps in **DATETIME** instead of string format.

Example

```
CREATE TABLE orders (
    id INT AUTO_INCREMENT PRIMARY KEY,
    customer_id INT,
    order_date DATETIME DEFAULT CURRENT_TIMESTAMP,
```

```
    amount DECIMAL(10,2)
);
```

Partition Large Tables

Partitioning improves query performance by splitting data into smaller chunks.

```
CREATE TABLE sales (
    id INT NOT NULL,
    sale_date DATE NOT NULL,
    amount DECIMAL(10,2),
    PRIMARY KEY (id, sale_date)
)
PARTITION BY RANGE (YEAR(sale_date)) (
    PARTITION p1 VALUES LESS THAN (2020),
    PARTITION p2 VALUES LESS THAN (2025)
);
```

18.3 MySQL Server Configuration Optimization

Optimize Buffer Sizes

Adjust key buffer sizes in **my.cnf** or **my.ini**:

```
key_buffer_size = 256M
query_cache_size = 64M
innodb_buffer_pool_size = 2G
innodb_log_file_size = 512M
```

- innodb_buffer_pool_size: Should be ~70% of RAM for InnoDB.
- key_buffer_size: Important for MyISAM tables.

Thread Management

Optimize thread handling for concurrency:

```
thread_cache_size = 8
max_connections = 500
```

Disable Unused Features

Turn off unnecessary logging:

general_log = 0
slow_query_log = 1
log_queries_not_using_indexes = 1

Enable slow query logging to detect slow queries.

Storage Engine Selection

Use InnoDB Over MyISAM

- **InnoDB**: Supports transactions, row-level locking, better performance.
- **MyISAM**: Good for read-heavy workloads but lacks transactions.

To check and convert storage engines:

SHOW TABLE STATUS WHERE Name = 'customers';
ALTER TABLE customers ENGINE = InnoDB;

18.4 Load Optimization

Use Bulk Inserts

Instead of inserting rows one by one, use bulk inserts:

INSERT INTO sales (id, amount) VALUES (1, 100), (2, 200), (3, 300);

Optimize Data Import/Export

For large datasets, use LOAD DATA INFILE:

LOAD DATA INFILE '/path/to/data.csv'
INTO TABLE customers
FIELDS TERMINATED BY ','
LINES TERMINATED BY '\n';

18.5 Backup and Replication Optimization

Use Proper Backup Strategies

- **mysqldump** for small databases:

  mysqldump -u root -p --all-databases > backup.sql

- **Percona XtraBackup** for large datasets.

Use Replication for Read Scaling

- **Master-Slave Replication**: Offload reads to slave servers.
- **Master-Master Replication**: For high availability setups.

To enable replication:

server-id = 1
log_bin = mysql-bin

Monitoring and Performance Tuning

Use MySQL Performance Schema

SELECT * FROM
performance_schema.events_statements_summary_by_digest;

Use Monitoring Tools

- **MySQL Workbench**
- **Percona Toolkit**
- **New Relic / Prometheus / Grafana**

MySQL performance optimization involves multiple factors, including query tuning, indexing, database design, server configuration, and monitoring. By systematically applying these optimizations, you can significantly improve MySQL's efficiency, scalability, and responsiveness.

Query Optimization Tips

Optimizing MySQL queries is essential for improving database performance, reducing execution time, and minimizing resource consumption. Below are detailed MySQL query optimization tips categorized into different aspects:

Indexing Strategies

Indexes speed up query performance by reducing the number of rows scanned.

Use Indexes Wisely

- Index **frequently queried** columns, especially those used in WHERE, JOIN, GROUP BY, and ORDER BY clauses.
- Avoid excessive indexing, as indexes consume disk space and slow down INSERT, UPDATE, and DELETE operations.

Types of Indexes

- **Primary Key**: Uniquely identifies each row.
- **Unique Index**: Ensures column values are unique.
- **Composite Index**: Indexes multiple columns together.
- **Full-Text Index**: Used for text searches.
- **Spatial Index**: Optimized for geographic data.

Best Practices for Indexing

- Use **EXPLAIN** to check if indexes are used.
- Avoid **redundant indexes** (multiple indexes on the same column).
- Use **covering indexes** (INDEX(col1, col2)) to cover query columns.
- For **high-cardinality** columns, indexes provide better benefits.

Optimizing Queries

Optimizing query structure reduces execution time.

Use EXPLAIN to Analyze Queries

Run:

EXPLAIN SELECT * FROM orders WHERE customer_id = 101;

It provides information about query execution plans, such as index usage and row scanning.

Optimize SELECT Queries

- Avoid SELECT *, specify only required columns:

  SELECT name, age FROM users WHERE country = 'USA';

- Use **LIMIT** to reduce result set size when appropriate:

  SELECT * FROM products ORDER BY price DESC LIMIT 10;

- Use **sub queries carefully**—prefer JOIN over correlated sub queries.

Optimize JOIN Queries

- Ensure indexed columns are used in ON conditions:

  SELECT o.order_id, c.name
  FROM orders o
  JOIN customers c ON o.customer_id = c.id;

- Use **INNER JOIN** instead of LEFT JOIN if possible.

Optimize GROUP BY and ORDER BY

- Use indexed columns for sorting:

  SELECT department, COUNT(*) FROM employees GROUP BY department;

- Avoid unnecessary sorting (ORDER BY without indexes is slow).

18.6 Query Caching

Caching avoids redundant query execution.

Enable Query Cache (for MySQL < 8.0)

SET GLOBAL query_cache_size = 1048576;

MySQL 8.0 removed query caching in favor of **external caching solutions** like Redis.

Use Prepared Statements for Repeated Queries

PREPARE stmt FROM 'SELECT * FROM orders WHERE customer_id = ?';
EXECUTE stmt USING @customer_id;

This avoids query parsing overhead.

Optimizing Table Structure

Well-structured tables improve query speed.

Choose the Right Data Types

- Use the **smallest possible** data type (TINYINT instead of INT if values are ≤ 255).
- Use **VARCHAR** instead of TEXT unless full-text search is required.
- Store **dates** as DATETIME or TIMESTAMP instead of VARCHAR.

Normalize and Denormalize Where Necessary

- **Normalization** reduces redundancy but can increase JOIN costs.
- **Denormalization** can improve read-heavy workloads.

Partition Large Tables

Partitioning can improve query speed:

```
ALTER TABLE sales PARTITION BY RANGE (year)
(
  PARTITION p1 VALUES LESS THAN (2020),
  PARTITION p2 VALUES LESS THAN (2025)
);
```

Avoiding Performance Bottlenecks

Reduce Lock Contention

- Use **InnoDB** for better concurrency.
- Use **row-level locking** instead of table-level locking.
- Use **SELECT FOR UPDATE** for transactions.

Optimize Transactions

- Use transactions efficiently:

```
START TRANSACTION;
UPDATE accounts SET balance = balance - 100 WHERE id = 1;
COMMIT;
```

- Keep transactions **short** to reduce locking time.

Use Connection Pooling

Using a connection pool (e.g., **MySQL's C3P0, HikariCP**) helps manage database connections efficiently.

Monitoring and Performance Tuning

Use SHOW PROCESSLIST **to Identify Slow Queries**

```
SHOW PROCESSLIST;
```

Find queries taking too long and optimize them.

Use SHOW VARIABLES **and** SHOW STATUS

Check MySQL settings:

```
SHOW VARIABLES LIKE 'query_cache_size';
SHOW STATUS LIKE 'Threads_connected';
```

Enable Slow Query Log

Identify slow queries:

```
SET GLOBAL slow_query_log = 1;
SET GLOBAL long_query_time = 2;  -- Log queries running > 2 seconds
```

18.7 Advanced Optimization Techniques

Use UNION ALL Instead of UNION

- UNION removes duplicates, making it slower.
- UNION ALL is faster:

```
SELECT id, name FROM users WHERE country = 'USA'
UNION ALL
SELECT id, name FROM customers WHERE country = 'USA';
```

Use HAVING Only When Necessary

Prefer WHERE over HAVING:

```
SELECT department, SUM(salary) FROM employees WHERE department = 'IT' GROUP BY department;
```

Avoid:

```
SELECT department, SUM(salary) FROM employees GROUP BY department HAVING department = 'IT';
```

Use Proper Storage Engines

- **InnoDB**: Best for transactions, row-level locking.
- **MyISAM**: Suitable for read-heavy applications.

Final Tip: Continuously Test & Improve

- Regularly **analyze query execution** using EXPLAIN.
- Optimize **schema** and **queries** as data grows.
- Use **profiling tools** like **pt-query-digest** for deep analysis.

By applying these optimizations, MySQL queries will run faster, be more efficient, and scale better!

Using EXPLAIN to Analyze Queries in MySQL

The EXPLAIN statement in MySQL is a powerful tool that helps database developers and administrators analyze and optimize queries. By using EXPLAIN, you can see how MySQL executes a query, including details about indexes, joins, sorting, and filtering. This allows you to identify performance bottlenecks and make improvements.

Understanding EXPLAIN

When you run EXPLAIN before a SELECT statement, MySQL returns a row of data for each table used in the query, showing how the query is executed.

Syntax:

EXPLAIN SELECT column_names FROM table_name WHERE conditions;

or

EXPLAIN FORMAT=JSON SELECT column_names FROM table_name WHERE conditions;

- The first form provides tabular output.
- The second form (FORMAT=JSON) provides a detailed JSON output.

2. Columns in EXPLAIN Output

When you run EXPLAIN, MySQL provides several columns of information that describe the execution plan:

Column Name	Description
id	The identifier for the query step. Higher values mean later execution in a multi-step query.
select_type	Describes the type of SELECT (e.g., SIMPLE, PRIMARY, SUBQUERY).
table	The name of the table being accessed.
partitions	Lists table partitions used (if any).
type	Shows the join type (e.g., ALL, INDEX, RANGE, REF, EQ_REF).
possible_keys	Lists potential indexes MySQL could use.
key	The actual index MySQL will use.
key_len	The length of the key used.
ref	Shows which columns/constants are compared to the indexed column.
rows	Estimated number of rows MySQL expects to examine.
filtered	Estimated percentage of rows that will be returned after applying the WHERE condition.
Extra	Additional information about query execution (e.g., Using where, Using index, Using temporary).

Interpreting Key EXPLAIN Columns

a) type (Join Type)

The type column is crucial in understanding query efficiency. Here are common values:

Type	Description
system	The table has only one row (fastest).
const	The query is using a constant comparison (id = 1).
eq_ref	A primary key or unique index is used (highly efficient).
ref	A non-unique index is used.
range	A range scan (BETWEEN, <, >, etc.).
index	Full index scan (less efficient than range).
ALL	Full table scan (least efficient).

Example:

EXPLAIN SELECT * FROM employees WHERE department_id = 5;

- If type = ALL, MySQL is scanning the entire table.
- If type = ref, MySQL is using an index (better performance).

b) Extra **Column**

The Extra column provides additional execution details:

Value	Meaning
Using where	MySQL filters rows using the WHERE clause.
Using index	The query uses an index only, avoiding table access (efficient).
Using temporary	A temporary table is created (can be slow).

Value	Meaning
Using filesort	MySQL is sorting data, which can be costly.

Example:

EXPLAIN SELECT * FROM employees ORDER BY salary DESC;

- If Extra = Using filesort, MySQL is sorting data manually.
- Adding an index on salary may remove the filesort.

Example Scenarios

a) Simple Query with Index

EXPLAIN SELECT * FROM employees WHERE emp_id = 10;

Output:

id	select_type	table	type	possible_keys	key	rows	Extra
1	SIMPLE	employees	const	PRIMARY	PRIMARY	1	NULL

Since emp_id is a primary key, MySQL uses const, which is the fastest method.

b) Query with Full Table Scan (Inefficient)

EXPLAIN SELECT * FROM employees WHERE salary > 50000;

Output:

id	select_type	table	type	possible_keys	key	rows	Extra
1	SIMPLE	employees	ALL	NULL	NULL	10000	Using where

- The ALL type indicates a full table scan, which is inefficient.

227

- To optimize, add an index on salary:

ALTER TABLE employees ADD INDEX (salary);

- Running EXPLAIN again should show range instead of ALL.

c) Query with Join Optimization

EXPLAIN SELECT e.name, d.department_name
FROM employees e
JOIN departments d ON e.department_id = d.department_id;

Output:

id	select_type	table	type	possible_keys	key	rows	Extra
1	SIMPLE	departments	ALL	PRIMARY	NULL	5	NULL
1	SIMPLE	employees	ref	dept_id_index	dept_id_index	100	NULL

- If the departments table lacks an index on department_id, it results in ALL (full table scan).
- Adding an index on department_id in departments will improve performance.

Using EXPLAIN FORMAT=JSON

For deeper insights, use the JSON format:

EXPLAIN FORMAT=JSON SELECT * FROM employees WHERE emp_id = 10;

- This returns a detailed execution plan, useful for complex queries.

Query Optimization Strategies

- **Use Indexes**: Add indexes on columns used in WHERE, JOIN, and ORDER BY.
- **Avoid SELECT ***: Fetch only the necessary columns.
- **Optimize Joins**: Ensure foreign keys are indexed.

- **Use LIMIT**: Fetch only the required rows.
- **Partition Large Tables**: If dealing with large datasets, consider partitioning.

EXPLAIN is a vital tool for diagnosing query performance issues in MySQL. By understanding its output and optimizing queries accordingly, you can significantly enhance database performance. Regular use of EXPLAIN helps prevent slow queries and ensures efficient data retrieval.

18.8 Index Optimization in MySQL

Indexes in MySQL play a crucial role in optimizing query performance. They allow MySQL to quickly locate data without scanning entire tables, significantly improving read efficiency. However, improper indexing can lead to unnecessary overhead, slowing down insert, update, and delete operations. This guide provides an in-depth look at index optimization techniques to maximize MySQL performance.

Understanding Indexes

An index is a data structure that MySQL uses to speed up searches and queries. It works like an index in a book: instead of scanning every page (row) in a book (table), you go directly to the page number (indexed column).

Types of Indexes in MySQL

1. **Primary Index (PRIMARY KEY)**
   o Automatically created on primary key columns.
   o Ensures unique and non-null values.
   o Uses a **clustered index** in InnoDB.
2. **Unique Index (UNIQUE)**
   o Prevents duplicate values in a column.
   o Speeds up queries where uniqueness is checked.
3. **Regular Index (INDEX)**
   o Speeds up queries but allows duplicates.
   o Useful for frequently searched columns.
4. **Full-Text Index (FULLTEXT)**
   o Used for text-based searches (e.g., MATCH() against large text fields).
   o Works well for searching natural language phrases.
5. **Spatial Index (SPATIAL)**
   o Used for geographic data (POINT, POLYGON, etc.).

        o   Only works with MyISAM and InnoDB (from MySQL 5.7+).
6. **Composite Index (Multi-Column Index)**
        o   Index created on multiple columns.
        o   Helps with queries filtering multiple conditions.
7. **Covering Index**
        o   An index that includes all the columns needed for a query.
        o   Avoids accessing the table data altogether.

Why Indexes Improve Performance

Indexes speed up queries by reducing the number of rows MySQL has to scan. Consider this:

SELECT * FROM employees WHERE last_name = 'Smith';

- Without an index: MySQL performs a **full table scan**, checking every row.
- With an index on last_name: MySQL quickly finds relevant rows, skipping unnecessary ones.

Creating and Managing Indexes

Creating an Index

You can create an index when creating a table or on an existing table.

On Table Creation

```
CREATE TABLE employees (
    id INT PRIMARY KEY,
    first_name VARCHAR(50),
    last_name VARCHAR(50),
    department_id INT,
    INDEX idx_lastname (last_name)  -- Creating an index on last_name
);
```

On an Existing Table

CREATE INDEX idx_lastname ON employees(last_name);

Composite Index

CREATE INDEX idx_name_dept ON employees(last_name, department_id);

- Useful for queries like:

  SELECT * FROM employees WHERE last_name = 'Smith' AND department_id = 5;

Unique Index

CREATE UNIQUE INDEX idx_email ON employees(email);

- Ensures email values remain unique.

Optimizing Index Usage

Indexes improve performance when used correctly. Follow these optimization techniques:

A) Choose the Right Columns for Indexing

- Index columns frequently used in WHERE, JOIN, ORDER BY, and GROUP BY.
- Avoid indexing columns that frequently change (UPDATE and DELETE slow down).

B) Use Composite Indexes Wisely

- If you frequently query multiple columns, a **composite index** is more efficient than multiple single-column indexes.

Example:

CREATE INDEX idx_name_dept ON employees(last_name, department_id);

- Efficient for:

SELECT * FROM employees WHERE last_name = 'Smith' AND department_id = 5;

- But **not** for:

SELECT * FROM employees WHERE department_id = 5;

  o Since last_name is the first column in the index, MySQL cannot use this index effectively.

C) Covering Indexes for Faster Queries

A **covering index** contains all the columns needed for a query, avoiding table lookups.

Example:

CREATE INDEX idx_name_salary ON employees(last_name, salary);

- Optimizes:

SELECT last_name, salary FROM employees WHERE last_name = 'Smith';

- MySQL retrieves results from the index **without accessing the table**.

D) Avoid Indexing Low-Cardinality Columns

- Indexing Boolean or gender fields (M/F) is **useless**.
- Indexing a column with only a few distinct values (e.g., status = 'Active' or Inactive') does not improve performance.

E) Optimize Index Order in Composite Indexes

- If querying **(last_name, department_id)**, ensure the first column in the index has the highest selectivity.
- The **order matters** in composite indexes.

Example:

CREATE INDEX idx_dept_lastname ON employees(department_id, last_name);

- Good for:

    SELECT * FROM employees WHERE department_id = 5 AND last_name = 'Smith';

- **Not** optimized for:

    SELECT * FROM employees WHERE last_name = 'Smith';

F) Remove Unused Indexes

- Unused indexes slow down INSERT, UPDATE, and DELETE operations.
- Find unused indexes:

    SELECT * FROM sys.schema_unused_indexes;

- Drop unnecessary indexes:

    DROP INDEX idx_unused ON employees;

Analyzing Index Performance with EXPLAIN

Use EXPLAIN to check if MySQL uses indexes.

Example:

EXPLAIN SELECT * FROM employees WHERE last_name = 'Smith';
Key Columns to Check in EXPLAIN Output

Column	Meaning
type	Should be ref, range, or const (avoid ALL).
key	Shows which index is used.

Column	Meaning
rows	The fewer rows scanned, the better.
Extra	Avoid Using filesort and Using temporary.

Maintaining Index Performance

A) Regularly Analyze and Optimize Indexes

- Use:

  ANALYZE TABLE employees;
  OPTIMIZE TABLE employees;

B) Monitor Slow Queries

- Enable the **slow query log** to detect inefficient queries:

  SET GLOBAL slow_query_log = 1;
  SET GLOBAL long_query_time = 2; -- Queries taking >2 seconds

When NOT to Use Indexes

- **Small Tables**: Scanning a small table is often faster than using an index.
- **Frequent Writes (INSERT/UPDATE/DELETE)**: Indexes slow down modifications.
- **Low-Cardinality Columns**: Indexing is_active (0/1) is inefficient.

Indexes are essential for MySQL query optimization, but **misusing them can hurt performance**. Key takeaways: ✅ Index columns frequently used in queries.

✅ Use composite indexes wisely.

✅ Avoid indexing low-cardinality columns.

✅ Regularly analyze and optimize indexes.

✅ Use EXPLAIN to check query execution plans.

18.9 Caching in MySQL

Caching is a critical optimization technique in MySQL that improves performance by storing frequently accessed data in memory, reducing the need for repeated disk reads and expensive computations. This guide will explore MySQL caching in detail, including query cache, InnoDB buffer pool, MySQL performance schema caching, application-level caching, and third-party caching mechanisms.

What is Caching in MySQL?

Caching is the process of storing frequently accessed or computed data in a temporary storage area (cache) to reduce access time and improve performance. When a request is made for data, MySQL first checks if the required data is available in cache before performing a disk read or computation.

Caching in MySQL helps in:

- Reducing query execution time
- Minimizing CPU and disk I/O load
- Improving database response times
- Enhancing scalability for high-traffic applications

Types of Caching in MySQL

MySQL provides several built-in caching mechanisms as well as external caching solutions:

1. Query Cache (Deprecated)
2. InnoDB Buffer Pool
3. Key Cache (for MyISAM)
4. Metadata and Table Definition Cache
5. Prepared Statement Cache
6. Performance Schema Caching
7. External Caching Solutions (e.g., Memcached, Redis, ProxySQL)

Query Cache (Deprecated since MySQL 8.0)

The MySQL **Query Cache** was used to store the results of SELECT queries so that identical queries could be served faster. However, due to high invalidation overhead, it was removed in MySQL 8.0.

How Query Cache Worked (Pre-MySQL 8.0)

- If an identical query was executed, MySQL would return the stored result instead of re-executing the query.
- Any modification to the underlying table (INSERT, UPDATE, DELETE) would invalidate all related cached queries.

Why Query Cache Was Removed?

- It often led to bottlenecks in multi-user environments.
- It did not scale well with high-write workloads.
- Alternative caching techniques (like InnoDB buffer pool and application-level caching) are more efficient.

InnoDB Buffer Pool (Most Important Caching Mechanism in MySQL)

The **InnoDB Buffer Pool** is the primary caching mechanism for InnoDB storage engine, responsible for storing frequently accessed pages from disk in memory.

How It Works?

- When a query is executed, MySQL first checks if the required data pages are in the buffer pool.
- If the data is found, MySQL reads from memory (fast access).
- If the data is not found, MySQL fetches it from disk (slow) and loads it into the buffer pool for future access.

Key Components of InnoDB Buffer Pool

1. **Data Pages Cache** – Stores frequently used table and index data.
2. **Change Buffer** – Caches changes to secondary indexes before flushing to disk.
3. **Adaptive Hash Index** – Improves query performance by maintaining frequently used index lookups.
4. **Flush List** – Keeps track of dirty pages that need to be written to disk.

Optimizing InnoDB Buffer Pool

- Increase the buffer pool size to fit most of the database in memory (innodb_buffer_pool_size).
- Use multiple buffer pool instances to reduce contention (innodb_buffer_pool_instances).
- Enable automatic flushing for better performance (innodb_flush_neighbors).

Key Cache (For MyISAM Storage Engine)

The **Key Cache** (or Key Buffer) is specific to the MyISAM storage engine and is used to cache index blocks.

How It Works?

- When a query searches an indexed column, MySQL first checks the key cache.
- If the required index page is found, MySQL reads from memory instead of disk.
- If not found, MySQL fetches the index page from disk and caches it.

Optimizing MyISAM Key Cache

- Increase key_buffer_size to store more index pages in memory.
- Use **table indexing efficiently** to minimize disk reads.

Metadata and Table Definition Cache

This cache stores metadata about tables, databases, stored procedures, and triggers to reduce the overhead of retrieving table definitions repeatedly.

How It Works?

- When a query accesses a table, MySQL retrieves its metadata (column names, indexes, constraints).
- Instead of fetching the metadata from disk each time, MySQL stores it in the **table definition cache** for quick access.

Optimizing Metadata Cache

- Increase table_open_cache and table_definition_cache to improve performance for databases with many tables.

Prepared Statement Cache

This cache stores the execution plans of prepared statements to avoid re-parsing and optimizing the same queries multiple times.

How It Works?

- When a **prepared statement** is executed multiple times with different values, MySQL caches the execution plan.
- This reduces the parsing and optimization overhead for repeated queries.

Optimizing Prepared Statement Cache

- Enable **prepared statements** for frequently used queries.
- Increase table_open_cache for efficient query execution.

Performance Schema Caching

The MySQL **Performance Schema** maintains caches for query execution statistics, memory allocation, and system performance metrics.

How It Works?

- Tracks query execution time, wait events, and I/O performance.
- Maintains cached statistics to improve query performance analysis.

Optimizing Performance Schema

- Enable performance_schema for advanced monitoring.
- Use query profiling to identify slow queries.

External Caching Solutions for MySQL

Since MySQL's built-in caches have limitations, external caching solutions are widely used for improving performance.

Common External Caching Techniques

Memcached

- Stores key-value pairs in memory.
- Used to cache entire query results.
- Best suited for read-heavy applications.

Redis

- Stores structured data (hashes, lists, sorted sets).
- Can act as a persistent caching layer.
- Used for caching session data, frequently accessed queries, and computed results.

ProxySQL

- An advanced MySQL proxy that caches queries and routes traffic intelligently.
- Reduces database load by caching frequently executed queries.
- Supports query rewriting and load balancing.

Application-Level Caching

- Applications can cache frequently accessed data in-memory instead of repeatedly querying MySQL.
- Common libraries: **Laravel Cache (PHP), Django Cache (Python), Spring Cache (Java).**

Best Practices for MySQL Caching

1. **Optimize InnoDB Buffer Pool** – Set innodb_buffer_pool_size to at least 70% of available RAM for better caching.
2. **Use External Caching (Redis, Memcached)** – Store frequently accessed queries outside MySQL.
3. **Enable Prepared Statements** – Reduce query parsing overhead.
4. **Optimize Indexing** – Proper indexing reduces disk I/O and improves cache hit rates.
5. **Use ProxySQL for Query Caching** – If your workload has repeated queries, ProxySQL can be an effective caching layer.
6. **Monitor Cache Performance** – Use SHOW STATUS LIKE '%cache%'; to analyze cache hit rates.

7. **Avoid Query Cache (If on Older MySQL Versions)** – It has significant performance issues.

Caching is essential for improving MySQL performance by reducing disk I/O and optimizing query execution. The **InnoDB Buffer Pool** is the most effective caching mechanism, while **external caches like Redis and Memcached** can further enhance performance. Proper cache tuning and monitoring can significantly boost database efficiency, especially in high-traffic applications.

Optimizing Data Types and Schema Design

Optimizing **Data Types** and **Schema Design** in MySQL is crucial for improving database performance, reducing storage costs, and ensuring efficient queries. Below is a comprehensive breakdown:

Understanding Data Types in MySQL

MySQL provides a variety of data types for storing different kinds of data. Choosing the right type can significantly impact **storage space, performance, and index efficiency.**

Numeric Data Types Optimization

Numeric data types should be chosen based on the expected range and precision.

Integer Types (TINYINT, SMALLINT, MEDIUMINT, INT, BIGINT)

- **TINYINT (1 byte)** → Range: -128 to 127 (signed) / 0 to 255 (unsigned)
- **SMALLINT (2 bytes)** → Range: -32,768 to 32,767 / 0 to 65,535
- **MEDIUMINT (3 bytes)** → Range: -8,388,608 to 8,388,607 / 0 to 16,777,215
- **INT (4 bytes)** → Range: -2,147,483,648 to 2,147,483,647 / 0 to 4,294,967,295
- **BIGINT (8 bytes)** → Range: Large numbers (useful for large IDs)

Optimization Tip:

- Choose the **smallest integer type** that accommodates your data.

- Use **UNSIGNED** where negative values are unnecessary, doubling the positive range.

Floating-Point Types (FLOAT, DOUBLE, DECIMAL)

- **FLOAT (4 bytes)** → Approximate values with ~7 decimal precision.
- **DOUBLE (8 bytes)** → Approximate values with ~15 decimal precision.
- **DECIMAL (variable bytes)** → Exact values with fixed-point arithmetic.

Optimization Tip:

- Use **FLOAT/DOUBLE** for approximate values (e.g., scientific calculations).
- Use **DECIMAL** for financial applications (exact precision is needed).

18.10 String Data Types Optimization

Efficiently choosing string data types can **reduce storage overhead** and **improve indexing**.

CHAR vs VARCHAR

- **CHAR(n)**: Fixed-length storage (good for uniform-length data like country codes, status flags).
- **VARCHAR(n)**: Variable-length storage (better for text fields with varying lengths).

Optimization Tip:

- Use **CHAR** for fixed-length data (e.g., 2-character country codes).
- Use **VARCHAR** for variable-length text to save space.

TEXT vs BLOB

- **TEXT**: Stores large textual data (not indexable efficiently).
- **BLOB**: Stores binary large objects (e.g., images, PDFs).

Optimization Tip:

- **Avoid using TEXT/BLOB** unless necessary; they **do not get indexed properly** and require special handling.

18.11 Date and Time Data Types Optimization

MySQL provides multiple date/time data types:

- **DATE (3 bytes)** → YYYY-MM-DD
- **DATETIME (8 bytes)** → YYYY-MM-DD HH:MM:SS
- **TIMESTAMP (4 bytes)** → Similar to DATETIME but optimized for indexing
- **TIME (3 bytes)** → HH:MM:SS
- **YEAR (1 byte)** → YYYY

Optimization Tip:

- Use **TIMESTAMP** instead of **DATETIME** when working with current timezones.
- Use **UNIX_TIMESTAMP()** (integer representation) if performance is a priority.

18.12 Schema Design Optimization

Schema design ensures **data integrity, normalization, indexing, and performance efficiency**.

Normalization vs Denormalization

- **Normalization** (Breaking data into multiple tables to remove redundancy)
    - ✅ **Pros**: Saves storage, avoids redundancy, improves consistency.
    - ✖ **Cons**: Requires complex queries (joins).
- **Denormalization** (Combining tables to reduce joins)
    - ✅ **Pros**: Speeds up read-heavy queries.
    - ✖ **Cons**: Increases redundancy and storage.

Optimization Tip:

- Normalize **until it hurts**, then denormalize **when necessary** for performance.

Choosing the Right Primary Key

- Use **INTEGER with AUTO_INCREMENT** for fast primary key indexing.
- Avoid **UUIDs as primary keys** (they are large and slow for indexing).
- Composite keys should be **avoided** if single-column keys work.

Proper Use of Indexes

Indexes speed up lookups but slow down writes.

Types of Indexes

- **Primary Key Index**: Implicitly created on the primary key.
- **Unique Index**: Prevents duplicate values.
- **Composite Index**: Indexes multiple columns (useful for WHERE conditions).
- **Full-Text Index**: Used for text searches.

Optimization Tip:

- Index **only the columns** used in searches (WHERE, JOIN, ORDER BY).
- Avoid over-indexing (too many indexes slow down inserts/updates).

Partitioning for Large Tables

Partitioning helps in scaling massive tables.

- **Range Partitioning**: Split data based on value ranges (e.g., date ranges).
- **List Partitioning**: Partition by predefined lists of values.
- **Hash Partitioning**: Distributes rows evenly across partitions.

Optimization Tip:

- Use **partitioning** for very large tables (millions of rows).

- Consider **shredding** for extremely large datasets.

Foreign Keys and Constraints

Foreign keys enforce referential integrity but can **slow down inserts/updates**.

Optimization Tip:

- Use **foreign keys** carefully in **high-write** tables.
- Consider **soft deletes** instead of cascading constraints.

Performance Tuning and Best Practices

Avoid NULLable Columns When Possible

- **NULL columns require extra storage** and complicate indexing.
- Instead, use **default values** where applicable.

Optimize Storage Engine Choice

- **InnoDB** (default): Best for transactional workloads (supports row-level locking).
- **MyISAM**: Fast reads but lacks transactions.
- **Memory Engine**: Stores data in RAM (fast but volatile).

Optimization Tip:

- Use **InnoDB** for most applications.

Optimize Query Performance

- Use **EXPLAIN ANALYZE** to diagnose slow queries.
- Optimize joins by **indexing foreign keys**.
- Use **LIMIT** to prevent fetching unnecessary rows.

Caching Strategies

- **Use MySQL Query Cache** (if available) for repetitive queries.
- **Leverage application-side caching** (e.g., Redis, Memcached).

Optimizing **data types** and **schema design** in MySQL is essential for building **efficient, scalable, and high-performance databases**. By carefully choosing data types, structuring schema intelligently, and applying indexing and partitioning strategies, you can significantly enhance your database's performance.

19 SECURITY IN MySQL

19.1 User Management and Privileges in MySQL- Creating & Managing User Accounts and Granting & Revoking Permissions

User management and privilege control are essential in MySQL to ensure database security, access control, and efficient resource allocation. MySQL provides robust mechanisms for creating users, granting permissions, revoking privileges, and maintaining security.

MySQL User Management

Creating Users

In MySQL, a user account consists of a **username** and a **host name** (which specifies where the user can connect from). The basic syntax to create a new user is:

CREATE USER 'username'@'host' IDENTIFIED BY 'password';

- 'username' – The name of the user.
- 'host' – The hostname or IP address from which the user can connect. Use '%' for any host.
- 'password' – The password for authentication.

Examples:

1. Create a user john who can connect from localhost:

   CREATE USER 'john'@'localhost' IDENTIFIED BY 'securepass';

2. Create a user maria who can connect from any host:

   CREATE USER 'maria'@'%' IDENTIFIED BY 'mypassword';

3. Create a user admin restricted to 192.168.1.100:

   CREATE USER 'admin'@'192.168.1.100' IDENTIFIED BY 'adminpass';

Viewing Users

To check existing MySQL users, run:

SELECT user, host FROM mysql.user;

This command lists all users along with their allowed hostnames.

Modifying User Passwords

To update a user's password, use:

ALTER USER 'username'@'host' IDENTIFIED BY 'newpassword';

Example

Change john's password:

ALTER USER 'john'@'localhost' IDENTIFIED BY 'newsecurepass';

Alternatively, if ALTER USER is not supported, use:

SET PASSWORD FOR 'john'@'localhost' = PASSWORD('newsecurepass');

Renaming Users

To rename an existing user:

RENAME USER 'oldname'@'host' TO 'newname'@'host';

Example

Rename john to john_doe:

RENAME USER 'john'@'localhost' TO 'john_doe'@'localhost';

Deleting Users

To remove a user from MySQL:

DROP USER 'username'@'host';

Example

Delete maria:

DROP USER 'maria'@'%';

MySQL Privileges Management

Understanding Privileges

Privileges define what actions a user can perform. Some common privileges include:

- **Global Privileges** – Apply to all databases.
- **Database Privileges** – Apply to a specific database.
- **Table Privileges** – Apply to specific tables.
- **Column Privileges** – Apply to specific columns.
- **Routine Privileges** – Apply to stored procedures and functions.

Privilege	Description
ALL PRIVILEGES	Grants all available privileges
SELECT	Allows reading data
INSERT	Allows inserting data
UPDATE	Allows modifying existing data
DELETE	Allows deleting data
CREATE	Allows creating databases or tables
DROP	Allows dropping databases or tables
ALTER	Allows modifying table structures
GRANT OPTION	Allows granting privileges to other users

Granting Privileges

To grant privileges to a user:

GRANT privileges ON database.table TO 'username'@'host';

Examples

1. Grant all privileges on all databases:

    GRANT ALL PRIVILEGES ON *.* TO 'admin'@'%';

2. Grant specific privileges on a database:

    GRANT SELECT, INSERT, UPDATE ON sales.* TO 'sales_user'@'localhost';

3. Grant privileges on a specific table:

    GRANT SELECT, UPDATE ON employees.salary TO 'hr_user'@'localhost';

4. Grant privileges with the ability to grant others:

    GRANT SELECT, INSERT ON reports.* TO 'manager'@'localhost' WITH GRANT OPTION;

Viewing User Privileges

To check user privileges:

SHOW GRANTS FOR 'username'@'host';

Example

View grants for john:

SHOW GRANTS FOR 'john'@'localhost';

Revoking Privileges

To revoke privileges from a user:

REVOKE privileges ON database.table FROM 'username'@'host';

Examples

1. Revoke all privileges:

   REVOKE ALL PRIVILEGES ON *.* FROM 'admin'@'%';

2. Revoke a specific privilege:

   REVOKE DELETE ON sales.* FROM 'sales_user'@'localhost';

Removing All Privileges

If you want to remove all privileges from a user, you can do:

REVOKE ALL PRIVILEGES, GRANT OPTION FROM 'username'@'host';

Managing Roles in MySQL

MySQL (version 8.0+) supports **roles**, which simplify privilege management.

Creating Roles

Roles group a set of privileges and can be assigned to users.

CREATE ROLE 'role_name';

Example

Create a developer role:

CREATE ROLE 'developer';

Granting Privileges to a Role

GRANT privileges ON database.table TO 'role_name';

Example

Grant SELECT and INSERT privileges to developer:

GRANT SELECT, INSERT ON projects.* TO 'developer';

Assigning Roles to Users

GRANT 'role_name' TO 'username'@'host';

Example

Assign the developer role to alice:

GRANT 'developer' TO 'alice'@'localhost';

To make the role active immediately:

SET DEFAULT ROLE 'developer' TO 'alice'@'localhost';

Viewing Roles and Assigned Users

To check roles granted to a user:

SHOW GRANTS FOR 'username'@'host';

To check all available roles:

SELECT * FROM mysql.roles_mapping;

Removing Roles

To revoke a role from a user:

REVOKE 'role_name' FROM 'username'@'host';

To drop a role entirely:

DROP ROLE 'role_name';

Best Practices for User Management

- **Use Least Privilege Principle** – Grant only necessary privileges.
- **Avoid Using 'root'** – Create separate admin users for better security.
- **Regularly Review Users & Privileges** – Use SHOW GRANTS and SELECT user, host FROM mysql.user;.
- **Use Roles for Efficient Management** – Group privileges into roles instead of assigning them individually.
- **Restrict Remote Access** – Limit user connections to necessary hosts/IPs.

MySQL provides a comprehensive user and privilege management system, allowing database administrators to securely manage access. By using **GRANT**, **REVOKE**, and **ROLES**, you can efficiently control database operations while maintaining security.

19.2 Protecting Your Database from SQL Injection Attacks in MySQL

SQL injection is one of the most common and dangerous security vulnerabilities that affect MySQL databases. It allows attackers to manipulate SQL queries and gain unauthorized access to data, modify it, or even delete it. Protecting your MySQL database from SQL injection requires a combination of best coding practices, proper input validation, and database security configurations.

Understanding SQL Injection

SQL injection occurs when an attacker inputs malicious SQL statements into a query through user inputs. If an application does not properly sanitize or parameterize these inputs, the attacker can manipulate the SQL query structure.

Example of an SQL Injection Attack

Consider the following PHP code that takes a username and password and queries the database to authenticate a user:

```php
<?php
$username = $_POST['username'];
$password = $_POST['password'];

$conn = new mysqli("localhost", "root", "", "users_db");

// Unsafe query
$sql = "SELECT * FROM users WHERE username = '$username' AND password = '$password'";

$result = $conn->query($sql);

if ($result->num_rows > 0) {
    echo "Login successful!";
} else {
    echo "Invalid username or password.";
}
?>
```

How an Attacker Can Exploit This

If an attacker enters the following username:

' OR '1'='1

The SQL query becomes:

SELECT * FROM users WHERE username = '' OR '1'='1' AND password = '';

Since '1'='1' always evaluates to true, the query returns all users, allowing the attacker to bypass authentication.

Best Practices to Prevent SQL Injection

Use Prepared Statements and Parameterized Queries

Prepared statements ensure that user input is treated as data, not SQL code.

Example: Using Prepared Statements in PHP (MySQLi)

```php
<?php
$conn = new mysqli("localhost", "root", "", "users_db");

$stmt = $conn->prepare("SELECT * FROM users WHERE username = ?
AND password = ?");
$stmt->bind_param("ss", $username, $password);

$username = $_POST['username'];
$password = $_POST['password'];

$stmt->execute();
$result = $stmt->get_result();

if ($result->num_rows > 0) {
   echo "Login successful!";
} else {
   echo "Invalid username or password.";
}
?>
```

This prevents SQL injection because user inputs are treated strictly as values, not executable SQL code.

Use Stored Procedures

Stored procedures help encapsulate SQL logic and prevent direct query manipulation.

Example of a MySQL Stored Procedure

```sql
DELIMITER //
CREATE PROCEDURE ValidateUser(IN username VARCHAR(50), IN
password VARCHAR(50))
BEGIN
   SELECT * FROM users WHERE username = username AND password
= password;
END //
DELIMITER ;
```

To execute this procedure securely in PHP:

```
$stmt = $conn->prepare("CALL ValidateUser(?, ?)");
$stmt->bind_param("ss", $username, $password);
$stmt->execute();
```

Escape User Inputs Using mysqli_real_escape_string (Only as a Last Resort)

If you cannot use prepared statements, ensure that inputs are escaped properly.

```
$username = mysqli_real_escape_string($conn, $_POST['username']);
$password = mysqli_real_escape_string($conn, $_POST['password']);
```

```
$sql = "SELECT * FROM users WHERE username = '$username' AND password = '$password'";
```

However, this is not as secure as prepared statements.

Implement Proper Input Validation

Sanitize and validate user inputs using regular expressions or built-in PHP functions.

Example of Validating Input in PHP

```
if (!preg_match("/^[a-zA-Z0-9_]+$/", $_POST['username'])) {
    die("Invalid username.");
}
```

Ensure that inputs match expected formats, such as email validation:

```
if (!filter_var($_POST['email'], FILTER_VALIDATE_EMAIL)) {
    die("Invalid email format.");
}
```

Limit Database Privileges

Follow the principle of least privilege. Do not use the root user for database operations. Instead, create a restricted user.

Example: Creating a Limited MySQL User

```
CREATE      USER      'app_user'@'localhost'      IDENTIFIED      BY
'secure_password';
GRANT SELECT, INSERT, UPDATE, DELETE ON users_db.* TO
'app_user'@'localhost';
FLUSH PRIVILEGES;
```

This ensures that even if SQL injection occurs, the damage is minimized.

Disable Dangerous SQL Functions

Certain SQL functions, like EXECUTE, DROP, and UNION, can be exploited. Disable them where possible.

Example: Revoking Dangerous Privileges

```
REVOKE      EXECUTE,      DROP,      ALTER      ON      users_db.*      FROM
'app_user'@'localhost';
FLUSH PRIVILEGES;
```

Use Web Application Firewalls (WAF)

A WAF can detect and block SQL injection attempts before they reach your database. Some popular options include:

- **ModSecurity** (Open-source)
- **Cloudflare WAF**
- **AWS WAF**

Monitor and Log SQL Activity

Enable MySQL logging to track suspicious queries.

Enable MySQL General Query Log

```
SET GLOBAL general_log = 'ON';
```

```
SET GLOBAL log_output = 'TABLE';
```

Check logs for unusual patterns:

```
SELECT * FROM mysql.general_log WHERE argument LIKE
'%UNION%';
```

Regularly Update MySQL and Software

Ensure your MySQL server, application framework, and libraries are always up-to-date to protect against known vulnerabilities.

Implement Captchas and Rate Limiting

To reduce brute-force attacks, implement reCAPTCHA or limit login attempts.

```
session_start();
if (!isset($_SESSION['attempts'])) {
    $_SESSION['attempts'] = 0;
}

if ($_SESSION['attempts'] > 3) {
    die("Too many login attempts. Please try again later.");
}

$_SESSION['attempts']++;
```

Protecting your MySQL database from SQL injection is crucial to maintaining data security. The best approach includes:
✓ Using **prepared statements**
✓ Validating and sanitizing inputs
✓ **Restricting database privileges**
✓ **Disabling dangerous SQL functions**
✓ **Monitoring and logging suspicious activities**

By implementing these strategies, you significantly reduce the risk of SQL injection attacks and keep your MySQL database secure.

19.3 Encryption in MySQL: A Comprehensive Guide

Encryption in MySQL is a crucial feature that helps protect sensitive data from unauthorized access. MySQL provides multiple ways to encrypt data, including **column-level encryption, tablespace encryption, and connection encryption (TLS/SSL)**. This guide explores these methods in great detail, covering their implementation, advantages, and considerations.

Types of Encryption in MySQL

Data-at-Rest Encryption

This encryption protects stored data by converting it into an unreadable format unless decrypted with a proper key. MySQL offers:

- Tablespace Encryption
- Column-Level Encryption
- Binary Log Encryption
- Redo/Undo Log Encryption

Data-in-Transit Encryption

This encryption ensures that data transmitted between MySQL clients and servers is secure from eavesdropping or man-in-the-middle attacks.

- **SSL/TLS Encryption**
- **Secure Connections via OpenSSL or GnuTLS**

Tablespace Encryption

What is Tablespace Encryption?

Tablespace encryption allows encryption of **entire InnoDB tablespaces**, ensuring that all data stored within a table is encrypted.

Implementation

Enable File-Per-Table Tablespaces:

SET GLOBAL innodb_file_per_table = ON;

This ensures that tables are stored separately in .ibd files, which can then be encrypted.

Create an Encrypted Table:

CREATE TABLE employees (id INT PRIMARY KEY, name VARCHAR(255), salary DECIMAL(10,2)) ENGINE=InnoDB ENCRYPTION='Y';

- o   ENCRYPTION='Y' enables tablespace encryption.

Check If a Table is Encrypted:

SELECT TABLE_NAME, CREATE_OPTIONS
FROM information_schema.tables
WHERE TABLE_SCHEMA = 'your_database_name';

This will display if encryption is enabled.

Key Management for Tablespace Encryption

- MySQL uses **MySQL Keyring** to store encryption keys securely.
- Supported Keyring Plugins:
    - o   keyring_file (stores keys in a local file)
    - o   keyring_encrypted_file (encrypts the key file)
    - o   keyring_hashicorp (uses HashiCorp Vault)
    - o   keyring_aws (Amazon KMS)

Example: Enabling Keyring File Plugin

early-plugin-load=keyring_file.so
keyring_file_data=/var/lib/mysql-keyring/keyring

Column-Level Encryption

Why Use Column-Level Encryption?

- More **granular control** over which data gets encrypted.
- Only specific sensitive columns (e.g., passwords, SSNs) are encrypted rather than the whole table.
- Provides an additional layer of security for critical information.

MySQL AES (Advanced Encryption Standard) Functions

MySQL provides built-in AES encryption functions:

- AES_ENCRYPT() – Encrypts a value using AES.
- AES_DECRYPT() – Decrypts an AES-encrypted value.

Implementation

Encrypting Data

```
INSERT INTO users (id, name, ssn)
VALUES (1, 'Alice', AES_ENCRYPT('123-45-6789', 'your_secret_key'));
```

Decrypting Data

```
SELECT id, name, AES_DECRYPT(ssn, 'your_secret_key') AS ssn
FROM users;
```

Considerations

- The **encryption key** (your_secret_key) should be stored securely, preferably outside the database.
- Use **random initialization vectors (IVs)** for added security.
- Encrypt before inserting, decrypt only when necessary.

Binary Log Encryption

Why Encrypt Binary Logs?

Binary logs store changes made to the database, including **INSERT, UPDATE, DELETE** statements. Encrypting these logs prevents unauthorized access to sensitive historical data.

Enabling Binary Log Encryption

```
binlog_encryption=ON
```

Verifying Binary Log Encryption

```
SHOW VARIABLES LIKE 'binlog_encryption';
```

Redo and Undo Log Encryption

Why Encrypt Redo and Undo Logs?

- Redo logs store changes before they are committed.
- Undo logs store old data for rollback operations.
- Encrypting these logs ensures that even temporary or rollback data remains secure.

Enabling Redo/Undo Log Encryption

```
innodb_redo_log_encrypt=ON
innodb_undo_log_encrypt=ON
```

Verifying Log Encryption

```
SHOW VARIABLES LIKE 'innodb_%_log_encrypt';
```

SSL/TLS Encryption for Data-in-Transit

Why Use SSL/TLS?

- Prevents **eavesdropping** by encrypting data transmitted between MySQL clients and servers.
- Ensures **secure authentication**.

Enabling SSL/TLS

Verify SSL Support

```
SHOW VARIABLES LIKE 'have_ssl';
```

If have_ssl is YES, SSL is enabled.

Generate SSL Certificates

```
openssl genrsa -out ca-key.pem 2048
openssl req -new -x509 -key ca-key.pem -out ca-cert.pem -days 365
openssl genrsa -out server-key.pem 2048
```

```
openssl req -new -key server-key.pem -out server-req.pem
openssl x509 -req -in server-req.pem -CA ca-cert.pem -CAkey ca-key.pem -
set_serial 01 -out server-cert.pem
```

Configure MySQL to Use SSL
```
ssl-ca=/path/to/ca-cert.pem
ssl-cert=/path/to/server-cert.pem
ssl-key=/path/to/server-key.pem
```

Force Clients to Use SSL
```
CREATE USER 'secure_user'@'%' IDENTIFIED BY 'password' REQUIRE SSL;
```

Verify SSL Connection

```
SHOW STATUS LIKE 'Ssl_cipher';
```

Best Practices for MySQL Encryption

Secure Key Management

- Use a **key management system (KMS)** (AWS KMS, Azure Key Vault).
- Store keys **outside** the database server.
- Rotate keys periodically.

Minimize Decryption

- Decrypt data **only when necessary**.
- Use **stored procedures** to handle decryption logic securely.

Enforce Access Controls

- Use **MySQL roles and privileges** to restrict who can access encrypted data.
- Example:

```
GRANT SELECT ON users TO 'app_user'@'%' IDENTIFIED BY 'password';
```

Audit Encrypted Data

- Enable **MySQL Audit Logs** to track access to sensitive information.
- Example:

```
audit_log_policy=ALL
```

MySQL provides multiple encryption methods to secure data at rest and in transit. **Tablespace encryption** is ideal for encrypting entire tables, while **column-level encryption** allows precise control over sensitive fields. **Binary log and redo/undo log encryption** ensure that temporary and historical data remain protected. For data in transit, **SSL/TLS encryption** is essential.

By following **best practices** such as secure key management, access control, and auditing, you can ensure that sensitive data in MySQL remains safe from unauthorized access.

20 MYSQL AND OTHER TECHNOLOGIES

MySQL is highly compatible with a variety of other databases and programming languages, making it a versatile and widely-used database management system (DBMS). Here's an overview of its compatibility:

Compatibility with Other Databases:

- **Database Interoperability:** MySQL can integrate with other databases like PostgreSQL, Oracle, or Microsoft SQL Server. Tools such as **MySQL Workbench** and **ODBC drivers** can help facilitate data exchange between different DBMS.
- **Replication:** MySQL supports replication, allowing it to copy data to other databases for redundancy or scaling purposes. This helps maintain compatibility with other systems where data sharing is needed.
- **Data Import/Export:** MySQL can import/export data in various formats (CSV, XML, JSON, SQL dump, etc.), making it easy to move data between different database systems.

Compatibility with Programming Languages:

- **PHP:** MySQL is most commonly used with PHP in web development. The combination of **PHP and MySQL** powers many websites and content management systems (e.g., WordPress, Joomla). PHP has built-in MySQL functions (mysqli and PDO).
- **Python:** Python can interact with MySQL through libraries like **MySQL Connector** or **PyMySQL**. These libraries allow developers to execute SQL queries and manage database connections efficiently.
- **Java:** MySQL is compatible with Java through JDBC (Java Database Connectivity). The **MySQL JDBC driver** enables Java applications to interact with MySQL databases by executing SQL queries and retrieving data.
- **Node.js:** MySQL can be accessed in Node.js applications via libraries like **mysql2** or **sequelize** (an ORM for Node.js). These libraries allow Node.js applications to work seamlessly with MySQL databases.
- **Ruby:** Ruby on Rails, a popular web development framework, integrates well with MySQL. The **mysql2 gem** allows Ruby programs to communicate with MySQL databases.
- **C/C++:** MySQL offers C and C++ connectors, allowing developers to interact directly with MySQL from these low-level languages for performance-sensitive applications.

Cross-Platform Compatibility:

- MySQL is cross-platform, meaning it runs on various operating systems, including **Linux, Windows, macOS**, and others. This ensures that MySQL-based applications can be developed and deployed on multiple platforms without compatibility issues.

API Support:

- **RESTful APIs**: MySQL can expose data via **REST APIs** (using technologies like PHP or Node.js), allowing it to interface with applications across different programming languages and platforms.

ORM (Object-Relational Mapping) Support:

- MySQL is supported by many **ORM frameworks** like **Hibernate** (Java), **Django ORM** (Python), **ActiveRecord** (Ruby), and **Sequelize** (Node.js). ORMs allow developers to interact with the database using objects and methods, abstracting away the need to write SQL queries directly.

In summary, MySQL's extensive support for various programming languages, its ability to integrate with other databases, and its cross-platform nature make it a highly compatible and adaptable choice for developers working across diverse technologies.

20.1 Integrating MySQL with PHP

Integrating MySQL with PHP is a common practice in web development, as it allows for dynamic interaction with databases. Here's a detailed breakdown of how to integrate MySQL with PHP, covering the essential concepts, steps, and examples:

Understanding MySQL and PHP Integration

MySQL is an open-source relational database management system (RDBMS), and PHP is a server-side scripting language commonly used for creating dynamic web pages. By integrating MySQL with PHP, you can store, retrieve, update, and delete data stored in a MySQL database through PHP scripts.

Setting up the Environment

To begin integrating MySQL with PHP, you need the following components installed:

- **MySQL Database**: Install MySQL server on your local machine or web server.
- **PHP**: Make sure PHP is installed, either locally for development or on a web server (like Apache or Nginx).
- **PHP MySQLi or PDO (PHP Data Objects)**: PHP supports two main methods for interacting with MySQL: MySQLi (MySQL Improved) and PDO. Both are capable of performing database operations securely, but PDO supports multiple database systems, while MySQLi is specifically for MySQL databases.

Connecting to MySQL Using PHP

To interact with MySQL, PHP must first establish a connection to the database server. You can use MySQLi or PDO to achieve this. Below are examples for both.

Using MySQLi (Procedural Style)

```php
<?php
// Connection details
$servername = "localhost";
$username = "root";
$password = "";
$dbname = "test_database";

// Create connection
$conn = mysqli_connect($servername, $username, $password, $dbname);

// Check connection
if (!$conn) {
    die("Connection failed: " . mysqli_connect_error());
}
echo "Connected successfully";
?>
```

Using MySQLi (Object-Oriented Style)

```php
<?php
```

```
// Connection details
$servername = "localhost";
$username = "root";
$password = "";
$dbname = "test_database";

// Create connection
$conn = new mysqli($servername, $username, $password, $dbname);

// Check connection
if ($conn->connect_error) {
    die("Connection failed: " . $conn->connect_error);
}
echo "Connected successfully";
?>
```

Using PDO (PHP Data Objects)

```
<?php
// Connection details
$servername = "localhost";
$username = "root";
$password = "";
$dbname = "test_database";

try {
    // Create PDO connection
    $conn = new PDO("mysql:host=$servername;dbname=$dbname", $username, $password);
    // Set PDO error mode to exception
    $conn->setAttribute(PDO::ATTR_ERRMODE, PDO::ERRMODE_EXCEPTION);
    echo "Connected successfully";
}
catch(PDOException $e) {
    echo "Connection failed: " . $e->getMessage();
}
?>
```

Performing CRUD Operations

Once you have established a connection to the MySQL database, you can perform Create, Read, Update, and Delete (CRUD) operations.

Create (Insert Data)

Inserting data into the database can be done using an INSERT INTO SQL query.

```
// MySQLi Example (Procedural Style)
$sql = "INSERT INTO users (username, email) VALUES ('JohnDoe',
'john@example.com')";
if (mysqli_query($conn, $sql)) {
    echo "New record created successfully";
} else {
    echo "Error: " . $sql . "<br>" . mysqli_error($conn);
}

// MySQLi Example (Object-Oriented Style)
$sql = "INSERT INTO users (username, email) VALUES ('JohnDoe',
'john@example.com')";
if ($conn->query($sql) === TRUE) {
    echo "New record created successfully";
} else {
    echo "Error: " . $sql . "<br>" . $conn->error;
}

// PDO Example
$sql = "INSERT INTO users (username, email) VALUES ('JohnDoe',
'john@example.com')";
$stmt = $conn->prepare($sql);
$stmt->execute();
echo "New record created successfully";
```

Read (Retrieve Data)

Fetching data from the database can be done using a SELECT query.

```
// MySQLi Example
$sql = "SELECT id, username, email FROM users";
$result = mysqli_query($conn, $sql);

if (mysqli_num_rows($result) > 0) {
    // Output data of each row
    while($row = mysqli_fetch_assoc($result)) {
```

```
    echo "id: " . $row["id"] . " - Name: " . $row["username"] . " - Email: " .
$row["email"] . "<br>";
    }
} else {
    echo "0 results";
}
```

```
// PDO Example
$sql = "SELECT id, username, email FROM users";
$stmt = $conn->prepare($sql);
$stmt->execute();
```

```
while ($row = $stmt->fetch(PDO::FETCH_ASSOC)) {
    echo "id: " . $row['id'] . " - Name: " . $row['username'] . " - Email: " .
$row['email'] . "<br>";
}
```

Update Data

Updating existing data in the database can be done with the UPDATE SQL query.

```
// MySQLi Example
$sql = "UPDATE users SET email='newemail@example.com' WHERE
username='JohnDoe'";
if (mysqli_query($conn, $sql)) {
    echo "Record updated successfully";
} else {
    echo "Error: " . $sql . "<br>" . mysqli_error($conn);
}
```

```
// PDO Example
$sql = "UPDATE users SET email='newemail@example.com' WHERE
username='JohnDoe'";
$stmt = $conn->prepare($sql);
$stmt->execute();
echo "Record updated successfully";
```

Delete Data

Deleting data from the database can be done using a DELETE query.

```
// MySQLi Example
```

```php
$sql = "DELETE FROM users WHERE username='JohnDoe'";
if (mysqli_query($conn, $sql)) {
    echo "Record deleted successfully";
} else {
    echo "Error: " . $sql . "<br>" . mysqli_error($conn);
}


// PDO Example
$sql = "DELETE FROM users WHERE username='JohnDoe'";
$stmt = $conn->prepare($sql);
$stmt->execute();
echo "Record deleted successfully";
```

Prepared Statements

Prepared statements are an important security feature that helps protect against SQL injection attacks. Both MySQLi and PDO support prepared statements.

Using Prepared Statements in MySQLi (Procedural Style)

```php
$sql = "INSERT INTO users (username, email) VALUES (?, ?)";
$stmt = mysqli_prepare($conn, $sql);
mysqli_stmt_bind_param($stmt, "ss", $username, $email);

$username = "JaneDoe";
$email = "jane@example.com";
mysqli_stmt_execute($stmt);
```

Using Prepared Statements in PDO

```php
$sql = "INSERT INTO users (username, email) VALUES (:username, :email)";
$stmt = $conn->prepare($sql);
$stmt->bindParam(':username', $username);
$stmt->bindParam(':email', $email);

$username = "JaneDoe";
$email = "jane@example.com";
$stmt->execute();
```

Closing the Connection

Once the operations are complete, it's good practice to close the database connection.

```
// For MySQLi
mysqli_close($conn);
```

```
// For PDO
$conn = null;
```

Error Handling

It is crucial to implement error handling to catch and report issues during database operations.

- For MySQLi, you can use mysqli_error() or mysqli_errno() to get error details.
- For PDO, errors can be caught by enabling exceptions with setAttribute(PDO::ATTR_ERRMODE, PDO::ERRMODE_EXCEPTION).

Integrating MySQL with PHP is a powerful combination for building dynamic, data-driven web applications. By using MySQLi or PDO, you can connect to a MySQL database, perform CRUD operations, and enhance security using prepared statements. Understanding how to handle connections, errors, and secure data access is key to creating robust web applications.

20.2 Connecting MySQL to Python

Connecting MySQL to Python involves using a Python library that allows Python to interact with MySQL databases. One of the most popular libraries for this purpose is mysql-connector-python, but others like PyMySQL and MySQLdb (part of the MySQL-python package) can also be used. Below is a step-by-step guide on how to connect MySQL to Python using the mysql-connector-python library.

Install the MySQL Connector Library

To interact with MySQL, the first thing you need to do is install the connector library. You can install it using pip:

```
pip install mysql-connector-python
```

Import the Connector in Your Python Code

Once the library is installed, you need to import it into your Python code to begin interacting with the database.

import mysql.connector

Create a Connection to the Database

To connect to MySQL, you will use the connect() function, providing it with the necessary credentials such as the host, user, password, and database name.

Establishing a connection to the MySQL server

db_connection = mysql.connector.connect(

host="localhost", # or the server IP if MySQL is on a remote machine

user="your_username", # the MySQL username

password="your_password", # the MySQL password

database="your_database" # the name of the database you want to use

)

Create a Cursor Object

Once the connection is established, you need a cursor object to execute SQL queries. A cursor is essentially a pointer that allows you to interact with the MySQL database.

cursor = db_connection.cursor()

Execute SQL Queries

With the cursor object, you can execute SQL queries such as SELECT, INSERT, UPDATE, or DELETE.

Example: Running a Simple Query

For example, to fetch all rows from a table, you can use the SELECT statement:

cursor.execute("SELECT * FROM your_table_name") # Fetching all results from the executed query

results = cursor.fetchall()

for row in results:

    print(row)

Example: Inserting Data into a Table

You can also insert data into your MySQL table using INSERT INTO statements:

insert_query = "INSERT INTO your_table_name (column1, column2) VALUES (%s, %s)" values = ("value1", "value2")

cursor.execute(insert_query, values) # Commit the transaction to the database

db_connection.commit()

Handling Errors

It's important to handle exceptions while working with MySQL to ensure your program doesn't crash unexpectedly. You can use Python's try and except blocks for error handling.

try:

cursor.execute("SELECT * FROM non_existent_table")

except mysql.connector.Error as err:

print(f"Error: {err}")

Closing the Connection

Once your operations are complete, you should always close the cursor and connection to release resources.

cursor.close()

db_connection.close()

Complete Example

Here is a complete example that connects to MySQL, retrieves data from a table, and inserts new data:

```python
import mysql.connector

try:

# Connect to MySQL server

db_connection = mysql.connector.connect(

host="localhost",user="root",password="password",database="my_database
")

# Create a cursor object

cursor = db_connection.cursor()

# Execute a SELECT query

cursor.execute("SELECT * FROM employees")

# Fetch and print all results

results = cursor.fetchall()

for row in results:

print(row)

# Insert a new row

insert_query = "INSERT INTO employees (name, position) VALUES (%s,
%s)"

values = ("John Doe", "Software Developer")

cursor.execute(insert_query, values)

# Commit the changes

db_connection.commit()
```

```
except mysql.connector.Error as err:
```

```
print(f"Error: {err}")
```

```
finally:
```

```
# Close the cursor and connection
```

```
if cursor:
```

```
    cursor.close()
```

```
if db_connection:
```

```
    db_connection.close()
```

Working with Transactions

In MySQL, transactions allow you to execute multiple SQL commands together as a single unit of work. You can use commit() to save changes and rollback() to undo them in case of errors.

```
# Begin a transaction
```

```
cursor.execute("START TRANSACTION")
```

```
# Execute SQL commands
```

```
cursor.execute("INSERT INTO employees (name, position) VALUES (%s, %s)", ("Jane Doe", "Data Scientist"))
```

```
# If no errors, commit the changes
```

```
db_connection.commit()
```

```
# If something goes wrong, rollback the transaction
```

```
db_connection.rollback()
```

Using Prepared Statements

Prepared statements are used to prevent SQL injection attacks and improve performance. Instead of embedding user input directly into SQL queries, you can use placeholders (%s) and pass the values separately.

query = "SELECT * FROM employees WHERE position = %s"

cursor.execute(query, ("Software Developer",))

```
# Fetch and print results
results = cursor.fetchall()
for row in results:
    print(row)
```

Using MySQL with Pandas

You can also combine mysql-connector with the pandas library to load MySQL data directly into a pandas DataFrame.

import pandas as pd

```
# Read MySQL data into a pandas DataFrame
df = pd.read_sql("SELECT * FROM employees", db_connection)
```

```
# Display the data
print(df.head())
```

Connecting MySQL to Python is a straightforward process with the mysql-connector-python library. It allows you to perform various database operations such as fetching data, inserting new records, handling errors, and even managing transactions. By following best practices like using prepared statements and committing or rolling back transactions appropriately, you can ensure secure and efficient database interactions in your Python projects.

20.3 Connecting MySQL to Java

Connecting MySQL to Java involves setting up a connection between your Java application and a MySQL database. This allows your Java program to interact with the database by executing SQL queries and retrieving results. To achieve this, you need the following components:

Install MySQL

First, ensure that MySQL is installed and running on your system. You can download it from the official MySQL website and follow the installation instructions for your platform.

Set Up MySQL Database

Before connecting, you should have a database set up in MySQL. You can create a database using the MySQL command line or a GUI like MySQL Workbench.

For example, to create a database:

CREATE DATABASE mydatabase;

Install MySQL Connector/J (JDBC Driver)

Java communicates with MySQL using a JDBC driver. MySQL provides a JDBC driver known as **MySQL Connector/J**, which is a Java library that allows Java applications to connect to MySQL databases.

To use it:

Download MySQL Connector/J: You can download it from the MySQL website or use Maven to manage it.

Maven Dependency:

```
<dependency>
  <groupId>mysql</groupId>
  <artifactId>mysql-connector-java</artifactId>
  <version>8.0.29</version>
</dependency>
```

If you're not using Maven, you can download the JAR file and add it to your Java project's classpath.

Java Program to Connect to MySQL

Step 1: Import JDBC classes

Import the necessary classes in your Java program.

```
import java.sql.Connection;
import java.sql.DriverManager;
import java.sql.Statement;
import java.sql.ResultSet;
import java.sql.SQLException;
```

Step 2: Load the JDBC Driver

Load the MySQL JDBC driver using Class.forName. This tells Java to use the MySQL driver when connecting to the database.

```
try {
    Class.forName("com.mysql.cj.jdbc.Driver");
} catch (ClassNotFoundException e) {
    System.out.println("MySQL JDBC Driver not found.");
    e.printStackTrace();
    return;
}
```

Step 3: Establish Connection

Use the DriverManager to establish a connection to the MySQL database. You'll need to provide the URL of the MySQL server, the username, and the password.

```
String url = "jdbc:mysql://localhost:3306/mydatabase";  // MySQL URL
with database name
String user = "root"; // Replace with your MySQL username
String password = "password"; // Replace with your MySQL password

Connection connection = null;

try {
    connection = DriverManager.getConnection(url, user, password);
    System.out.println("Connected to the database successfully!");
} catch (SQLException e) {
    System.out.println("Connection failed.");
    e.printStackTrace();
}
```

Step 4: Create and Execute Queries

Once the connection is established, you can execute SQL queries.

Creating a Statement:

```
Statement statement = connection.createStatement();
```

Executing a Query: Here's an example where we query all records from a table:

```
String query = "SELECT * FROM users";  // Example SQL query

try (ResultSet resultSet = statement.executeQuery(query)) {
    while (resultSet.next()) {
        int id = resultSet.getInt("id");
        String name = resultSet.getString("name");
        System.out.println("ID: " + id + ", Name: " + name);
    }
} catch (SQLException e) {
    e.printStackTrace();
}
```

Step 5: Close the Connection

After executing the query and fetching results, it's important to close the connection to free up resources.

```
try {
    if (connection != null) {
        connection.close();
    }
} catch (SQLException e) {
    e.printStackTrace();
}
```

Full Example Code:

```
import java.sql.Connection;
import java.sql.DriverManager;
import java.sql.Statement;
import java.sql.ResultSet;
import java.sql.SQLException;

public class MySQLConnectionExample {
    public static void main(String[] args) {
        String url = "jdbc:mysql://localhost:3306/mydatabase";  // MySQL
URL with database name
        String user = "root";  // Replace with your MySQL username
        String password = "password";  // Replace with your MySQL password

        Connection connection = null;
```

```
try {
    Class.forName("com.mysql.cj.jdbc.Driver");  // Load MySQL JDBC Driver
    connection = DriverManager.getConnection(url, user, password);  // Establish connection
    System.out.println("Connected to the database successfully!");

    Statement statement = connection.createStatement();
    String query = "SELECT * FROM users";  // Example SQL query

    try (ResultSet resultSet = statement.executeQuery(query)) {
        while (resultSet.next()) {
            int id = resultSet.getInt("id");
            String name = resultSet.getString("name");
            System.out.println("ID: " + id + ", Name: " + name);
        }
    } catch (SQLException e) {
        e.printStackTrace();
    }
} catch (ClassNotFoundException e) {
    System.out.println("MySQL JDBC Driver not found.");
    e.printStackTrace();
} catch (SQLException e) {
    System.out.println("Connection failed.");
    e.printStackTrace();
} finally {
    try {
        if (connection != null) {
            connection.close();  // Close connection
        }
    } catch (SQLException e) {
        e.printStackTrace();
    }
}
}
}
```

Error Handling

When working with databases, you should handle possible errors like SQL exceptions, incorrect credentials, or missing driver libraries.

- **SQLException:** Handles issues related to database access or connection errors.
- **ClassNotFoundException:** This exception is thrown if the JDBC driver is not found.

Additional Tips

- **Use PreparedStatement for Security:** For queries involving user input (like INSERT, UPDATE, etc.), use PreparedStatement to prevent SQL injection.

  Example:

  String insertQuery = "INSERT INTO users (name, email) VALUES (?, ?)";
  try   (PreparedStatement   preparedStatement   = connection.prepareStatement(insertQuery)) {
      preparedStatement.setString(1, "John Doe");
      preparedStatement.setString(2, "john.doe@example.com");
      preparedStatement.executeUpdate();
  } catch (SQLException e) {
      e.printStackTrace();
  }

- **Connection Pooling:** For applications that need to handle a large number of connections, use connection pooling (via libraries like HikariCP or Apache DBCP) to manage connections efficiently.

This process establishes a solid foundation for connecting MySQL to Java, allowing you to build more complex applications that interact with the database.

20.4 Connecting MySQL to C

C provides several libraries that allow communication with MySQL databases. The most common and widely used library is the **MySQL C API**, which is part of the **MySQL Connector/C** package.

Steps to connect MySQL with C:

Install MySQL Connector/C:

Download and install the MySQL Connector/C from the official website: MySQL Connector/C.

Include the MySQL header file: In your C program, include the MySQL header file to access the necessary functions.

#include <mysql/mysql.h>

Initialize the MySQL library: Call mysql_library_init() to initialize the MySQL library.

mysql_library_init(0, NULL, NULL);

Create a MySQL connection: Initialize a MYSQL object and use the mysql_real_connect() function to establish a connection.

MYSQL *conn;

conn = mysql_init(NULL);

if (conn == NULL) {fprintf(stderr, "mysql_init() failed\n");

exit(1); }

if (mysql_real_connect(conn, "localhost", "user", "password", "database", 0, NULL, 0) == NULL) { fprintf(stderr, "mysql_real_connect() failed\n"); mysql_close(conn); exit(1); }

Perform a query: Once connected, you can execute SQL queries using mysql_query().

if (mysql_query(conn, "SELECT * FROM table_name")) { fprintf(stderr, "SELECT failed. Error: %s\n", mysql_error(conn)); exit(1); }

Retrieve results: After executing a query, retrieve the results using mysql_store_result() or mysql_use_result().

MYSQL_RES *res = mysql_store_result(conn);

if (res == NULL) { fprintf(stderr, "mysql_store_result() failed. Error: %s\n", mysql_error(conn)); exit(1); }

MYSQL_ROW row;

while ((row = mysql_fetch_row(res)) != NULL) { printf("%s\n", row[0]); // Assuming the first column is of interest }

Close the connection: Finally, close the connection when you're done with it.

mysql_free_result(res);

mysql_close(conn);

Compile and Link: When compiling, link with the MySQL client library:

gcc -o mysql_program mysql_program.c -lmysqlclient

20.5 Connecting MySQL to C++

In C++, the process is similar to C, but C++ provides the **MySQL Connector/C++** library, which offers object-oriented features for managing database connections.

Steps to connect MySQL with C++:

Step 1: Install MySQL Connector/C++: Install the MySQL Connector/C++ from the official site: MySQL Connector/C++.

Step 2: Include necessary headers: **Include the relevant C++ header files to** interact with MySQL.

```
#include <mysql_driver.h>
#include <mysql_connection.h>
```

Step 3: Create a MySQL connection object: Use the get_driver_instance() method to get an instance of the MySQL driver and then use connect() to establish a connection.
```
sql::mysql::MySQL_Driver *driver;
sql::Connection *con;
driver = sql::mysql::get_mysql_driver_instance();
con = driver->connect("tcp://127.0.0.1:3306", "user", "password");
con->setSchema("database_name");
```

Step 4: Perform queries: After establishing the connection, use the sql::Statement object to execute queries.

```
sql::Statement *stmt;
stmt = con->createStatement();
stmt->execute("SELECT * FROM table_name");
```

Step 5: Retrieve results: To fetch the query results, use a sql::ResultSet.

```
sql::ResultSet *res;
res = stmt->executeQuery("SELECT * FROM table_name");
while (res->next()) {
    std::cout << res->getString("column_name") << std::endl;
}
```

Step 6: Close the connection: Close the connection and free resources after use.

```
delete res;
delete stmt;
delete con;
```

Step 7: Compile and Link: Link the MySQL Connector/C++ libraries while compiling.

```
g++ -o mysql_program mysql_program. -lmysqlconn
```

20.6 Connecting MySQL to PEARL

PEARL (Process and Experiment Automation Realtime Language) is a high-level programming language used mainly for real-time systems, and it isn't commonly used for database interaction. However, if you want to connect PEARL to a MySQL database, it might require an external library or API.

One way to interface PEARL with MySQL is by using **C-based libraries** or **shell calls** that run SQL commands, as PEARL doesn't natively support database interaction.

Steps to connect MySQL with PEARL:

Using C or Shell calls:

You can invoke system commands from PEARL, such as using the system()

function to run shell commands that interface with MySQL.

Example:

system("mysql -u user -p'password' -e 'SELECT * FROM database_name.table_name'");

PEARL's system() function: The system() function executes shell commands, so you can pass in the MySQL client commands to interact with the database.

SYSTEM("mysql -u user -p'password' -e 'SELECT column_name FROM table_name'");

Processing results: PEARL doesn't have built-in functionality for processing query results directly. You could instead capture the output into a file and then read it into PEARL using file I/O operations.

General Considerations

- **Security**: Ensure that your database credentials are securely managed (e.g., using environment variables instead of hardcoding them).
- **Error handling**: Always check for errors when connecting, executing queries, and retrieving data to handle potential issues gracefully.
- **Data Types**: Be mindful of data types when retrieving results and passing data between MySQL and your program. Ensure that you correctly handle types like strings, integers, and dates.

- Using MySQL with Web Frameworks (e.g., Django, Laravel)

Using MySQL with different web frameworks is a common practice when building dynamic websites and web applications. MySQL is a powerful relational database management system (RDBMS), while web frameworks provide the structure to develop applications in a specific programming language, such as Python, JavaScript, PHP, Ruby, etc. Let's dive into how MySQL integrates with different web frameworks, covering the basics, configuration, and some examples.

20.7 MySQL Integration with Python Web Frameworks

Django

Django is a high-level Python web framework that encourages rapid development. It uses an ORM (Object Relational Mapping) to manage database queries, making it easy to interact with MySQL without needing to write raw SQL queries.

Configuration: Django's settings.py file holds the database configuration. To use MySQL, you'll need the mysqlclient package (a MySQL database adapter for Python).

```
ip install mysqlclient
```

Example settings.py configuration:

```
DATABASES = {
    'default': {
        'ENGINE': 'django.db.backends.mysql',
        'NAME': 'your_db_name',
        'USER': 'your_db_user',
        'PASSWORD': 'your_db_password',
        'HOST': 'localhost',
        'PORT': '3306',
    }
}
```

Models and Queries: Django allows you to define models as Python classes. Once the model is defined, Django automatically generates the appropriate SQL statements to interact with the MySQL database. Example model:

```
class Book(models.Model):
    title = models.CharField(max_length=100)
    author = models.CharField(max_length=100)
    published_date = models.DateField()
```

Example query:
```
books = Book.objects.all()
```

Flask

Flask is a lightweight and flexible web framework in Python. It doesn't come with an ORM by default, but it can integrate easily with MySQL using extensions like Flask-MySQLdb or SQLAlchemy.

Configuration: You typically use Flask-MySQLdb to connect Flask with MySQL:

```
pip install Flask-MySQLdb
```

Example configuration in Flask:

```
app.config['MYSQL_HOST'] = 'localhost'
app.config['MYSQL_USER'] = 'your_db_user'
app.config['MYSQL_PASSWORD'] = 'your_db_password'
app.config['MYSQL_DB'] = 'your_db_name'

mysql = MySQL(app)
```

Using SQLAlchemy: For more complex applications, you might choose SQLAlchemy as an ORM. Flask integrates easily with SQLAlchemy, which allows you to interact with MySQL through Python objects.

```
pip install flask-sqlalchemy
```

Example Flask app with SQLAlchemy:

```
from flask import Flask

from flask_sqlalchemy import SQLAlchemy

app = Flask(__name__)

app.config['SQLALCHEMY_DATABASE_URI']=
'mysql://your_db_user:your_db_password@localhost/your_db_name'

db = SQLAlchemy(app)

class User(db.Model):
```

```
id = db.Column(db.Integer, primary_key=True)

name = db.Column(db.String(80), unique=True, nullable=False)

email = db.Column(db.String(120), unique=True, nullable=False)

db.create_all()
```

MySQL Integration with JavaScript (Node.js)

Express.js is a minimalistic web framework for Node.js, and MySQL is commonly used with it to store data for web applications.

Configuration: You typically use the mysql package to connect to MySQL in Express.js.

```
npm install mysql
```

Example MySQL connection configuration:

```
const mysql = require('mysql');

const connection = mysql.createConnection({

host: 'localhost', user: 'your_db_user', password: 'your_db_password',
database: 'your_db_name' });

connection.connect((err) => {

if (err) throw err; console.log('Connected to MySQL database'); });
```

Performing Queries: Example query in Express.js to fetch all users:

```
app.get('/users', (req, res) => {

connection.query('SELECT * FROM users', (err, results) => {

if (err) throw err;

        res.json(results);
      });
    });
```

Sequelize ORM

Sequelize is a promise-based ORM for Node.js that supports MySQL. It abstracts raw SQL queries, allowing developers to interact with the database using JavaScript objects.

Configuration:

npm install sequelize mysql2

Example Sequelize setup:

```
const { Sequelize, DataTypes } = require('sequelize');

const sequelize = new
Sequelize('mysql://your_db_user:your_db_password@localhost/your_db_na
me');

const User = sequelize.define('User', {

name: {

        type: DataTypes.STRING,
        allowNull: false
      },
      email: {
      type: DataTypes.STRING,
      unique: true,
      allowNull: false
      }
    });

    sequelize.sync().then(() => {
      console.log('Database & tables created!');
    });
```

Laravel

Laravel is a popular PHP framework that comes with built-in support for MySQL. Laravel uses an ORM called Eloquent, which provides an easy-to-use interface for interacting with the database.

- **Configuration**: The database connection is configured in the .env file of your Laravel project:

```
DB_CONNECTION=mysql
DB_HOST=127.0.0.1
DB_PORT=3306
DB_DATABASE=your_db_name
DB_USERNAME=your_db_user
DB_PASSWORD=your_db_password
```

- **Models and Queries**: Laravel uses Eloquent to manage database queries. Example model:

```
class Post extends Model {
    protected $fillable = ['title', 'content'];
}
```

Example query:

```
$posts = Post::all();
```

CodeIgniter

CodeIgniter is another PHP framework that allows for easy integration with MySQL. It provides a simple database class that simplifies query building and executing.

Configuration: In application/config/database.php, you'll set up your MySQL connection:

```
$db['default'] = array(
 'dsn'   => '',
 'hostname' => 'localhost',
 'username' => 'your_db_user',
 'password' => 'your_db_password',
 'database' => 'your_db_name',
 'dbdriver' => 'mysqli',
 'dbprefix' => '',
 'pconnect' => FALSE,
 'db_debug' => (ENVIRONMENT !== 'production'),
 'cache_on' => FALSE,
 'cachedir' => '',
 'char_set' => 'utf8',
```

```
'dbcollat' => 'utf8_general_ci',
'swap_pre' => ",
'encrypt' => FALSE,
'compress' => FALSE,
'stricton' => FALSE,
'failover' => array(),
'save_queries' => TRUE
);
```

Query Building: You can build queries using CodeIgniter's Query Builder:
```
$query = $this->db->get('users');
```

Ruby on Rails

Rails is a web application framework written in Ruby. MySQL is supported out of the box in Rails.

Configuration: In the config/database.yml file, you set up the MySQL connection:

```
development:
adapter: mysql2
encoding: utf8
database: your_db_name
username: your_db_user
password: your_db_password
host: localhost
```

Models and Queries: ActiveRecord is Rails' ORM for interacting with MySQL. Example model:
```
class Post < ApplicationRecord
end
```

Example query:

```
posts = Post.all
```

Using MySQL with web frameworks depends on the specific framework you're working with, but most modern frameworks provide tools to seamlessly integrate with MySQL databases, either through raw SQL or through an ORM. Whether you're using Django's ORM in Python, Sequelize in Node.js, or Eloquent in Laravel, MySQL remains a powerful database option for web development. Each framework has its own strengths, and your choice depends on your programming language preference and project requirements.

20.8 Using MySQL in Cloud Environments

Using MySQL in cloud environments has become increasingly popular because of the flexibility, scalability, and cost-efficiency cloud platforms offer. Cloud environments enable users to deploy MySQL databases in a highly available and fault-tolerant manner, with easy management and automated backups.

Overview of MySQL in Cloud Environments

MySQL is an open-source relational database management system (RDBMS) that can run on cloud infrastructures. Major cloud providers like Amazon Web Services (AWS), Google Cloud Platform (GCP), and Microsoft Azure offer MySQL as a service (often referred to as Database-as-a-Service or DBaaS), or allow users to install and manage MySQL on cloud virtual machines.

The cloud environment abstracts the underlying infrastructure, making it easier to manage MySQL databases without worrying about hardware, network configurations, or scalability limits. Cloud-based MySQL databases often come with features such as automatic backups, high availability, monitoring tools, and managed updates.

Cloud Services Offering MySQL

Some key cloud services for MySQL include:

- **Amazon RDS (Relational Database Service) for MySQL**: AWS offers managed MySQL database instances that handle tasks like backups, patching, and scaling automatically.
- **Google Cloud SQL for MySQL**: Google Cloud's managed database service for MySQL provides automated management and scaling, including automatic failover and backups.
- **Azure Database for MySQL**: Microsoft Azure's managed MySQL offering integrates with other Azure services and provides built-in high availability and automated scaling.
- **Self-managed MySQL on Virtual Machines**: All cloud providers allow you to install MySQL manually on a virtual machine, giving you full control over configuration and management.

Advantages of Using MySQL in Cloud Environments

- **Scalability**: Cloud platforms offer on-demand resource scaling, so you can adjust the compute and storage resources allocated to your MySQL instance based on your application's needs.
- **High Availability**: Most cloud providers' offer managed MySQL services with built-in high availability and automated failover mechanisms. In the event of a failure, traffic is automatically redirected to standby instances.
- **Cost-Efficiency**: With cloud environments, you only pay for the resources you use. There are no upfront costs, and the flexible pricing models allow you to choose between on-demand, reserved, or spot instances.
- **Automated Maintenance**: Managed MySQL services in the cloud provide automatic backups, patching, and software upgrades. This reduces the operational overhead of database management.
- **Security**: Cloud platforms provide built-in encryption, secure access controls, and integration with identity management systems like AWS IAM, Google Cloud Identity, or Azure Active Directory to help secure your MySQL database.

Example: Deploying MySQL on Amazon RDS

Let's go through an example of deploying a MySQL database on **Amazon RDS** to see how you can use MySQL in a cloud environment.

Step 1: Setting up MySQL in AWS RDS

1. **Log into AWS Console**: Start by logging into your AWS Management Console.
2. **Navigate to RDS Service**: From the AWS Console, search for "RDS" and select it.
3. **Create a New Database Instance**:
   - Click on "Create database."
   - Choose "MySQL" as the database engine.
   - Select a template (Production or Dev/Test based on your use case).
   - Choose your desired MySQL version.
4. **Database Instance Configuration**:
   - Set up your DB instance identifier, username, and password for the MySQL database.
   - Choose the instance size (e.g., db.t3.micro for small workloads or db.m5.large for larger production workloads).

o For scalability, enable the "Multi-AZ deployment" option for high availability.

5. **Storage**:
    o Set the allocated storage, and choose whether to enable storage auto-scaling to ensure that the storage can grow automatically as your database grows.

6. **VPC and Security**:
    o Select a Virtual Private Cloud (VPC) where your database will be deployed.
    o Configure the security group to control inbound/outbound traffic to/from your MySQL instance. You'll need to allow access from trusted IP addresses or security groups.

7. **Backup and Maintenance**:
    o Enable automated backups and set a retention period.
    o Set up automatic minor version upgrades to keep the database up-to-date with the latest patches.

8. **Launch the Instance**: Once configured, click on "Create database."

Step 2: Connecting to Your MySQL Database

After the instance is created, you will be provided with an endpoint and port number to connect to your MySQL instance. You can use MySQL command-line tools, MySQL Workbench, or any application that supports MySQL connections to interact with the database.

For example, using the command-line:

```
mysql -h <RDS-endpoint> -u <username> -p
```

You will be prompted to enter the password you set during the database creation.

Step 3: Performing Operations

Once connected, you can perform regular SQL operations on your MySQL database. For example:

- **Creating a Database**:

```
CREATE DATABASE test_db;
```

- **Creating a Table**:

```
CREATE TABLE users (
  id INT PRIMARY KEY,
  name VARCHAR(100),
  email VARCHAR(100)
);
```

- **Inserting Data**:

```
INSERT INTO users (id, name, email) VALUES (1, 'John Doe',
'john.doe@example.com');
```

- **Querying Data**:

```
SELECT * FROM users;
```

Step 4: Automating Backup and Maintenance

Amazon RDS provides automated backups by default. You can configure the backup retention period (up to 35 days) and enable Point-in-Time Recovery (PITR) to restore your database to any point in time within the retention period.

RDS also allows you to configure automated patching, so your MySQL database will stay up-to-date with the latest security patches.

Best Practices for Using MySQL in Cloud Environments

- **Scaling**: Use horizontal scaling techniques, such as read replicas, to offload read-heavy workloads from your primary database and improve performance.
- **Monitoring**: Use cloud-native monitoring tools such as Amazon CloudWatch, Google Stackdriver, or Azure Monitor to track database performance, set up alarms for specific metrics (e.g., CPU utilization, storage space), and gain insights into query performance.
- **Security**: Leverage the cloud provider's security features, including encryption at rest and in transit, network isolation using VPCs, and role-based access controls.
- **Cost Optimization**: Choose the appropriate instance type based on your workload, and enable auto-scaling or reserve instances for cost savings in predictable workloads.

Using MySQL in cloud environments like AWS, GCP, or Azure provides a range of benefits, including automatic management, scalability, security, and cost efficiency. Cloud services take care of infrastructure management tasks such as backups, patches, and failover, allowing you to focus on application development. With features like automated scaling, monitoring, and high availability, deploying MySQL on the cloud ensures that your database can grow seamlessly as your application scales.

21 TROUBLE SHOOTING ERRORS IN MySQL

21.1 Different types of errors and their trouble shooting techniques.

1. Error 1045 (28000): Access Denied for User

Cause:

This error occurs when MySQL denies access due to incorrect username, password, or insufficient privileges.

Example:

mysql -u root -p

If you enter the wrong password, you'll see:

ERROR 1045 (28000): Access denied for user 'root'@'localhost' (using password: YES)

Solution:

- Ensure you are using the correct username and password.
- Reset the root password:

ALTER USER 'root'@'localhost' IDENTIFIED WITH mysql_native_password BY 'newpassword';
FLUSH PRIVILEGES;

- If you've lost access, restart MySQL in **safe mode**:

sudo systemctl stop mysql
sudo mysqld_safe --skip-grant-tables &
mysql -u root

Then reset the password as above.

2. Error 1049 (42000): Unknown Database

Cause:

Occurs when trying to connect to or use a non-existent database.

Example:

mysql -u root -p mydatabase

If mydatabase does not exist:

pgsql

ERROR 1049 (42000): Unknown database 'mydatabase'

Solution:

- Verify the database exists:

SHOW DATABASES;

- If the database does not exist, create it:

CREATE DATABASE mydatabase;

- Ensure correct spelling and case sensitivity.

3. Error 1064 (42000): You Have an Error in Your SQL Syntax

Cause:

This is a syntax error, often due to:

- Missing or misplaced keywords
- Unescaped special characters
- Incorrect function usage

Example:

SELECT * FROM users WHERE name = 'John;

Error:

ERROR 1064 (42000): You have an error in your SQL syntax

Solution:

- Check for missing quotes:

SELECT * FROM users WHERE name = 'John';

- Use correct MySQL functions:

SELECT NOW(); -- Correct usage

- Verify column and table names.

4. Error 1146 (42S02): Table Doesn't Exist

Cause:

Trying to access a table that does not exist.

Example:

SELECT * FROM customers;

Error:

ERROR 1146 (42S02): Table 'mydatabase.customers' doesn't exist

Solution:

- Check available tables:

SHOW TABLES;

- Ensure the table is created:

CREATE TABLE customers (id INT PRIMARY KEY, name VARCHAR(255));

- Verify spelling and database selection:

USE mydatabase;

5. Error 1054 (42S22): Unknown Column in Field List

Cause:

Trying to select or insert into a column that does not exist.

Example:

SELECT age FROM users;

Error:

ERROR 1054 (42S22): Unknown column 'age' in 'field list'
Solution:

- Verify columns exist:

DESCRIBE users;

- If missing, add the column:

ALTER TABLE users ADD COLUMN age INT;

- Check for typos.

6. Error 1062 (23000): Duplicate Entry for Primary Key

Cause:

Occurs when inserting duplicate values into a unique column.

Example:

INSERT INTO users (id, name) VALUES (1, 'Alice');
INSERT INTO users (id, name) VALUES (1, 'Bob');

Error:

ERROR 1062 (23000): Duplicate entry '1' for key 'PRIMARY'

Solution:

- Use IGNORE to skip duplicates:

INSERT IGNORE INTO users (id, name) VALUES (1, 'Bob');

- Use ON DUPLICATE KEY UPDATE:

INSERT INTO users (id, name) VALUES (1, 'Bob')
ON DUPLICATE KEY UPDATE name = 'Bob';

- Ensure proper auto-incrementing.

7. Error 2002 (HY000): Can't Connect to MySQL Server

Cause:

- MySQL server is not running
- Incorrect hostname or port
- Firewall restrictions

Solution:

- Start MySQL service:

sudo systemctl start mysql

- Check the port:

mysql -u root -p --port=3306

- Verify MySQL is listening:

netstat -tulnp | grep mysql

- Restart the service:

sudo systemctl restart mysql

8. Error 1215 (HY000): Cannot Add Foreign Key Constraint

Cause:

Occurs when foreign key constraints are invalid.

Example:

```
CREATE TABLE orders (
    id INT PRIMARY KEY,
    user_id INT,
    FOREIGN KEY (user_id) REFERENCES users(id)
);
```

If users.id does not exist or has a different type, you get:

ERROR 1215 (HY000): Cannot add foreign key constraint

Solution:

- Ensure both columns have the same type and indexing:

ALTER TABLE users ADD PRIMARY KEY (id);

- Enable INNODB storage engine:

SHOW ENGINES;

9. Error 1452 (23000): Cannot Add or Update a Child Row

Cause:

Foreign key constraint failure when inserting a non-existent value.

Example:

INSERT INTO orders (id, user_id) VALUES (1, 999);

Error:

ERROR 1452 (23000): Cannot add or update a child row: a foreign key constraint fails

Solution:

- Ensure the referenced value exists:

SELECT * FROM users WHERE id = 999;

- Disable foreign key checks temporarily:

SET FOREIGN_KEY_CHECKS = 0;

- Use CASCADE on deletion:

ALTER TABLE orders ADD CONSTRAINT fk_user FOREIGN KEY (user_id) REFERENCES users(id) ON DELETE CASCADE;

10. Error 2013 (HY000): Lost Connection to MySQL Server

Cause:

- Timeout exceeded
- Large query execution
- Network issues

Solution:

- Increase timeout:

SET GLOBAL wait_timeout = 28800;
SET GLOBAL interactive_timeout = 28800;

- Optimize queries:

EXPLAIN SELECT * FROM large_table;

- Ensure proper indexing.

Final Tips for Debugging MySQL Errors

- Use SHOW WARNINGS; after running a query to see warnings.
- Check logs:

sudo tail -f /var/log/mysql/error.log

- Use SHOW ENGINE INNODB STATUS; for storage engine issues.
- Validate your queries using:

EXPLAIN SELECT * FROM table_name;

21.2 Debugging Queries in MySQL

Debugging queries in MySQL is an essential skill for database developers and administrators. It involves identifying, analyzing, and fixing errors or performance issues in SQL statements. Debugging can be categorized into **syntax errors, logical errors, and performance issues**. Below, we explore various debugging techniques, tools, and real-world examples.

Understanding Common MySQL Errors

Before diving into debugging techniques, let's understand some common types of errors:

1. Syntax Errors

Occur due to incorrect SQL syntax.

Example:

SELECT * FORM users;

Error: #1064 - You have an error in your SQL syntax **Fix:** The correct syntax is:

SELECT * FROM users;

2. Logical Errors

Queries run without syntax errors but return incorrect results.

Example:

SELECT name FROM users WHERE age > 50;

If this always returns an empty result despite users over 50 existing, you may need to check data types or conditions.

3. Performance Issues

Queries may be correct but execute slowly due to inefficient indexing or joins.

Example:

SELECT * FROM orders WHERE order_date > '2023-01-01';

If order_date is not indexed, this query will perform a **full table scan**, making it slow.

21.3 Debugging Techniques in MySQL

To debug SQL queries, you can use the following techniques:

Checking Syntax Errors

MySQL provides error messages that help identify syntax issues.

Example:

SELECT name, age FROM users WHERE name = 'John

Error: #1064 - You have an error in your SQL syntax (Missing closing quote)
Fix: Ensure proper string termination:

SELECT name, age FROM users WHERE name = 'John';

Using EXPLAIN to Analyze Query Execution Plan

The EXPLAIN statement helps analyze how MySQL executes a query.

Example: Slow Query

SELECT * FROM orders WHERE customer_id = 101;

If customer_id is not indexed, this query scans the entire table.

Using EXPLAIN

EXPLAIN SELECT * FROM orders WHERE customer_id = 101;

CREATE INDEX idx_customer_id ON orders(customer_id);

Now, re-running EXPLAIN should show a faster query execution.

Checking for NULL Values

- If a query returns unexpected results, check for NULL values.
- Example:

SELECT * FROM users WHERE email = 'john@example.com';

If this does not return results, but NULL values exist, try:

SELECT * FROM users WHERE email IS NULL;

Fix: Ensure the column does not allow NULL values or handle NULL properly.

Debugging Joins

- Joins can cause issues if they involve mismatched keys or missing data.

Example: Inner Join Missing Matches

SELECT orders.id, customers.name
FROM orders
JOIN customers ON orders.customer_id = customers.id;

If some expected records are missing, check for missing customer IDs.

Fix Using LEFT JOIN

SELECT orders.id, customers.name
FROM orders
LEFT JOIN customers ON orders.customer_id = customers.id;

This ensures all orders are returned, even if they don't have matching customers.

Using SHOW WARNINGS

- If MySQL executes a query but with minor errors, SHOW WARNINGS helps debug.
- Example:

INSERT INTO users (id, name) VALUES (1, 'Alice'), (1, 'Bob');
SHOW WARNINGS;

This will show duplicate key warnings if id is a primary key.

Using SHOW ERRORS

- If a query fails, SHOW ERRORS provides detailed messages.
- Example:

CREATE TABLE users (id INT PRIMARY KEY, name VARCHAR(50));
INSERT INTO users (id, name) VALUES ('abc', 'John');
SHOW ERRORS;

Fix: Ensure correct data types.

Enabling General Query Log

- Logs all queries for debugging purposes.
- Enable it:

SET GLOBAL general_log = 'ON';

- View logs:

SELECT * FROM mysql.general_log;

Debugging Performance Issues

Checking Index Usage

- Ensure indexes are used with:

  SHOW INDEX FROM orders;

Identifying Slow Queries

- Enable the slow query log:

  SET GLOBAL slow_query_log = 'ON';

- View slow queries:

  SELECT * FROM mysql.slow_log;

21.4 Optimizing Queries

Example: Optimizing Aggregations

SELECT COUNT(*) FROM orders WHERE status = 'Completed';

If slow, use:

ALTER TABLE orders ADD INDEX idx_status(status);

This speeds up the query.

21.5 Debugging Tools

MySQL Workbench

- Provides an **SQL editor** with error highlighting.
- Has an **EXPLAIN execution plan** tool.

phpMyAdmin

- Displays query errors with details.
- Supports query profiling.

Third-Party Profilers

- **Percona Toolkit**: Identifies slow queries.
- **MySQL Performance Schema**: Helps debug query execution.

21.6 Debugging Case Study

Problem: Slow Query on Large Table

SELECT * FROM sales WHERE region = 'North America' AND year = 2023;

Steps to Debug

Check EXPLAIN Output

EXPLAIN SELECT * FROM sales WHERE region = 'North America' AND year = 2023;

If it shows a **full table scan**, indexes are missing.

Add an Index

CREATE INDEX idx_region_year ON sales(region, year);

Check Improvement

EXPLAIN SELECT * FROM sales WHERE region = 'North America' AND year = 2023;

Now it should use an **index scan**, improving performance.

Debugging MySQL queries involves checking syntax, logical issues, and performance bottlenecks. Techniques like using EXPLAIN, SHOW WARNINGS, indexing, and query logs help resolve problems efficiently. Mastering these techniques ensures optimized and error-free MySQL queries.

21.7 Server Performance Monitoring and Tuning in MySQL

Server performance monitoring and tuning in MySQL are crucial to ensuring efficient database operations, minimizing response times, and optimizing resource usage. This involves identifying bottlenecks, optimizing queries, tuning system configurations, and ensuring hardware resources are used optimally.

MySQL Performance Monitoring

Monitoring MySQL performance involves tracking key metrics such as CPU usage, memory utilization, disk I/O, and query execution times. The following tools and techniques help in this process:

Monitoring Tools

Several tools and commands help monitor MySQL performance:

MySQL Performance Schema

The **Performance Schema** is an advanced monitoring tool that provides detailed insights into MySQL internals.

Enable the Performance Schema:

SHOW VARIABLES LIKE 'performance_schema';

If it is disabled (OFF), enable it by modifying the my.cnf file:

performance_schema=ON

Query active threads:

SELECT * FROM performance_schema.threads WHERE PROCESSLIST_STATE IS NOT NULL;

Find the top 10 slow queries:

SELECT sql_text, timer_wait FROM performance_schema.events_statements_history_long ORDER BY timer_wait DESC

LIMIT 10;

MySQL Slow Query Log

The **Slow Query Log** helps identify queries that take longer than a specified threshold.

Enable the slow query log:

SET GLOBAL slow_query_log = 'ON';

SET GLOBAL long_query_time = 2; -- Log queries taking more than 2 seconds

View logged slow queries:

SELECT * FROM mysql.slow_log ORDER BY start_time DESC LIMIT 10;

MySQL SHOW Commands

MySQL provides several SHOW commands to monitor performance:

Check currently running queries:

SHOW PROCESSLIST;

View MySQL server status:

SHOW STATUS LIKE 'Threads%';

Check InnoDB engine statistics:

SHOW ENGINE INNODB STATUS;

MySQL Workbench Performance Reports

MySQL Workbench provides built-in performance monitoring tools like:

- Performance Schema Reports
- Server Status Dashboard
- Query Analyzer

MySQL Performance Tuning

Tuning MySQL involves optimizing queries, indexing, memory allocation, and database configuration.

Query Optimization

Use EXPLAIN to Analyze Queries

The EXPLAIN statement shows how MySQL executes a query, helping identify inefficiencies.

Example:

EXPLAIN SELECT * FROM orders WHERE customer_id = 1001;

Output might show:

id	select_type	table	type	possible_keys	key	rows	Extra
1	SIMPLE	orders	ALL	NULL	NULL	1000	Using where

- The ALL type indicates a **full table scan**, which is slow. Adding an index on customer_id improves performance.

Using Indexes

Indexes improve query performance by reducing the number of scanned rows.

- Create an index:

    CREATE INDEX idx_customer_id ON orders(customer_id);

- Verify index usage:

    EXPLAIN SELECT * FROM orders WHERE customer_id = 1001;

After adding an index, the type should change from ALL to INDEX or REF, improving efficiency.

Configuration Tuning

Tuning MySQL server parameters enhances performance. Adjust these settings in my.cnf or my.ini:

Buffer Pool Size (innodb_buffer_pool_size**)**

This setting controls how much memory is allocated for caching InnoDB data and indexes.

- Recommended: **Set it to 70-80% of available RAM** for dedicated MySQL servers.
- Check current setting:

  SHOW VARIABLES LIKE 'innodb_buffer_pool_size';

- Update value:

  innodb_buffer_pool_size = 2G

Query Cache (query_cache_size**)**

Caching query results can improve performance but can cause lock contention in high-write workloads.

- Check current setting:

  SHOW VARIABLES LIKE 'query_cache_size';

- Adjust value:

  query_cache_size = 128M

Connection Pool (max_connections**)**

This parameter controls the number of simultaneous connections MySQL allows.

- Check current setting:

  SHOW VARIABLES LIKE 'max_connections';

- Increase for high-load systems:

max_connections = 500

Thread Concurrency (innodb_thread_concurrency**)**

Defines the number of threads used for query execution.

- Recommended setting: **CPU cores × 2**
- Example:

innodb_thread_concurrency = 16

Disk and Storage Optimization

Optimize Tables

Periodically running OPTIMIZE TABLE improves performance by defragmenting tables.

OPTIMIZE TABLE orders;

Choosing Storage Engines

- **InnoDB:** Best for high-performance transactions and ACID compliance.
- **MyISAM:** Faster for read-heavy workloads but lacks transactions.

To check storage engine:

SHOW TABLE STATUS WHERE Name = 'orders';

To convert a table to InnoDB:

ALTER TABLE orders ENGINE = InnoDB;

Performance Monitoring and Tuning Workflow

1. **Identify Slow Queries:** Use the slow query log and EXPLAIN.
2. **Optimize Queries:** Add indexes, rewrite queries, and avoid unnecessary joins.

3. **Tune MySQL Configuration:** Adjust memory, cache, and connection limits.
4. **Monitor System Resources:** Track CPU, RAM, and disk usage.
5. **Optimize Storage Engine:** Use InnoDB for transactional workloads.
6. **Regular Maintenance:** Run OPTIMIZE TABLE and ANALYZE TABLE.

Monitoring and tuning MySQL performance is essential for handling large databases efficiently. By leveraging tools like EXPLAIN, the Slow Query Log, and Performance Schema, along with tuning memory allocation and indexing, MySQL can handle high workloads with optimal speed. Regular maintenance and proactive monitoring ensure continued performance improvements.

22. REAL-WORLD PROJECTS

22.1 Building a Simple Library Management System

Creating a **Simple Library Management System (LMS) using MySQL** involves several key steps:

Project Scope and Features

The LMS should support the following functionalities:

1. **User Management** (Admin, Librarian, Members)
2. **Book Management** (Add, Update, Delete, Search)
3. **Membership Management** (Issue & Return Books, Fines)
4. **Transaction Management** (Book Borrowing, Returning)
5. **Reports & Logs** (Issued Books, Overdue Books, Fine Collection)

Step 1: Entity-Relationship (ER) Diagram

Entities & Relationships:

1. **Users** (UserID, Name, Role, Email, Password)
2. **Books** (BookID, Title, Author, Genre, ISBN, CopiesAvailable)
3. **Members** (MemberID, Name, Email, Phone, Address, JoinDate)
4. **Transactions** (TransactionID, MemberID, BookID, IssueDate, ReturnDate, Fine)
5. **Fines** (FineID, TransactionID, Amount, PaidStatus)

Relationships:

- A **Member** can borrow multiple **Books**.
- A **Book** can be issued multiple times.
- A **Transaction** records the book issuance and return.

Step 2: MySQL Database Schema

CREATE DATABASE LibraryDB;
USE LibraryDB;

-- Users Table
CREATE TABLE Users (
    UserID INT AUTO_INCREMENT PRIMARY KEY,

```
    Name VARCHAR(100),
    Role ENUM('Admin', 'Librarian'),
    Email VARCHAR(100) UNIQUE,
    Password VARCHAR(255)
);

-- Books Table
CREATE TABLE Books (
    BookID INT AUTO_INCREMENT PRIMARY KEY,
    Title VARCHAR(255),
    Author VARCHAR(100),
    Genre VARCHAR(50),
    ISBN VARCHAR(20) UNIQUE,
    CopiesAvailable INT DEFAULT 1
);

-- Members Table
CREATE TABLE Members (
    MemberID INT AUTO_INCREMENT PRIMARY KEY,
    Name VARCHAR(100),
    Email VARCHAR(100) UNIQUE,
    Phone VARCHAR(20),
    Address TEXT,
    JoinDate DATE DEFAULT CURDATE()
);

-- Transactions Table (Issue & Return)
CREATE TABLE Transactions (
    TransactionID INT AUTO_INCREMENT PRIMARY KEY,
    MemberID INT,
    BookID INT,
    IssueDate DATE DEFAULT CURDATE(),
    ReturnDate DATE DEFAULT NULL,
    Fine DECIMAL(5,2) DEFAULT 0.00,
    FOREIGN KEY (MemberID) REFERENCES Members(MemberID),
    FOREIGN KEY (BookID) REFERENCES Books(BookID)
);

-- Fines Table
CREATE TABLE Fines (
    FineID INT AUTO_INCREMENT PRIMARY KEY,
    TransactionID INT,
    Amount DECIMAL(5,2),
    PaidStatus ENUM('Unpaid', 'Paid') DEFAULT 'Unpaid',
```

   FOREIGN KEY (TransactionID) REFERENCES
Transactions(TransactionID)
);

Step 3: Implementing Core Functions (Queries)

1. Adding Books

```
INSERT INTO Books (Title, Author, Genre, ISBN, CopiesAvailable)
VALUES ('The Alchemist', 'Paulo Coelho', 'Fiction', '978-0061122415', 5);
```

2. Adding Members

```
INSERT INTO Members (Name, Email, Phone, Address)
VALUES ('John Doe', 'john@example.com', '1234567890', '123 Street, City');
```

3. Issuing a Book

```
INSERT INTO Transactions (MemberID, BookID)
VALUES (1, 2); -- Assuming MemberID=1, BookID=2
UPDATE Books SET CopiesAvailable = CopiesAvailable - 1 WHERE
BookID = 2;
```

4. Returning a Book & Calculating Fine

```
UPDATE Transactions
SET ReturnDate = CURDATE(), Fine = (DATEDIFF(CURDATE(),
IssueDate) - 14) * 1.00
WHERE TransactionID = 1 AND ReturnDate IS NULL;
```

```
UPDATE Books SET CopiesAvailable = CopiesAvailable + 1 WHERE
BookID = 2;
```

5. Paying Fines

```
UPDATE Fines SET PaidStatus = 'Paid' WHERE FineID = 1;
```

6. List of Issued Books

SELECT Members.Name, Books.Title, Transactions.IssueDate,
Transactions.ReturnDate
FROM Transactions
JOIN Members ON Transactions.MemberID = Members.MemberID
JOIN Books ON Transactions.BookID = Books.BookID
WHERE Transactions.ReturnDate IS NULL;

7. Checking Overdue Books

SELECT Members.Name, Books.Title, Transactions.IssueDate,
Transactions.ReturnDate, Transactions.Fine
FROM Transactions
JOIN Members ON Transactions.MemberID = Members.MemberID
JOIN Books ON Transactions.BookID = Books.BookID
WHERE Transactions.ReturnDate IS NULL AND
DATEDIFF(CURDATE(), IssueDate) > 14;

Step 4: ER Diagram Representation

Here's a simplified ER diagram of the **Library Management System**:

Tables and Relationships

- **Books** (BookID) → **Transactions** (BookID)
- **Members** (MemberID) → **Transactions** (MemberID)
- **Transactions** (TransactionID) → **Fines** (TransactionID)

Step 5: User Interface Considerations

You can integrate this database with a **frontend** using:

- **PHP & MySQL** (For Web-Based LMS)
- **Python Flask/Django** (For a Web App)
- **Java Swing/JDBC** (For a Desktop App)

Step 6: Enhancements & Features

Advanced Features to Consider:

✅ Email Notifications for Due Books

✅ Barcode Scanning for Book Entry
✅ Multi-User Roles (Librarian/Admin)
✅ Graphical Reports (Books Issued, Fines Collected)

You have two main options for the GUI/Web Interface:

1. **Web-Based Interface (Recommended)**
   o **Frontend:** HTML, CSS, JavaScript (with frameworks like React or Vue)
   o **Backend:** Python (Flask/Django) or PHP
   o **Database:** MySQL
   o **Features:** User authentication, book search, issue/return books, fine payment system
2. **Desktop GUI**
   o **Tech Stack:** Java (Swing/JavaFX), Python (Tkinter/PyQt)
   o **Database Connectivity:** JDBC (for Java) or MySQL Connector (for Python)
   o **Features:** Local desktop app with login, book management, transactions, reports

For a **desktop application** using **MySQL**, you have two strong options:

1. **Java (Swing/JavaFX) + JDBC**
   o Best for a structured, enterprise-style application
   o Uses **JDBC** to connect to MySQL
   o JavaFX provides a modern UI
   o Can package as an executable (.jar/.exe)
2. **Python (Tkinter/PyQt) + MySQL Connector**
   o Easier for rapid development
   o PyQt offers a sleek GUI
   o Tkinter is lightweight but basic
   o Can be compiled into an executable (.exe using PyInstaller)

Key Features in Desktop LMS

✅ Login System (Admin/Librarian)
✅ Book Management (Add, Update, Delete)
✅ Member Management
✅ Borrow & Return Books
✅ Fine Calculation
✅ Reports & Logs

22.2 Creating an E-Commerce Database

Building a comprehensive e-commerce database system involves designing a well-structured relational database using MySQL. Here's an outline of the project development process:

1. Requirements Analysis

Identify the key components of an e-commerce platform, including:

- User management (customers, admins, sellers)
- Product management
- Order management
- Payment processing
- Inventory management
- Reviews & ratings
- Shipping & delivery
- Promotions & discounts
- Reports & analytics

2. Entity-Relationship (ER) Diagram

The ER diagram should capture the relationships between various entities. Here are the primary entities and their relationships:

1. **Users (Customers, Admins, Sellers)**
2. **Products** (Belonging to Categories)
3. **Orders** (Linked to Users and Products)
4. **Payments** (Linked to Orders)
5. **Shipments** (Tracking delivery status)
6. **Reviews & Ratings** (Linked to Users and Products)
7. **Cart** (Temporary order storage)
8. **Discounts** (Coupons, Offers)

3. Database Schema (Tables & Relationships)

Here's a basic schema with key tables:

1. Users Table

```
CREATE TABLE users (
    user_id INT PRIMARY KEY AUTO_INCREMENT,
```

```
  username VARCHAR(50) UNIQUE NOT NULL,
  email VARCHAR(100) UNIQUE NOT NULL,
  password_hash VARCHAR(255) NOT NULL,
  role ENUM('customer', 'admin', 'seller') NOT NULL,
  created_at TIMESTAMP DEFAULT CURRENT_TIMESTAMP
);
```

2. Products Table

```
CREATE TABLE products (
  product_id INT PRIMARY KEY AUTO_INCREMENT,
  name VARCHAR(255) NOT NULL,
  description TEXT,
  price DECIMAL(10,2) NOT NULL,
  stock INT NOT NULL,
  category_id INT,
  seller_id INT,
  created_at TIMESTAMP DEFAULT CURRENT_TIMESTAMP,
  FOREIGN KEY (category_id) REFERENCES categories(category_id),
  FOREIGN KEY (seller_id) REFERENCES users(user_id)
);
```

3. Orders Table

```
CREATE TABLE orders (
  order_id INT PRIMARY KEY AUTO_INCREMENT,
  user_id INT,
  total_price DECIMAL(10,2) NOT NULL,
  status ENUM('pending', 'shipped', 'delivered', 'cancelled') DEFAULT
'pending',
  created_at TIMESTAMP DEFAULT CURRENT_TIMESTAMP,
  FOREIGN KEY (user_id) REFERENCES users(user_id)
);
```

4. Order Items Table

```
CREATE TABLE order_items (
  order_item_id INT PRIMARY KEY AUTO_INCREMENT,
  order_id INT,
  product_id INT,
  quantity INT NOT NULL,
  price DECIMAL(10,2) NOT NULL,
  FOREIGN KEY (order_id) REFERENCES orders(order_id),
```

```
    FOREIGN KEY (product_id) REFERENCES products(product_id)
);
```

5. Payments Table

```
CREATE TABLE payments (
    payment_id INT PRIMARY KEY AUTO_INCREMENT,
    order_id INT,
    payment_method ENUM('credit_card', 'paypal', 'cod') NOT NULL,
    payment_status ENUM('pending', 'completed', 'failed') DEFAULT
'pending',
    transaction_id VARCHAR(100),
    created_at TIMESTAMP DEFAULT CURRENT_TIMESTAMP,
    FOREIGN KEY (order_id) REFERENCES orders(order_id)
);
```

6. Shipments Table

```
CREATE TABLE shipments (
    shipment_id INT PRIMARY KEY AUTO_INCREMENT,
    order_id INT,
    tracking_number VARCHAR(100) UNIQUE,
    status ENUM('pending', 'shipped', 'delivered') DEFAULT 'pending',
    estimated_delivery DATE,
    created_at TIMESTAMP DEFAULT CURRENT_TIMESTAMP,
    FOREIGN KEY (order_id) REFERENCES orders(order_id)
);
```

7. Reviews Table

```
CREATE TABLE reviews (
    review_id INT PRIMARY KEY AUTO_INCREMENT,
    user_id INT,
    product_id INT,
    rating INT CHECK (rating BETWEEN 1 AND 5),
    review_text TEXT,
    created_at TIMESTAMP DEFAULT CURRENT_TIMESTAMP,
    FOREIGN KEY (user_id) REFERENCES users(user_id),
    FOREIGN KEY (product_id) REFERENCES products(product_id)
);
```

8. Categories Table

```
CREATE TABLE categories (
    category_id INT PRIMARY KEY AUTO_INCREMENT,
    name VARCHAR(255) NOT NULL UNIQUE,
    parent_category INT NULL,
    FOREIGN        KEY        (parent_category)        REFERENCES
categories(category_id)
);
```

9. Cart Table

```
CREATE TABLE cart (
    cart_id INT PRIMARY KEY AUTO_INCREMENT,
    user_id INT,
    product_id INT,
    quantity INT NOT NULL,
    added_at TIMESTAMP DEFAULT CURRENT_TIMESTAMP,
    FOREIGN KEY (user_id) REFERENCES users(user_id),
    FOREIGN KEY (product_id) REFERENCES products(product_id)
);
```

10. Discounts Table

```
CREATE TABLE discounts (
    discount_id INT PRIMARY KEY AUTO_INCREMENT,
    code VARCHAR(50) UNIQUE NOT NULL,
    percentage DECIMAL(5,2) NOT NULL,
    expiry_date DATE NOT NULL
);
```

4. Implementation Plan

- **Phase 1:** Database Design & MySQL Implementation
- **Phase 2:** Backend API Development
  (Node.js/Python/Django/Flask)
- **Phase 3:** Frontend Development (React.js/Angular)
- **Phase 4:** Payment Gateway Integration (PayPal, Stripe)
- **Phase 5:** Testing & Security Enhancements
- **Phase 6:** Deployment (AWS, DigitalOcean, or Shared Hosting)

22.3 Data Analytics with MySQL

Data Analytics with MySQL: A Comprehensive Guide with Real-World Examples

Data analytics is the process of examining raw data to uncover patterns, trends, and insights that aid in decision-making. MySQL, a powerful relational database management system (RDBMS), is widely used in data analytics due to its robustness, scalability, and SQL querying capabilities.

This guide will provide a deep dive into data analytics with MySQL, covering concepts, techniques, and real-world applications.

1. Understanding Data Analytics in MySQL

Data analytics in MySQL involves various steps, including:

1. **Data Collection:** Storing structured data in MySQL tables.
2. **Data Cleaning:** Removing duplicates, handling missing values, and ensuring data integrity.
3. **Exploratory Data Analysis (EDA):** Using SQL queries to uncover patterns, distributions, and anomalies.
4. **Data Transformation:** Using joins, aggregations, and subqueries to structure data for analysis.
5. **Data Visualization:** Exporting data for visualization in tools like Power BI, Tableau, or Python libraries.
6. **Reporting and Decision-Making:** Extracting meaningful insights to drive business decisions.

2. Setting Up MySQL for Data Analytics

Installation and Configuration

1. Download and install MySQL Server from MySQL Official Site.
2. Use MySQL Workbench or command line for database management.
3. Load datasets using LOAD DATA INFILE or INSERT INTO.

Creating a Sample Database

Let's consider a **real-world example**: an **E-commerce Sales Database**.

Step 1: Create a Database

```
CREATE DATABASE ECommerce;
USE ECommerce;
Step 2: Create Tables

CREATE TABLE Customers (
    customer_id INT PRIMARY KEY AUTO_INCREMENT,
    name VARCHAR(100),
    email VARCHAR(100) UNIQUE,
    city VARCHAR(50),
    country VARCHAR(50),
    signup_date DATE
);

CREATE TABLE Orders (
    order_id INT PRIMARY KEY AUTO_INCREMENT,
    customer_id INT,
    order_date DATE,
    total_amount DECIMAL(10,2),
    status ENUM('Pending', 'Shipped', 'Delivered', 'Cancelled'),
    FOREIGN KEY (customer_id) REFERENCES Customers(customer_id)
);

CREATE TABLE Products (
    product_id INT PRIMARY KEY AUTO_INCREMENT,
    name VARCHAR(100),
    category VARCHAR(50),
    price DECIMAL(10,2),
    stock INT
);

CREATE TABLE OrderDetails (
    order_detail_id INT PRIMARY KEY AUTO_INCREMENT,
    order_id INT,
    product_id INT,
    quantity INT,
    subtotal DECIMAL(10,2),
    FOREIGN KEY (order_id) REFERENCES Orders(order_id),
    FOREIGN KEY (product_id) REFERENCES Products(product_id)
);
```

Step 3: Insert Sample Data

INSERT INTO Customers (name, email, city, country, signup_date) VALUES
('Alice Johnson', 'alice@example.com', 'New York', 'USA', '2023-01-15'),
('Bob Smith', 'bob@example.com', 'Los Angeles', 'USA', '2023-02-20');

INSERT INTO Products (name, category, price, stock) VALUES
('Laptop', 'Electronics', 1200.00, 50),
('Headphones', 'Electronics', 150.00, 200),
('Desk Chair', 'Furniture', 250.00, 30);

INSERT INTO Orders (customer_id, order_date, total_amount, status) VALUES
(1, '2023-03-01', 1350.00, 'Shipped'),
(2, '2023-03-05', 250.00, 'Delivered');

INSERT INTO OrderDetails (order_id, product_id, quantity, subtotal) VALUES
(1, 1, 1, 1200.00),
(1, 2, 1, 150.00),
(2, 3, 1, 250.00);

3. Data Analytics Queries with MySQL

A. Basic Data Exploration

1. View Customer Data

SELECT * FROM Customers;

2. Count Total Orders

SELECT COUNT(*) AS total_orders FROM Orders;

B. Analyzing Sales Trends

1. Total Revenue Generated

SELECT SUM(total_amount) AS total_revenue FROM Orders;

2. Revenue by Product Category

```
SELECT p.category, SUM(od.subtotal) AS revenue
FROM OrderDetails od
JOIN Products p ON od.product_id = p.product_id
GROUP BY p.category;
```

3. Monthly Sales Trend

```
SUM(total_amount) AS monthly_revenue
FROM Orders
GROUP BY month
ORDER BY month;
```

C. Customer Behavior Analysis

1. Top 5 Customers by Spending

```
SELECT c.name, SUM(o.total_amount) AS total_spent
FROM Orders o
JOIN Customers c ON o.customer_id = c.customer_id
GROUP BY c.name
ORDER BY total_spent DESC
LIMIT 5;
```

2. Repeat Customer Rate

```
SELECT COUNT(DISTINCT customer_id) / (SELECT COUNT(*) FROM
Customers) AS repeat_customer_rate
FROM Orders
GROUP BY customer_id
HAVING COUNT(order_id) > 1;
```

D. Inventory Management

1. Most Sold Products

```
SELECT p.name, SUM(od.quantity) AS total_sold
FROM OrderDetails od
JOIN Products p ON od.product_id = p.product_id
GROUP BY p.name
ORDER BY total_sold DESC;
```

2. Low Stock Alerts

```
SELECT name, stock
FROM Products
WHERE stock < 10;
```

E. Customer Segmentation

1. Customer Orders by Country

```
SELECT c.country, COUNT(o.order_id) AS order_count
FROM Orders o
JOIN Customers c ON o.customer_id = c.customer_id
GROUP BY c.country;
```

2. Customer Retention Analysis

```
SELECT customer_id, COUNT(order_id) AS order_count
FROM Orders
GROUP BY customer_id
HAVING order_count > 1;
```

5. Advanced Data Analytics in MySQL

A. Using Window Functions

1. Running Total Sales

```
SELECT order_date, SUM(total_amount) OVER (ORDER BY order_date)
AS running_total
FROM Orders;
```

2. Ranking Customers by Spending

```
SELECT customer_id,
    SUM(total_amount) AS total_spent,
    RANK() OVER (ORDER BY SUM(total_amount) DESC) AS rank
FROM Orders
GROUP BY customer_id;
```

B. Predictive Analytics with MySQL

While MySQL itself lacks built-in machine learning capabilities, we can prepare data for predictive modeling by exporting it to Python (Pandas, Scikit-Learn) or other tools.

Example: Identifying High-Value Customers for Targeted Marketing

```
SELECT c.customer_id, c.name, SUM(o.total_amount) AS total_spent
FROM Customers c
JOIN Orders o ON c.customer_id = o.customer_id
GROUP BY c.customer_id
HAVING total_spent > 1000;
```

Export this data to Python for deeper analysis:

```
import pandas as pd
df = pd.read_sql("SELECT * FROM high_value_customers", connection)
```

6. Visualization and Reporting

MySQL does not provide built-in visualization, but data can be exported to:

- **Tableau, Power BI** for dashboards.
- **Python (Matplotlib, Seaborn)** for statistical charts.
- **Excel, Google Sheets** for reporting.

Data analytics with MySQL is essential for deriving business insights. By leveraging SQL queries, aggregations, and advanced functions, businesses can optimize operations, improve customer retention, and forecast trends. For deeper analytics, MySQL data can be integrated with Python or BI tools.

22.4 Collaborative Project: Building a Blog Database

A **Blog Database System** is essential for managing users, posts, comments, and categories efficiently. This project involves designing and implementing a **relational database** to store and manage blog-related data, ensuring scalability, security, and ease of retrieval.

Project Overview

Objective

To design and develop a fully functional **Blog Database System** using **MySQL**. The system should support multiple users, allow content creation and management, and provide a structured approach to storing posts, categories, comments, and user details.

Project Scope

The project will cover:

- **Database Design**: ER Diagram, Schema, and Normalization
- **Database Implementation**: Tables, Relationships, and Constraints
- **User Management**: Roles (Admin, Author, Reader)
- **Content Management**: Posts, Categories, Tags
- **Interaction Management**: Comments, Likes, Ratings
- **Security Measures**: Authentication, Authorization, Data Privacy
- **Performance Optimization**: Indexing, Query Optimization

Project Team & Responsibilities

Role	Responsibilities
Database Architect	Designs the ER Diagram, schema, and normalization
Backend Developer	Implements CRUD operations, stored procedures
Frontend Developer	Builds the UI (React, Vue, or Django/Flask templates)
Security Expert	Manages encryption, authentication, and access control
QA Tester	Tests for bugs, performance, and security vulnerabilities
Project Manager	Oversees project execution and team collaboration

Step 1: Requirements Gathering

Before designing the database, we identify key **functional and non-functional requirements**:

Functional Requirements

✅ User Registration & Authentication
✅ Blog Post Creation, Editing, and Deletion
✅ Categorization of Blog Posts
✅ Comments, Likes, and User Engagement
✅ Role-Based Access Control
✅ Search and Filtering

Non-Functional Requirements

✅ Scalability for High Traffic
✅ Data Integrity and Security
✅ Performance Optimization
✅ Backup & Recovery Plan

Step 2: ER Diagram & Database Design

Entities & Relationships

1. **Users** (Authors, Readers, Admins)
2. **Posts** (Written by Authors)
3. **Categories** (Organize Posts)
4. **Comments** (Users can Comment on Posts)
5. **Tags** (Additional Labeling for Posts)
6. **Likes** (Users can Like Posts)
7. **Roles & Permissions** (Admins, Authors, Readers)

ER Diagram

The **Entity-Relationship Diagram (ERD)** defines relationships between tables:

Users 1:M Posts
Users 1:M Comments

Users M:N Likes
Posts 1:M Comments
Posts M:N Tags
Posts M:1 Categories

Step 3: Database Schema

Below is the **MySQL schema** for the blog system.

```
-- Users Table
CREATE TABLE Users (
    user_id INT PRIMARY KEY AUTO_INCREMENT,
    username VARCHAR(50) UNIQUE NOT NULL,
    email VARCHAR(100) UNIQUE NOT NULL,
    password_hash VARCHAR(255) NOT NULL,
    role ENUM('Admin', 'Author', 'Reader') DEFAULT 'Reader',
    created_at TIMESTAMP DEFAULT CURRENT_TIMESTAMP
);
```

```
-- Categories Table
CREATE TABLE Categories (
    category_id INT PRIMARY KEY AUTO_INCREMENT,
    category_name VARCHAR(50) UNIQUE NOT NULL
);
```

```
-- Posts Table
CREATE TABLE Posts (
    post_id INT PRIMARY KEY AUTO_INCREMENT,
    title VARCHAR(255) NOT NULL,
    content TEXT NOT NULL,
    user_id INT,
    category_id INT,
    created_at TIMESTAMP DEFAULT CURRENT_TIMESTAMP,
    FOREIGN KEY (user_id) REFERENCES Users(user_id) ON DELETE CASCADE,
    FOREIGN KEY (category_id) REFERENCES Categories(category_id) ON DELETE SET NULL
);
```

```
-- Tags Table
CREATE TABLE Tags (
    tag_id INT PRIMARY KEY AUTO_INCREMENT,
    tag_name VARCHAR(50) UNIQUE NOT NULL
);
```

-- Post_Tags Table (Many-to-Many Relationship)

```
CREATE TABLE Post_Tags (
    post_id INT,
    tag_id INT,
    PRIMARY KEY (post_id, tag_id),
    FOREIGN KEY (post_id) REFERENCES Posts(post_id) ON DELETE
CASCADE,
    FOREIGN KEY (tag_id) REFERENCES Tags(tag_id) ON DELETE
CASCADE
);
```

-- Comments Table

```
CREATE TABLE Comments (
    comment_id INT PRIMARY KEY AUTO_INCREMENT,
    post_id INT,
    user_id INT,
    comment_text TEXT NOT NULL,
    created_at TIMESTAMP DEFAULT CURRENT_TIMESTAMP,
    FOREIGN KEY (post_id) REFERENCES Posts(post_id) ON DELETE
CASCADE,
    FOREIGN KEY (user_id) REFERENCES Users(user_id) ON DELETE
CASCADE
);
```

-- Likes Table (Users Liking Posts)

```
CREATE TABLE Likes (
    like_id INT PRIMARY KEY AUTO_INCREMENT,
    post_id INT,
    user_id INT,
    created_at TIMESTAMP DEFAULT CURRENT_TIMESTAMP,
    FOREIGN KEY (post_id) REFERENCES Posts(post_id) ON DELETE
CASCADE,
    FOREIGN KEY (user_id) REFERENCES Users(user_id) ON DELETE
CASCADE
);
```

Step 4: Query Examples

Basic Queries

1. Insert Data

```
INSERT INTO Users (username, email, password_hash, role)
```

VALUES ('john_doe', 'john@example.com', 'hashed_password', 'Author');

INSERT INTO Categories (category_name) VALUES ('Technology');

INSERT INTO Posts (title, content, user_id, category_id)
VALUES ('My First Blog Post', 'This is the content...', 1, 1);

2. Retrieve All Blog Posts

SELECT p.post_id, p.title, u.username, c.category_name, p.created_at
FROM Posts p
JOIN Users u ON p.user_id = u.user_id
JOIN Categories c ON p.category_id = c.category_id
ORDER BY p.created_at DESC;

3. Get Comments for a Specific Post

SELECT c.comment_text, u.username, c.created_at
FROM Comments c
JOIN Users u ON c.user_id = u.user_id
WHERE c.post_id = 1;

4. Get Popular Posts (Most Likes)

SELECT p.title, u.username, COUNT(l.like_id) AS like_count
FROM Posts p
JOIN Users u ON p.user_id = u.user_id
LEFT JOIN Likes l ON p.post_id = l.post_id
GROUP BY p.post_id
ORDER BY like_count DESC;

5. Search Posts by Keyword

SELECT * FROM Posts
WHERE title LIKE '%keyword%' OR content LIKE '%keyword%';

Step 5: Security Measures

User Authentication: Use bcrypt for password hashing
SQL Injection Prevention: Use prepared statements
Access Control: Role-based permissions
Backup Strategy: Daily database backups
Data Privacy: Encrypt sensitive information

Step 6: Frontend & Backend Integration

- **Frontend Options**: React.js, Vue.js, or Django Templates
- **Backend API**: Flask, Django REST, or Node.js
- **Database Connection**: SQLAlchemy (Python), Sequelize (Node.js)
- **Deployment**: AWS RDS / DigitalOcean MySQL

Step 7: Testing & Deployment

Testing Plan

✅ **Unit Tests**: Test individual CRUD operations
✅ **Integration Tests**: Ensure frontend and backend work together
✅ **Load Testing**: Test performance under high traffic

Deployment

Use Docker for containerization
Host Database on AWS RDS
Automate Backups using cron jobs
Monitor Performance with MySQL Workbench

This collaborative **Blog Database System** provides a structured, scalable, and secure platform for blogging. The project covers **database design, implementation, security, and optimization**, ensuring smooth **content management and user interaction**.

APPENDIX A-MySQL COMMAND LINE CHEAT SHEET

Here's a detailed MySQL Command Line Cheatsheet that covers some of the most commonly used commands:

1. Basic Commands

- **Connect to MySQL Server:**

  mysql -u [username] -p

- **Exit MySQL:**

  exit;

- **Show Databases:**

  SHOW DATABASES;

- **Create a Database:**

  CREATE DATABASE [database_name];

- **Use a Database:**

  USE [database_name];

- **Show Tables in the Current Database:**

  SHOW TABLES;

- **Show Table Structure:**

  DESCRIBE [table_name];

2. Creating, Altering, and Dropping Tables

- **Create a Table:**

  CREATE TABLE [table_name] (
      column1 datatype [constraints],

```
column2 datatype [constraints],
  ...
);
```

- **Alter Table to Add Column:**

  ALTER TABLE [table_name] ADD COLUMN [column_name] [datatype];

- **Alter Table to Modify Column:**

  ALTER TABLE [table_name] MODIFY COLUMN [column_name] [new_datatype];

- **Drop a Table:**

  DROP TABLE [table_name];

- **Rename a Table:**

  RENAME TABLE [old_table_name] TO [new_table_name];

3. Inserting and Managing Data

- **Insert Data into a Table:**

  INSERT INTO [table_name] (column1, column2, ...)
  VALUES (value1, value2, ...);

- **Insert Multiple Rows:**

  INSERT INTO [table_name] (column1, column2, ...)
  VALUES (value1, value2, ...), (value1, value2, ...), ...;

- **Select Data from a Table:**

  SELECT * FROM [table_name];

- **Select Specific Columns:**

  SELECT column1, column2 FROM [table_name];

- **Where Clause to Filter Results:**

  SELECT * FROM [table_name] WHERE column1 = value;

- **Update Data in a Table:**

  UPDATE [table_name] SET column1 = value1, column2 = value2 WHERE condition;

- **Delete Data from a Table:**

  DELETE FROM [table_name] WHERE condition;

4. Sorting and Limiting Data

- **Order by Clause:**

  SELECT * FROM [table_name] ORDER BY column1 [ASC|DESC];

- **Limit the Number of Rows:**

  SELECT * FROM [table_name] LIMIT [number];

- **Limit with Offset:**

  SELECT * FROM [table_name] LIMIT [offset], [number];

5. Joins

- **Inner Join:**

  SELECT columns
  FROM table1
  INNER JOIN table2 ON table1.column = table2.column;

- **Left Join:**

  SELECT columns
  FROM table1
  LEFT JOIN table2 ON table1.column = table2.column;

- **Right Join:**

```
SELECT columns
FROM table1
RIGHT JOIN table2 ON table1.column = table2.column;
```

6. Aggregation Functions

- **COUNT():** Counts rows.

```
SELECT COUNT(*) FROM [table_name];
```

- **SUM():** Calculates the sum of a column.

```
SELECT SUM(column_name) FROM [table_name];
```

- **AVG():** Calculates the average value of a column.

```
SELECT AVG(column_name) FROM [table_name];
```

- **MAX():** Finds the maximum value in a column.

```
SELECT MAX(column_name) FROM [table_name];
```

- **MIN():** Finds the minimum value in a column.

```
SELECT MIN(column_name) FROM [table_name];
```

7. Grouping Data

- **GROUP BY Clause:**

```
SELECT column1, COUNT(*)
FROM [table_name]
GROUP BY column1;
```

- **HAVING Clause (after GROUP BY):**

```
SELECT column1, COUNT(*)
FROM [table_name]
GROUP BY column1
HAVING COUNT(*) > 5;
```

8. Indexing

- **Create an Index:**

  CREATE INDEX [index_name] ON [table_name] (column_name);

- **Drop an Index:**

  DROP INDEX [index_name] ON [table_name];

9. Transactions

- **Start a Transaction:**

  START TRANSACTION;

- **Commit a Transaction:**

  COMMIT;

- **Rollback a Transaction:**

  ROLLBACK;

10. User and Privileges

- **Create a User:**

  CREATE USER '[username]'@'[hostname]' IDENTIFIED BY '[password]';

- **Grant Privileges:**

  GRANT [privileges] ON [database_name].* TO '[username]'@'[hostname]';

- **Revoke Privileges:**

  REVOKE [privileges] ON [database_name].* FROM '[username]'@'[hostname]';

- **Show Users:**

SELECT user, host FROM mysql.user;

11. Backup and Restore

- **Backup a Database (Command Line):**

mysqldump -u [username] -p [database_name] > [backup_file].sql

- **Restore a Database (Command Line):**

mysql -u [username] -p [database_name] < [backup_file].sql

12. Miscellaneous

- **Show Current User:**

SELECT USER();

- **Show Current Date and Time:**

SELECT NOW();

- **Show Server Version:**

SELECT VERSION();

This cheatsheet includes a wide range of MySQL commands that will help you work effectively from the command line

APPENDIX B-MySQL FUNCTION REFERENCE

Here's a detailed MySQL functions reference to guide you through some of the most useful functions available in MySQL. These functions can be categorized into several groups such as string, numeric, date/time, and aggregate functions.

1. String Functions

These functions help you manipulate strings and text data.

- **CONCAT(str1, str2, ...)**
  Combines multiple strings into one string.

  SELECT CONCAT('Hello ', 'World');
  -- Output: Hello World

- **LENGTH(str)**
  Returns the length of the string in bytes.

  SELECT LENGTH('Hello');
  -- Output: 5

- **LOWER(str) / UPPER(str)**
  Converts the string to lowercase/uppercase.

  SELECT LOWER('HELLO');
  -- Output: hello

- **SUBSTRING(str, start, length)**
  Extracts a substring from a string.

  SELECT SUBSTRING('abcdef', 2, 3);
  -- Output: bcd

- **REPLACE(str, old_substring, new_substring)**
  Replaces occurrences of a substring within a string.

  SELECT REPLACE('Hello World', 'World', 'Everyone');
  -- Output: Hello Everyone

- **TRIM([remstr FROM] str)**
  Removes leading and trailing spaces (or other characters).

  SELECT TRIM(' Hello ');
  -- Output: Hello

2. Numeric Functions

These functions perform operations on numeric data.

- **ABS(x)**
  Returns the absolute value of x.

  SELECT ABS(-5);
  -- Output: 5

- **CEIL(x) / FLOOR(x)**
  Returns the smallest integer greater than or equal to x (CEIL) or the largest integer less than or equal to x (FLOOR).

  SELECT CEIL(5.4), FLOOR(5.4);
  -- Output: 6, 5

- **ROUND(x, d)**
  Rounds x to d decimal places.

  SELECT ROUND(5.678, 2);
  -- Output: 5.68

- **RAND()**
  Returns a random floating-point value between 0 and 1.

  SELECT RAND();
  -- Output: 0.567 (random)

- **POW(x, y) / POWER(x, y)**
  Returns x raised to the power of y.

  SELECT POW(2, 3);
  -- Output: 8

- **MOD(x, y)**
  Returns the remainder of x divided by y.

  SELECT MOD(10, 3);
  -- Output: 1

3. Date and Time Functions

These functions help you work with date and time values.

- **CURDATE() / CURRENT_DATE()**
  Returns the current date.

  SELECT CURDATE();
  -- Output: 2025-02-17

- **NOW()**
  Returns the current date and time.

  SELECT NOW();
  -- Output: 2025-02-17 12:45:00

- **DATE_ADD(date, INTERVAL expr unit)**
  Adds a time interval to a date.

  SELECT DATE_ADD('2025-02-17', INTERVAL 10 DAY);
  -- Output: 2025-02-27

- **DATE_SUB(date, INTERVAL expr unit)**
  Subtracts a time interval from a date.

  SELECT DATE_SUB('2025-02-17', INTERVAL 5 DAY);
  -- Output: 2025-02-12

- **YEAR(date) / MONTH(date) / DAY(date)**
  Extracts the year, month, or day part of a date.

  SELECT YEAR('2025-02-17');
  -- Output: 2025

- **DATE_FORMAT(date, format)**
  Formats a date value according to the specified format.

```
SELECT DATE_FORMAT('2025-02-17', '%W, %M %d, %Y');
-- Output: Monday, February 17, 2025
```

4. Aggregate Functions

These functions operate on a set of values to return a single value.

- **COUNT(*)**
  Returns the number of rows in a result set.

  ```
  SELECT COUNT(*) FROM employees;
  ```

- **SUM(column)**
  Returns the sum of values in a numeric column.

  ```
  SELECT SUM(salary) FROM employees;
  ```

- **AVG(column)**
  Returns the average value of a numeric column.

  ```
  SELECT AVG(salary) FROM employees;
  ```

- **MAX(column) / MIN(column)**
  Returns the maximum or minimum value of a column.

  ```
  SELECT MAX(salary), MIN(salary) FROM employees;
  ```

5. Conditional Functions

These functions allow for conditional logic in queries.

- **IF(condition, true_value, false_value)**
  Returns a value based on a condition.

  ```
  SELECT IF(salary > 5000, 'High', 'Low') FROM employees;
  ```

- **CASE WHEN condition THEN result ELSE alternative END**
  Conditional expression with multiple conditions.

  ```
  SELECT CASE WHEN salary > 5000 THEN 'High' ELSE 'Low'
  END FROM employees;
  ```

6. JSON Functions

MySQL supports functions to handle JSON data.

- **JSON_OBJECT(key1, value1, key2, value2, ...)**
  Creates a JSON object from key-value pairs.

  SELECT JSON_OBJECT('name', 'John', 'age', 30);
  -- Output: {"name": "John", "age": 30}

- **JSON_EXTRACT(json_doc, path)**
  Extracts data from a JSON document.

  SELECT JSON_EXTRACT('{"name": "John", "age": 30}', '$.name');
  -- Output: "John"

- **JSON_ARRAY(value1, value2, ...)**
  Creates a JSON array.

  SELECT JSON_ARRAY(1, 'Hello', TRUE);
  -- Output: [1, "Hello", true]

7. Window Functions

MySQL 8.0 introduced window functions to perform calculations across a set of table rows.

- **ROW_NUMBER()**
  Assigns a unique row number to each row within the result set.

  SELECT ROW_NUMBER() OVER (ORDER BY salary DESC) FROM employees;

- **RANK()**
  Provides a rank to rows in the result set, with gaps in ranking.

  SELECT RANK() OVER (ORDER BY salary DESC) FROM employees;

- **NTILE(n)**
  Divides the result set into n groups and assigns a group number.

SELECT NTILE(4) OVER (ORDER BY salary DESC) FROM employees;

Here's a deeper dive into **string comparison functions** and **encryption functions** in MySQL, along with examples for each:

1. String Comparison Functions

MySQL provides several functions to compare strings, check for equality, or perform case-insensitive comparisons.

- LIKE

The LIKE operator is used to search for a specified pattern in a column. It supports wildcard characters (% for any sequence of characters and _ for a single character).

SELECT * FROM employees WHERE name LIKE 'J%n';
-- This will match names starting with 'J' and ending with 'n', e.g., "John", "Jen".

- = (Equality Operator)

Compares two strings for exact equality. This is case-sensitive.

SELECT * FROM employees WHERE name = 'John';
-- This will only match rows where the name is exactly 'John'.

- COLLATE

You can use COLLATE to specify a specific collation for string comparison, which determines case-sensitivity and accent-sensitivity.

- **Case-insensitive comparison:**

  SELECT * FROM employees WHERE name COLLATE UTF8_GENERAL_CI = 'john';
  -- This will return rows where the name is 'John', 'JOHN', or 'john' (case-insensitive).

- BINARY

This forces a case-sensitive comparison, overriding the collation.

SELECT * FROM employees WHERE BINARY name = 'john';
-- This will match 'john' but not 'John' or 'JOHN'.

- STRCMP(str1, str2)

Compares two strings. Returns:

- 0 if the strings are equal
- 1 if str1 is greater than str2
- -1 if str1 is less than str2

SELECT STRCMP('apple', 'banana');
-- Output: -1 (because 'apple' is less than 'banana')

2. Encryption Functions

MySQL provides several encryption and decryption functions to secure data.

- MD5(str)

This function returns a 32-character MD5 hash of the input string. It's commonly used to store passwords securely.

SELECT MD5('password123');
-- Output: 482c811da5d5b4bc6d497ffa98491e38

Note: MD5 is considered cryptographically broken and unsuitable for further use, especially for sensitive data. However, it can be used for basic non-sensitive tasks.

- SHA1(str)

Returns the SHA-1 hash of the string, which is more secure than MD5 (but still considered weak by modern standards).

SELECT SHA1('password123');
-- Output: 5baa61e4c9b93f3f0682250b6cf8331b7ee68fd8

- AES_ENCRYPT(str, key)

Encrypts a string using AES encryption. You can use a user-supplied key to encrypt the data. The encrypted data can be safely stored in the database.

SELECT HEX(AES_ENCRYPT('SensitiveData', 'encryptionKey'));
-- Output: A hex-encoded encrypted version of 'SensitiveData'

- AES_DECRYPT(encrypted_str, key)

Decrypts an AES-encrypted string back to its original form.

SELECT AES_DECRYPT(UNHEX('encrypted_data_in_hex'),
'encryptionKey');
-- Output: SensitiveData

- PASSWORD(str)

This function returns a hashed password. It's mainly used for password hashing in MySQL user accounts, but it's deprecated and not recommended for use in applications.

SELECT PASSWORD('mySecurePassword');
-- Output: A hashed version of the password

- DES_ENCRYPT(str, key)

Encrypts a string using the DES algorithm. This is a less secure option compared to AES.

SELECT HEX(DES_ENCRYPT('SensitiveData', 'key123'));
-- Output: A hex-encoded encrypted version

- DES_DECRYPT(encrypted_str, key)

Decrypts a string encrypted with the DES_ENCRYPT function.

SELECT DES_DECRYPT(UNHEX('encrypted_data_in_hex'), 'key123');
-- Output: SensitiveData

- HMAC(key, str)

Computes a hash value for the string using a keyed hash message authentication code (HMAC), typically for verification of integrity.

```
SELECT HMAC('key', 'message');
-- Output: The HMAC of 'message' using 'key' as the secret key
```

- BASE64_ENCODE(str) and BASE64_DECODE(str)

Encode and decode data using Base64 encoding, commonly used for transferring binary data as ASCII text.

```
SELECT TO_BASE64('Hello World');
-- Output: SGVsbG8gV29ybGQ=
```

```
SELECT FROM_BASE64('SGVsbG8gV29ybGQ=');
-- Output: Hello World
```

3. Additional Useful String Functions

- CONCAT_WS(separator, str1, str2, ...)

Concatenates strings with a specified separator between them.

```
SELECT CONCAT_WS('-', '2025', '02', '17');
-- Output: 2025-02-17
```

- CHAR_LENGTH(str) / LENGTH(str)

CHAR_LENGTH counts the number of characters, while LENGTH counts the number of bytes. This is important if you're dealing with multibyte characters.

```
SELECT CHAR_LENGTH('hello'), LENGTH('hello');
-- Output: 5, 5 (same for single-byte characters)
```

```
SELECT CHAR_LENGTH('你好'), LENGTH('你好');
-- Output: 2, 6 (2 characters, but 6 bytes due to UTF-8 encoding)
```

- REVERSE(str)

Reverses the string.

```
SELECT REVERSE('Hello');
-- Output: olleH
```

To conclude.

- **String Comparison Functions** allow for various ways to compare, match, and filter string data in MySQL, including using LIKE, STRCMP(), and handling case-sensitivity with COLLATE and BINARY.
- **Encryption Functions** enable secure storage and transmission of sensitive data, such as passwords, using techniques like hashing (MD5, SHA1), and encryption/decryption (AES, DES).
- **Base64 Encoding/Decoding** can be very useful when you need to handle binary data as text.

APPENDIX C- LEARNING THROUGH CASE STUDY.

Case study on how SQL queries can be used to analyze and derive insights from the data.

Case Study 1: Online Retail Store

Let's consider a fictitious online retail store that sells various products to customers worldwide. The store maintains a database with the following tables:

1. products: Contains information about the products available for sale.

2.customers: Stores details about the customers who have made purchases.

3.orders: Records information about individual orders placed by customers.

4.order_items: Contains the details of items purchased in each order.

Objective:

The objective of this case study is to analyze the sales data to gain insights into the performance of the online retail store.

Example Queries:

Total Revenue:

SELECT SUM(unit_price * quantity) AS total_revenue

FROM orders

JOIN order_items ON orders.order_id = order_items.order_id;

Top Selling Products:

SELECT product_id, product_name, SUM(quantity) AS total_sold

FROM order_items

JOIN products ON order_items.product_id = products.product_id

GROUP BY product_id, product_name

ORDER BY total_sold DESC

LIMIT 10;

Monthly Revenue Trend:

SELECT YEAR(order_date) AS year, MONTH(order_date) AS month, SUM(unit_price * quantity) AS monthly_revenue

FROM orders

JOIN order_items ON orders.order_id = order_items.order_id

GROUP BY YEAR(order_date), MONTH(order_date)

ORDER BY year, month;

Customer Distribution by Country:

SELECT country, COUNT(*) AS customer_count

FROM customers

GROUP BY country

ORDER BY customer_count DESC;

Average Order Value:

SELECT AVG(order_total) AS average_order_value

FROM (

   SELECT order_id, SUM(unit_price * quantity) AS order_total

   FROM order_items

   GROUP BY order_id

) AS order_totals;

Repeat Customers:

SELECT customer_id, COUNT(*) AS order_count

FROM orders

GROUP BY customer_id

HAVING order_count > 1;

These are just a few examples of SQL queries that can be used to analyze the data in our hypothetical online retail store case study. Depending on the specific requirements and objectives of the analysis, additional queries and aggregations can be formulated to derive deeper insights into the business performance and customer behavior.

Case Study 2: Health Industry (Hospital Database)

This is a hypothetical case study from health industry focusing on a hospital's database. We'll create a simplified schema and demonstrate SQL queries that could be used to analyze patient data, medical records, and hospital operations.

Database Schema:

We'll define the following tables:

1. Patients: Stores patient information.

•Columns: patient_id, first_name, last_name,gender, date_of_birth, address, city, state, zip_code.

2. Doctors: Contains details of doctors working at the hospital.

•Columns: doctor_id, first_name, last_name,This specialization, department.

3.Appointments: Records appointments scheduled by patients with doctors.

•Columns:appointment_id,patient_id,   doctor_id,   appointment_date, appointment_time.

4.Medical_Records: Stores medical records for each patient.

•Columns: record_id, patient_id, doctor_id, diagnosis, prescription, date.

Objective:

The objective of this case study is to analyze patient demographics, appointment scheduling, doctor performance, and medical treatments within the hospital.

Example Queries:

Total Number of Patients:

SELECT COUNT(*) AS total_patients

FROM Patients;

Top Specializations among Doctors:

SELECT specialization, COUNT(*) AS doctor_count

FROM Doctors

GROUP BY specialization

ORDER BY doctor_count DESC

LIMIT 5;

Patient Age Distribution:

SELECT YEAR(CURRENT_DATE) - YEAR(date_of_birth) -
(DATE_FORMAT(CURRENT_DATE, '%m%d') <
DATE_FORMAT(date_of_birth, '%m%d')) AS age_group,

COUNT(*) AS patient_count

FROM Patients

GROUP BY age_group

ORDER BY age_group;

Busiest Doctors (Based on Appointment Count):

SELECT d.doctor_id, CONCAT(d.first_name, ' ', d.last_name) AS doctor_name, COUNT(a.appointment_id) AS appointment_count

FROM Doctors d

```
LEFT JOIN Appointments a ON d.doctor_id = a.doctor_id

GROUP BY d.doctor_id, doctor_name

ORDER BY appointment_count DESC

LIMIT 5;
```

Most Common Diagnoses:

```
SELECT diagnosis, COUNT(*) AS diagnosis_count

FROM Medical_Records

GROUP BY diagnosis

ORDER BY diagnosis_count DESC

LIMIT 5;
```

Average Appointment Wait Time:

```
SELECT     AVG(TIMESTAMPDIFF(MINUTE,     appointment_date,
appointment_time)) AS avg_wait_time_minutes

FROM Appointments;
```

Patients with Chronic Conditions (Based on Diagnosis):

```
SELECT  p.patient_id,  CONCAT(p.first_name,  ' ',  p.last_name)  AS
patient_name, m.diagnosis

FROM Patients p

JOIN Medical_Records m ON p.patient_id = m.patient_id

WHERE m.diagnosis IN ('diabetes', 'hypertension', 'asthma');
```

These queries demonstrate how SQL can be used to extract valuable insights from the hospital's database, helping hospital administrators, doctors, and healthcare professionals make informed decisions and improve patient care. Depending on specific requirements, additional queries can be formulated to explore various aspects of hospital operations and patient health outcomes.

Case Study 3: Air Flight Operations

This is a hypothetical case study from the airline industry focusing on a database for managing flight operations, passenger information, and booking details. We'll design a simplified schema and provide SQL queries for analyzing flight schedules, passenger demographics, and booking trends.

Database Schema:

We'll define the following tables:

1. Flights: Stores information about flights operated by the airline.

• Columns:flight_id,flight_number, departure_airport,arrival_airport, departure_time, arrival_time, aircraft_type.

2. Passengers: Contains details of passengers traveling on the airline.

• Columns: passenger_id, first_name,last_name,gender, date_of_birth, nationality.

3. Bookings: Records booking information for passengers.

• Columns:booking_id, passenger_id, flight_id, booking_date, booking_status.

Objective:

The objective of this case study is to analyze flight schedules, passenger demographics, booking trends, and flight occupancy to optimize airline operations and improve customer satisfaction.

Example Queries:

Total Number of Flights:

SELECT COUNT(*) AS total_flights

FROM Flights;

Busiest Routes (Based on Number of Flights):

SELECT departure_airport, arrival_airport, COUNT(*) AS flight_count

FROM Flights

GROUP BY departure_airport, arrival_airport

ORDER BY flight_count DESC

LIMIT 5;

Top Aircraft Types Used:

SELECT aircraft_type, COUNT(*) AS aircraft_count

FROM Flights

GROUP BY aircraft_type

ORDER BY aircraft_count DESC

LIMIT 5;

Passenger Age Distribution:

SELECT YEAR(CURRENT_DATE) - YEAR(date_of_birth) - (DATE_FORMAT(CURRENT_DATE, '%m%d') < DATE_FORMAT(date_of_birth, '%m%d')) AS age_group,

COUNT(*) AS passenger_count

FROM Passengers

GROUP BY age_group

ORDER BY age_group;

Top Nationalities of Passengers:

SELECT nationality, COUNT(*) AS passenger_count

FROM Passengers

GROUP BY nationality

ORDER BY passenger_count DESC

LIMIT 5;

Booking Trends Over Time:

SELECT YEAR(booking_date) AS year, MONTH(booking_date) AS month, COUNT(*) AS booking_count

FROM Bookings

GROUP BY year, month

ORDER BY year, month;

Flight Occupancy Rate:

SELECT f.flight_number, COUNT(b.booking_id) AS booked_seats,

(COUNT(b.booking_id) / MAX(seats_per_flight)) * 100 AS occupancy_rate

FROM Flights f

LEFT JOIN Bookings b ON f.flight_id = b.flight_id

GROUP BY f.flight_number;

These queries demonstrate how SQL can be used to analyze flight schedules, passenger demographics, and booking trends in the airline industry. By leveraging data insights, airlines can optimize operations, improve customer experience, and make data-driven decisions to enhance overall efficiency and profitability.

APPENDIX D- MORE PROJECTS

1. Online Book Store project in SQL

This is a simplified example of a project involving an online bookstore database. We'll create tables for books, authors, customers, and orders, along with some sample data and example SQL queries with outputs.

Database Schema:

1. Books: Stores information about books.

• Columns: book_id, title, author_id, price, publication_date.

2. Authors: Contains details of authors.

• Columns: author_id, author_name.

3. Customers: Stores customer information.

• Columns: customer_id, first_name, last_name, email, address.

4. Orders: Records order information.

• Columns: order_id, customer_id, book_id, order_date, quantity.

Sample Data:

-- Authors Table

INSERT INTO Authors (author_id, author_name) VALUES

(1, 'J.K. Rowling'),

(2, 'Stephen King'),

(3, 'Agatha Christie');

-- Books Table

INSERT INTO Books (book_id, title, author_id, price, publication_date) VALUES

(1, 'Harry Potter and the Philosopher''s Stone', 1, 10.99, '1997-06-26'),

(2, 'The Shining', 2, 12.50, '1977-01-28'),

(3, 'Murder on the Orient Express', 3, 8.99, '1934-01-01');

-- Customers Table

INSERT INTO Customers (customer_id, first_name, last_name, email, address) VALUES

(1, 'John', 'Doe', 'john@example.com', '123 Main St, Anytown, USA'),

(2, 'Jane', 'Smith', 'jane@example.com', '456 Elm St, Anytown, USA');

-- Orders Table

INSERT INTO Orders (order_id, customer_id, book_id, order_date, quantity) VALUES

(1, 1, 1, '2024-01-15', 2),

(2, 2, 2, '2024-01-20', 1),

(3, 1, 3, '2024-02-05', 3);

Example Queries with Outputs:

List all books along with their authors:

SELECT b.title, a.author_name

FROM Books b

JOIN Authors a ON b.author_id = a.author_id;

Output:

title	author_name
Harry Potter and the Philosopher's Stone	J.K. Rowling
The Shining	Stephen King
Murder on the Orient Express	Agatha Christie

Calculate total revenue generated from book sales:

SELECT SUM(b.price * o.quantity) AS total_revenue

FROM Books b

JOIN Orders o ON b.book_id = o.book_id;

Output:

| total_revenue |

|------------------|

| 70.45 |

List customers who made orders along with the total number of books they purchased:

SELECT   c.first_name,   c.last_name,   COUNT(o.book_id)   AS total_books_purchased

FROM Customers c

JOIN Orders o ON c.customer_id = o.customer_id

GROUP BY c.customer_id, c.first_name, c.last_name;

Output:

first_name	last_name	total_books_purchased
John	Doe	5
Jane	Smith	1

List books ordered along with the corresponding order dates and quantities:

SELECT b.title, o.order_date, o.quantity

FROM Books b

JOIN Orders o ON b.book_id = o.book_id;

Output:

title	order_date	quantity
Harry Potter and the Philosopher's Stone	2024-01-15	2
The Shining	2024-01-20	1
Murder on the Orient Express	2024-02-05	3

This example provides a basic framework for a SQL project involving an online bookstore database, demonstrating table creation, data insertion, and various SQL queries along with their outputs. Depending on your specific requirements and interests, you can expand upon this project by adding more tables, data, and complex queries.

2 Automobile Industry database project

Let's design a more detailed SQL project for an automobile industry database. We'll include more tables to cover various aspects such as customers, employees, inventory, sales, and maintenance. I'll also provide sample data and queries.

Tables:

CarModels: Stores information about different car models.

•Columns: ModelID (Primary Key), Brand, ModelName, Year, EngineType, Price

CREATE TABLE CarModels (

ModelID INT PRIMARY KEY,

Brand VARCHAR(50),

ModelName VARCHAR(50),

Year INT,

EngineType VARCHAR(50),

Price DECIMAL(10, 2)

    );

Customers: Stores information about customers who purchase cars.

• Columns: CustomerID (Primary Key), Name, Email, Phone

CREATE TABLE Customers (

CustomerID INT PRIMARY KEY,

Name VARCHAR(100),

Email VARCHAR(100),

Phone VARCHAR(20)

    );

Employees: Stores information about employees involved in sales and maintenance.

• Columns: EmployeeID (Primary Key), Name, Position, Department, Salary

CREATE TABLE Employees (

EmployeeID INT PRIMARY KEY,

Name VARCHAR(100),

Position VARCHAR(100),

Department VARCHAR(100),

Salary DECIMAL(10, 2)

    );

Sales: Tracks sales transactions.

• Columns: SaleID (Primary Key), ModelID (Foreign Key to CarModels), CustomerID (Foreign Key to Customers), SaleDate, EmployeeID (Foreign

Key to Employees)

CREATE TABLE Sales (

SaleID INT PRIMARY KEY,

ModelID INT,

CustomerID INT,

SaleDate DATE,

EmployeeID INT,

FOREIGN KEY (ModelID) REFERENCES CarModels(ModelID),

FOREIGN KEY (CustomerID) REFERENCES Customers(CustomerID),

FOREIGN KEY (EmployeeID) REFERENCES Employees(EmployeeID)

    );

Inventory: Tracks the available quantity of each car model.

• Columns: InventoryID (Primary Key), ModelID (Foreign Key to CarModels), Quantity

CREATE TABLE Inventory (

  InventoryID INT PRIMARY KEY,

  ModelID INT,

  Quantity INT,

  FOREIGN KEY (ModelID) REFERENCES CarModels(ModelID)

    );

Maintenance: Records maintenance tasks for each car.

• Columns: MaintenanceID (Primary Key), ModelID (Foreign Key to CarModels), Description, MaintenanceDate, Cost

CREATE TABLE Maintenance (

MaintenanceID INT PRIMARY KEY,

ModelID INT,

Description TEXT,

MaintenanceDate DATE,

Cost DECIMAL(10, 2),

FOREIGN KEY (ModelID) REFERENCES CarModels(ModelID)

);

Sample Data:

-- CarModels

INSERT INTO CarModels (ModelID, Brand, ModelName, Year, EngineType, Price) VALUES

(1, 'Toyota', 'Camry', 2023, 'Petrol', 25000.00),

(2, 'Honda', 'Accord', 2023, 'Hybrid', 28000.00),

(3, 'Ford', 'Mustang', 2022, 'Petrol', 35000.00),

(4, 'Chevrolet', 'Camaro', 2022, 'Petrol', 32000.00);

-- Customers

INSERT INTO Customers (CustomerID, Name, Email, Phone) VALUES

(1, 'John Doe', 'john@example.com', '123-456-7890'),

(2, 'Jane Smith', 'jane@example.com', '456-789-0123'),

(3, 'Bob Johnson', 'bob@example.com', '789-012-3456');

-- Employees

INSERT INTO Employees (EmployeeID, Name, Position, Department, Salary) VALUES

(1, 'Alice Johnson', 'Sales Manager', 'Sales', 60000.00),

(2, 'Bob Smith', 'Sales Representative', 'Sales', 45000.00),

(3, 'Charlie Brown', 'Mechanic', 'Maintenance', 50000.00);

-- Sales

INSERT INTO Sales (SaleID, ModelID, CustomerID, SaleDate, EmployeeID) VALUES

(1, 1, 1, '2023-01-15', 2),

(2, 2, 2, '2023-02-20', 1),

(3, 3, 3, '2022-05-10', 2),

(4, 4, 1, '2022-07-05', 1);

-- Inventory

INSERT INTO Inventory (InventoryID, ModelID, Quantity) VALUES

(1, 1, 10),

(2, 2, 5),

(3, 3, 8),

(4, 4, 12);

-- Maintenance

INSERT INTO Maintenance (MaintenanceID, ModelID, Description, MaintenanceDate, Cost) VALUES

(1, 1, 'Oil change and filter replacement', '2023-01-20', 80.00),

(2, 2, 'Brake pad replacement', '2023-03-05', 120.00),

(3, 3, 'Tire rotation and alignment', '2022-06-01', 100.00),

(4, 4, 'Engine tune-up', '2022-08-10', 200.00);

Queries:

Retrieve all car models with their respective prices.

SELECT * FROM CarModels;

Retrieve the total sales amount for each model.

SELECT cm.ModelName, SUM(cm.Price) AS TotalSalesAmount

FROM CarModels cm

JOIN Sales s ON cm.ModelID = s.ModelID

GROUP BY cm.ModelName;

Find out which customers bought a car in 2023.

SELECT c.Name, cm.Brand, cm.ModelName, s.SaleDate

FROM Customers c

JOIN Sales s ON c.CustomerID = s.CustomerID

JOIN CarModels cm ON s.ModelID = cm.ModelID

WHERE YEAR(s.SaleDate) = 2023;

Retrieve the top-selling car model.

SELECT cm.ModelName, COUNT(*) AS TotalSales

FROM CarModels cm

JOIN Sales s ON cm.ModelID = s.ModelID

GROUP BY cm.ModelName

ORDER BY TotalSales DESC

LIMIT 1;

Calculate the total cost of maintenance for each car model.

SELECT cm.ModelName, SUM(m.Cost) AS TotalMaintenanceCost

FROM CarModels cm

JOIN Maintenance m ON cm.ModelID = m.ModelID

GROUP BY cm.ModelName;

These queries provide a comprehensive view of the automobile industry database, covering sales, inventory, maintenance, and customer data.

3. Pharmaceutical Industry database project

Consider the following pharmaceutical company database including tables, sample data, and some example queries with outputs.

Tables:

Products: Stores information about pharmaceutical products.

• Columns: ProductID (Primary Key), ProductName, Manufacturer, ExpiryDate, PricePerUnit

CREATE TABLE Products (

ProductID INT PRIMARY KEY,

ProductName VARCHAR(100),

Manufacturer VARCHAR(100),

ExpiryDate DATE,

PricePerUnit DECIMAL(10, 2)

);

Customers: Stores information about customers purchasing pharmaceutical products.

• Columns: CustomerID (Primary Key), Name, Email, Phone

CREATE TABLE Customers (

CustomerID INT PRIMARY KEY,

Name VARCHAR(100),

Email VARCHAR(100),

Phone VARCHAR(20)

);

Employees: Stores information about employees working in the pharmaceutical company.

• Columns: EmployeeID (Primary Key), Name, Position, Department, Salary

CREATE TABLE Employees (

EmployeeID INT PRIMARY KEY,

Name VARCHAR(100),

Position VARCHAR(100),

Department VARCHAR(100),

Salary DECIMAL(10, 2)

);

Sales: Tracks sales transactions of pharmaceutical products.

• Columns: SaleID (Primary Key), ProductID (Foreign Key to Products), CustomerID (Foreign Key to Customers), SaleDate, Quantity, TotalAmount

CREATE TABLE Sales (

SaleID INT PRIMARY KEY,

ProductID INT,

CustomerID INT,

SaleDate DATE,

Quantity INT,

TotalAmount DECIMAL(10, 2),

FOREIGN KEY (ProductID) REFERENCES Products(ProductID),

FOREIGN KEY (CustomerID) REFERENCES Customers(CustomerID)

   );

Suppliers: Stores information about suppliers providing pharmaceutical products.

• Columns: SupplierID (Primary Key), Name, ContactInfo

CREATE TABLE Suppliers (

SupplierID INT PRIMARY KEY,

Name VARCHAR(100),

ContactInfo TEXT

   );

Sample Data:

-- Products

INSERT INTO Products (ProductID, ProductName, Manufacturer, ExpiryDate, PricePerUnit) VALUES

(1, 'Paracetamol', 'ABC Pharma', '2024-12-31', 5.00),

(2, 'Amoxicillin', 'XYZ Pharmaceuticals', '2023-10-15', 10.00),

(3, 'Omeprazole', 'DEF Labs', '2023-09-30', 8.00),

(4, 'Aspirin', 'PQR Drugs', '2023-08-31', 3.50);

-- Customers

INSERT INTO Customers (CustomerID, Name, Email, Phone) VALUES

(1, 'John Doe', 'john@example.com', '123-456-7890'),

(2, 'Jane Smith', 'jane@example.com', '456-789-0123'),

(3, 'Bob Johnson', 'bob@example.com', '789-012-3456');

-- Employees

INSERT INTO Employees (EmployeeID, Name, Position, Department, Salary) VALUES

(1, 'Alice Johnson', 'Sales Manager', 'Sales', 60000.00),

(2, 'Bob Smith', 'Sales Representative', 'Sales', 45000.00),

(3, 'Charlie Brown', 'Pharmacist', 'Pharmacy', 55000.00);

-- Sales

INSERT INTO Sales (SaleID, ProductID, CustomerID, SaleDate, Quantity, TotalAmount) VALUES

(1, 1, 1, '2024-02-10', 2, 10.00),

(2, 2, 2, '2023-09-20', 1, 10.00),

(3, 3, 3, '2023-07-05', 3, 24.00),

(4, 4, 1, '2023-05-15', 5, 17.50);

-- Suppliers

INSERT INTO Suppliers (SupplierID, Name, ContactInfo) VALUES

(1, 'PharmaCorp', 'info@pharmacorp.com'),

(2, 'MediCare Suppliers', 'contact@medicare.com'),

(3, 'HealthLink Pharmaceuticals', 'support@healthlinkpharma.com');

Example Queries with Outputs:

Retrieve all products along with their expiry dates and prices.

SELECT * FROM Products;

Output

ProductID	ProductName	Manufacturer	ExpiryDate	PricePerUnit
1	Paracetamol	ABC Pharma	2024-12-31	5.00
2	Amoxicillin	XYZ Pharmaceuticals	2023-10-15	10.00
3	Omeprazole	DEF Labs	2023-09-30	8.00
4	Aspirin	PQR Drugs	2023-08-31	3.50

Retrieve the total sales amount for each product.

SELECT p.ProductName, SUM(s.TotalAmount) AS TotalSalesAmount

FROM Sales s

JOIN Products p ON s.ProductID = p.ProductID

GROUP BY p.ProductName;

Output

ProductName	TotalSalesAmount
Paracetamol	10.00
Amoxicillin	10.00
Omeprazole	24.00
Aspirin	17.50

Find out which customers purchased products in 2023.

SELECT c.Name AS CustomerName, p.ProductName, s.SaleDate

FROM Customers c

JOIN Sales s ON c.CustomerID = s.CustomerID

JOIN Products p ON s.ProductID = p.ProductID

WHERE YEAR(s.SaleDate) = 2023;

Output

CustomerName	ProductName	SaleDate
Bob Johnson	Omeprazole	2023-07-05
John Doe	Aspirin	2023-05-15

Retrieve the top-selling product.

SELECT p.ProductName, SUM(s.Quantity) AS TotalQuantitySold

FROM Sales s

JOIN Products p ON s.ProductID = p.ProductID

GROUP BY p.ProductName

ORDER BY TotalQuantitySold DESC

LIMIT 1;

Output

ProductName	TotalQuantitySold
Omeprazole	3

Find out which supplier provides the highest number of products.

SELECT sp.Name AS SupplierName, COUNT(p.ProductID) AS NumberOfProductsSupplied

FROM Suppliers sp

JOIN Products p ON sp.SupplierID = p.SupplierID

GROUP BY sp.Name

ORDER BY NumberOfProductsSupplied DESC

LIMIT 1;

Output

SupplierName	NumberOfProductsSupplied
XYZ Pharmaceuticals	1
DEF Labs	1
ABC Pharma	1
PQR Drugs	1

These queries provide insights into sales, inventory, customers, employees, and suppliers in the pharmaceutical industry database. You can further customize and expand these queries based on specific requirements.

4 Garment Industry database project

Consider following garment industry database, including tables, sample data, and example queries with outputs.

Tables:

Products: Stores information about garments.

• Columns: ProductID (Primary Key), ProductName, Brand, Category, Size, Color, Price

CREATE TABLE Products (

ProductID INT PRIMARY KEY,

ProductName VARCHAR(100),

Brand VARCHAR(100),

Category VARCHAR(100),

Size VARCHAR(10),

Color VARCHAR(50),

Price DECIMAL(10, 2)

);

Customers: Stores information about customers purchasing garments.

• Columns: CustomerID (Primary Key), Name, Email, Phone

CREATE TABLE Customers (

CustomerID INT PRIMARY KEY,

Name VARCHAR(100),

Email VARCHAR(100),

Phone VARCHAR(20)

);

Employees: Stores information about employees working in the garment company.

• Columns: EmployeeID (Primary Key), Name, Position, Department, Salary

CREATE TABLE Employees (

EmployeeID INT PRIMARY KEY,

Name VARCHAR(100),

Position VARCHAR(100),

Department VARCHAR(100),

Salary DECIMAL(10, 2)

);

Sales: Tracks sales transactions of garments.

• Columns: SaleID (Primary Key), ProductID (Foreign Key to Products), CustomerID (Foreign Key to Customers), SaleDate, Quantity, TotalAmount

CREATE TABLE Sales (

SaleID INT PRIMARY KEY,

ProductID INT,

CustomerID INT,

SaleDate DATE,

Quantity INT,

TotalAmount DECIMAL(10, 2),

FOREIGN KEY (ProductID) REFERENCES Products(ProductID),

FOREIGN KEY (CustomerID) REFERENCES Customers(CustomerID)

  );

Sample Data:

-- Products

INSERT INTO Products (ProductID, ProductName, Brand, Category, Size, Color, Price) VALUES

(1, 'T-shirt', 'Nike', 'Tops', 'M', 'Black', 25.00),

(2, 'Jeans', 'Levi's', 'Bottoms', '32x32', 'Blue', 50.00),

(3, 'Dress', 'Zara', 'Dresses', 'S', 'Red', 40.00),

(4, 'Sweater', 'Adidas', 'Outerwear', 'L', 'Gray', 60.00);

-- Customers

INSERT INTO Customers (CustomerID, Name, Email, Phone) VALUES

(1, 'John Doe', 'john@example.com', '123-456-7890'),

(2, 'Jane Smith', 'jane@example.com', '456-789-0123'),

(3, 'Bob Johnson', 'bob@example.com', '789-012-3456');

-- Employees

INSERT INTO Employees (EmployeeID, Name, Position, Department, Salary) VALUES

(1, 'Alice Johnson', 'Sales Manager', 'Sales', 60000.00),

(2, 'Bob Smith', 'Sales Representative', 'Sales', 45000.00),

(3, 'Charlie Brown', 'Store Manager', 'Inventory', 55000.00);

-- Sales

INSERT INTO Sales (SaleID, ProductID, CustomerID, SaleDate, Quantity, TotalAmount) VALUES

(1, 1, 1, '2024-02-10', 2, 50.00),

(2, 2, 2, '2023-09-20', 1, 50.00),

(3, 3, 3, '2023-07-05', 3, 120.00),

(4, 4, 1, '2023-05-15', 1, 60.00);

Example Queries with Outputs:

Retrieve all products along with their details.

SELECT * FROM Products;

Output:

ProductID	ProductName	Brand	Category	Size	Color	Price
1	T-shirt	Nike	Tops	M	Black	25.00
2	Jeans	Levi's	Bottoms	32x32	Blue	50.00
3	Dress	Zara	Dresses	S	Red	40.00
4	Sweater	Adidas	Outerwear	L	Gray	60.00

Retrieve the total sales amount for each product.

SELECT p.ProductName, SUM(s.TotalAmount) AS TotalSalesAmount

FROM Sales s

JOIN Products p ON s.ProductID = p.ProductID

GROUP BY p.ProductName;

Output:

ProductName	TotalSalesAmount
T-shirt	50.00
Jeans	50.00
Dress	120.00
Sweater	60.00

Find out which customers purchased products in 2023.

SELECT c.Name AS CustomerName, p.ProductName, s.SaleDate

FROM Customers c

JOIN Sales s ON c.CustomerID = s.CustomerID

JOIN Products p ON s.ProductID = p.ProductID

WHERE YEAR(s.SaleDate) = 2023;

Output:

CustomerName	ProductName	SaleDate
Bob Johnson	Dress	2023-07-05
John Doe	Sweater	2023-05-15

Retrieve the top-selling product.

SELECT p.ProductName, SUM(s.Quantity) AS TotalQuantitySold

FROM Sales s

JOIN Products p ON s.ProductID = p.ProductID

GROUP BY p.ProductName

ORDER BY TotalQuantitySold DESC

LIMIT 1;

Output:

ProductName	TotalQuantitySold
Dress	3

Find out which employee has the highest salary.

SELECT Name, Salary

FROM Employees

ORDER BY Salary DESC

LIMIT 1;

Output:

Name	Salary
Alice Johnson	60000.00

These queries provide insights into sales, inventory, customers, employees, and products in the garment industry database. You can further customize and expand these queries based on specific requirements.

APPENDIX E- Quick Reference of Syntaxes, Examples and Data Types of SQL commands

1 SQL Command Syntax
• DDL Commands

1. Command: CREATE DATABASE

Syntax: CREATE DATABASE <databasename>;

Purpose: Creates a database with the specified name.

2. Command: CREATE TABLE

Syntax: CREATE TABLE <tablename>(<column name1><data type1>[,<column name2><data type2>,

.

.

<column nameN><data typeN>]

);

Purpose: Creates a table with the specified name.

3. Command: ALTER TABLE

Syntax: ALTER TABLE <tablename> ADD <columnname><datatype>;

ALTER TABLE <tablename> DROP <columnname>;

ALTER TABLE <tablename> MODIFY <column><new_definition>;

ALTER TABLE <tablename> ADD PRIMARY KEY(<column>);

ALTER TABLE <tablename> DROP PRIMARY KEY;

ALTER TABLE<tablename> ADD FOREIGN KEY(<column>) REFERENCES<tablename>(primarykeycolumn of other table);

ALTER TABLE <tablename> MODIFY <column><definition> NULL;

ALTER TABLE <tablename> MODIFY <column><definition> NOT NULL;

Purpose: Modifies the structure of a table

4. Command: DROP

Syntax: DROP TABLE <tablename>;

DROP DATABASE <databasename>;

Purpose: To remove table or database from MySQL DBMS.

5. Purpose: Creating table from existing table

Syntax: CREATE TABLE <tablename> AS (SELECT * FROM <tablename>);

6. Command: DESCRIBE

Syntax: DESCRIBE <tablename>;   or   DESC <tablename>

Purpose: To view structure of table.

7. Command: SHOW

Syntax: SHOW TABLES;

SHOW DATABASES;

Purpose: To see names of all the tables in the database OR to see names of all the databases in MySQL

8. Command: USE

Syntax: USE<databasename>;

Purpose: To open a database and start working in it.

9. Purpose: To reorder columns in the table

Syntax: ALTER   TABLE   <tablename>   MODIFY <columnname><datatype> FIRST

ALTER TABLE <tablename> MODIFY <columnname><datatype> AFTER <column name>;

10. Purpose: Changing a column name

Syntax: ALTER TABLE <tablename> CHANGE <oldcolumnname><newcolumnname><datatype>;

• DML Commands

1. Command: INSERT

Syntax: INSERT INTO <tablename> [<column1>, <column2>, ..., <column3>] VALUES (<value1>, <value2>, ... <value n>);

Purpose: Inserts data into a table

b. Purpose: Inserting data from another table

Syntax: INSERT INTO Empl(Empno ,Ename, Sal) SELECT Enum, Name, Salary FROM

Employees WHERE Salary>10000;

2. Command: SELECT DATABASE()

Syntax: SELECT DATABASE();

Purpose: Shows the name of the current database

3. Command: SELECT

Syntax: SELECT <* / column name / expression> FROM <table name> [WHERE<condition>] [ORDER BY <column name / expression> [ASC/DESC]];

Purpose: Retrieves data from a table

4. Command: UPDATE

Syntax: UPDATE <tablename> SET <column name> = <value> [,<column name> = <value>, ...] [WHERE <condition>];

Purpose: Updates/Modifies data in a table

5. Command: DELETE

Syntax: DELETE FROM < tablename> [Where < condition>];

Purpose: Deletes data from a table where condition is met.

Syntax: DELETE FROM < tablename>;

Purpose: Deletes full data from a table.

Database integrity using constraints.

• A constraint is a condition or check on a field or set of fields.

• The constraints applied to maintain data integrity are also known as integrity constraints. Few of them are:

1.Primary Key   2. Foreign Key

4. Check 5. Default   6. NOT NULL

Let us see an example of each:

1. Primary Key

   Example: CREATE TABLE EMP(ecode int(4) PRIMARY KEY, ename varchar(20)

NOT NULL, gender char(1), grade char(1), gross decimal(7,2));

   Example: CREATE TABLE EMP(ecode int(4), ename varchar(20) NOT NULL,gender char(1),grade

char(1), gross decimal(7,2), PRIMARY KEY(ecode));

Example: CREATE TABLE EMP(ecode int(4) CONSTRAINT ecode_pk PRIMARY KEY,ename varchar(20) NOT NULL, gender char(1), grade char(1), gross decimal(7,2));

2. Foreign Key

   Example: CREATE TABLE DEPT(depcode varchar(4) PRIMARY KEY, hodcode int(4) REFERENCES

EMP(ecode) ON DELETE CASCADE ON UPDATE CASCADE, dname varchar(30));

Example: CREATE TABLE DEPT(depcode varchar(4) PRIMARY KEY, hodcode int(4), dname varchar(30)),FOREIGN KEY (hodcode) REFERENCES EMP(ecode) ON DELETE CASCADE ON UPDATE CASCADE) ;

3.Unique constraint

Example: CREATE TABLE EMP(ecode int(4) UNIQUE, ename varchar(20) NOT NULL, gender char(1), grade char(1), gross decimal(7,2));

4. Check constraint

Example: CREATE TABLE EMP(ecode int(4) PRIMARY KEY, ename varchar(20),gender char(1), grade char(1), gross decimal(7,2) CHECK(gross>5000);

5. Default constraint

Example: CREATE TABLE EMP(ecode int(4) PRIMARY KEY, ename varchar(20) NOT NULL, gender char(1), grade char(1) DEFAULT 'E', gross decimal(7,2));

6. NOT NULL constraint

Example: CREATE TABLE EMP(ecode int(4) PRIMARY KEY, ename varchar(20)NOT NULL, gender char(1), grade char(1), gross decimal(7,2));

Extracting data from a table using SELECT statements.

Command: SELECT

Syntax: SELECT <* / column name / expression> ,[<column name/Expression list>]

FROM <table name>[WHERE <condition>] [ORDER BY <column name / expression> [ASC/DESC]];

Purpose: Retrieves data from a table

Following are the clauses which can be used with SELECT command:

a. DISTINCT -Used to display distinct values from a column of a table.

b. WHERE -Used to specify the condition based on which rows of a table are displayed.

c. BETWEEN-Used to define the range of values within which the column values must fall to make a condition true. Range includes both the upper and the lower values. NOT BETWEEN can be used to make a condition true when the column values must not fall in the range

d. IN is used to select values that match any value in a list of Specified values. NOT IN can be used to select values that does not match any value in a list of Specified values.

e. LIKE is used for pattern matching of string data using wildcard characters % and_. NOT LIKE   is used for pattern not matching of string data using wildcard characters % and_.

f. IS NULL is used to select rows in which the specified column is NULL. IS NOT NULL is used to select rows in which the specified column is NOT NULL.

g. ORDER BY used to display the selected rows in ascending or in descendingorder of the specified column/expression.

Data Types in SQL

There are many data types available in MySQL, but a few which are used most often are:

1. For Text data we use CHAR(size)-Fixed length

For Text data we use VARCHAR(size)-Variable length

2. For Numeric data with decimal we use DECIMAL(M,D)   FLOAT(M,D), DOUBLE(M,D).

3. For normal sized numeric data upto 11 digits without decimal(whole number) we use INT(size) or INTEGER(size)

For numeric data upto 4 digits without decimal(whole number) we useTINY INT(size).

For numeric data upto 5 digits without decimal(whole number) we use SMALLINT(size).

For numeric data upto 9 digits without decimal(whole number) we use MEDIUMINT(size).

For large numeric data up to 11 digits without decimal(whole number) we use BIGINT(size).

4. For date data we use DATE

For date and time combination data we use DATETIME

For time stamp between midnight Jan 1,1970 and 2038 we use TIMESTAMP

For storing time in HH:MM:SS format we use TIME

For storing year in two digits or four digits we use YEAR(2) OR YEAR(4). By default it is four.

5. For storing binary large objects like binary data such as images or other types of files we use TEXT or BLOB. The difference between the two is that the sort and comparisons on stored data are not case sensitive in TEXT but it is case sensitive in BLOBs. The maximum length of data could be 65535 characters and no need to specify length.

ABOUT THE BOOK AND AUTHOR

"THE MYSQL ENGINEER- *Step-by-Step Learning of Essential Techniques for Efficient MySQL Database Development and Administration.*" is written by Sohail Mohammed, a professional who has 15 years of industry and academics experience. The author has taught MySQL Database Management System, Java Netbeans, Python, Networking, Emerging Technologies and Web Applications. He has also worked as a Software Quality Assurance Engineer on different projects.

The salient features of the book are:

1. This book is for Step-by-Step Learning of Essential Techniques for Efficient MySQL Database Development and Administration.
2. Comprehensive coverage of basic to advanced topics taught and practiced in MySQL Data Base Management System and Structured Query Language.
3. Explanation is provided with adequate amount of examples and syntax.
4. The book is written in easy to understand lucid language.
5. Though the commands taught are from MySQL RDBMS, comprehensive explanation of commands from other RDBMS software also included where found necessary.
6. Learning through Case Studies
7. Learning through Real World Projects
8. Quick Reference of Syntaxes, Examples and Data Types of SQL commands.

His other publications of Computer Sciences are:

"Networks Unraveled- A Comprehensive Guide to Modern Computer Networking"

"The Cyber Crime Frontier-Understanding Cyber Crime, Cyber Forensics, U.S. Federal Cyber Laws, Cyber Security Techniques, Digital Forensics and Encryption"

"SQL SUCCESS-A Beginner's and High Schooler's Guide to Professional Database Management"

His publications on self-help are:

"Health Care In DigiWorld And Ergonomics - A Health Care Guide for Parents, Adolescents and Adults for understanding and preventing the Negative Health effects of Technology Overuse Ergonomically."

"Holistic Healing Through Mindfulness & Meditation - A comprehensive guide on mindfulness and meditation techniques for holistic healing."

"Transforming Suffering Into Spiritual Growth And Holistic Healing - A book that examines how personal suffering can lead to Spiritual Awakening and deeper empathy leading to Holistic Healing."

"A GUIDE TO BOLD LIVING- BREAKING APPREHENSION'S GRIP. A JOURNEY TO OVERCOMING FEAR AND EMBRACING LIFE."

"HEALTHY STOMACH FOR HEALTHY BRAIN - Exploring How Gut Health Influences Anxiety, Depression and Brain Function" - by Adam Abraham (Pen Name)

"Enhancing Your Potentials Through Personality Development - A handbook to excel in your life by discovering and developing your true self."